The Fruits of Empirical Linguistics
Volume 1: Process

Studies in Generative Grammar 101

Mouton de Gruyter
Berlin · New York

The Fruits of Empirical Linguistics

Volume 1: Process

Edited by

Sam Featherston
Susanne Winkler

Mouton de Gruyter
Berlin · New York

Mouton de Gruyter (formerly Mouton, The Hague)
is a Division of Walter de Gruyter GmbH & Co. KG, Berlin.

The series Studies in Generative Grammar was formerly published by
Foris Publications Holland.

♾ Printed on acid-free paper which falls within the guidelines
of the ANSI to ensure permanence and durability.

Library of Congress Cataloging-in-Publication Data

The fruits of empirical linguistics / edited by Sam Featherston, Susanne Winkler.
2 v. cm.
Includes bibliographical references and index.
Contents: v. 1. Process – v. 2. Product.
ISBN 978-3-11-021338-6 (vol. 1 : hardcover : alk. paper)
ISBN 978-3-11-021347-8 (vol. 2 : hardcover)
1. Computational linguistics – Methodology. 2. Discourse analysis – Data processing. I. Featherston, Sam II. Winkler, Susanne, 1960–
P98.F78 2009
410.285–dc22
2009016914

Bibliographic information published by the Deutsche Nationalbibliothek

The Deutsche Nationalbibliothek lists this publication in the Deutsche Nationalbibliografie; detailed bibliographic data are available in the Internet at http://dnb.d-nb.de.

ISBN 978-3-11-021338-6
ISSN 0167-4331

Cover design: Christopher Schneider, Laufen.
Printed in Germany.

Table of contents

Empirical linguistics: Process and product vii

Linguistic choices vs. probabilities – how much and what can linguistic theory explain?
Antti Arppe 1

How to provide exactly one interpretation for every sentence, or what eye movements reveal about quantifier scope
Oliver Bott and Janina Radó 25

A scale for measuring well-formedness: Why syntax needs boiling and freezing points
Sam Featherston 47

The thin line between facts and fiction
Hubert Haider 75

Annotating genericity: How do humans decide? (A case study in ontology extraction)
Aurelie Herbelot and Ann Copestake 103

Canonicity in argument realization and verb semantic deficits in Alzheimer's disease
Christina Manouilidou and Roberto G. de Almeida 123

Automated collection and analysis of phonological data
James Myers 151

Semantic evidence and syntactic theory
Frederick J. Newmeyer 177

Automated support for evidence retrieval in documents with nonstandard orthography
Thomas Pilz and Wolfram Luther 211

Scaling issues in the measurement of linguistic acceptability
Thomas Weskott and Gisbert Fanselow 229

Conjoint analysis in linguistics – Multi-factorial analysis of Slavonic possessive adjectives
Tim Züwerink 247

Volume 2: Table of contents

German verb-first conditionals as unintegrated clauses:
A case study in converging synchronic and diachronic evidence
Katrin Axel and Angelika Wöllstein 1

Optionality in verb cluster formation
Markus Bader, Tanja Schmid and Jana Häussler 37

Clitic placement in Serbian: Corpus and experimental evidence
Molly Diesing, Dušica Filipović Đurđević and Draga Zec 59

Explorations in ellipsis: The grammar and processing of silence
Lyn Frazier 75

Comparatives and types of *þonne* in Old English:
Towards an integrated analysis of the data types
in comparatives derivations
Remus Gergel 103

Context effects in the formation of adjectival resultatives
Helga Gese, Britta Stolterfoht and Claudia Maienborn 125

New data on an old issue:
Subject/object asymmetries in long extractions in German
Tanja Kiziak 157

Parallelism and information structure:
Across-the-board-extraction from coordinate ellipsis
Andreas Konietzko 179

An empirical perspective on positive polarity items in German
Mingya Liu and Jan-Philipp Soehn 197

First-mention definites: More than exceptional cases
Marta Recasens, M. Antònia Martí and Mariona Taulé 217

Partial agreement in German: A processing issue?
Ilona Steiner 239

Index 261

Empirical linguistics: Process and product

The collaborative research centre *SFB 441* 'Linguistic Data Structures' came into being in 1999 as part of an academic sea change in the practice of linguistics: a shift towards a more data-driven approach. In fact this development is only the most recent symptom of a long-lasting tension within the study of language; in earlier stages of linguistics too there was often a degree of ambiguity about the branch of academic study that it most readily belongs to: the Arts, the Humanities, the Social Sciences, or even the Natural Sciences.

Some examples may illustrate this: Paul Passy, the founder of the International Phonetics Association, was a Christian Socialist, and would probably have regarded himself primarily as social reformer; his work on phonetics was intended to improve language education. Thomas Young, who invented the the term 'Indo-European' to describe a language family, was first and foremost a physicist; while the Grimm brothers, whose work covered folk tales, German phonology, and lexicography, are perhaps best characterized as Germanic philologists. The term 'philologist' is symptomatic of this phenomenon; it has as its first meaning in the Oxford English Dictionary 'one devoted to learning or literature; a scholar'; and as it second meaning 'a person versed in the science of language'. The Grimm brothers would perhaps have felt happiest with the first description, but most modern linguists would tend toward the second.

This between-stools nature of linguistics has often led to the development of different schools within branches of linguistics. A current example is the distinction between those syntacticians and semanticists who are primarily descriptive and those who aspire to be explanatory. The first group see their central aim as describing what speakers and listeners, writers and readers actually do, and construct accounts of this. They avoid speculation and deliver sound results, well-motivated in data. Their critics might regard these solid findings as rather dull, however, or worse: taxonomic. The second group regard theory building as their ultimate aim, and value innovative analyses and explanatory breadth more highly. Their critics might regard this work as castles in the air, relying heavily on crucial but untested hypothetical assumptions.

The recent trend towards a more empirical linguistics largely concerns these two adjacent fields of syntax and semantics. The new approach might be characterized as the attempt to integrate the data collection and analysis techniques and competence of the more descriptively adequate school of linguistics with the explanatory ambitions and sophisticated theoretical architecture of the more rationalist school. The international conference *Linguistic Evidence 2008*, like its predecessors in 2004 and 2006, provided, amongst other things, but perhaps above all, a forum for researchers who subscribe to this goal. Let us note here that this objective is not easily attained: joining the two approaches requires the linguist to adhere to many or most of the constraints of both the fields. The data must be valid and reliable, the statistical analysis performed and reported, but at the same time the linguistic evidence gathered should not merely relate to simple descriptive questions – it will ideally be of relevance to the wider systemic questions which are of interest to linguists in search of explanation.

The volumes of *The Fruits of Empirical Linguistics: Process* and *Product* contain the proceedings of this most recent conference. In the call for papers we announced that, while work from all branches of linguistics were welcome, there would be a special session on experimental methods in syntax and semantics, since these are the areas of linguistics where the paradigm shift towards a more empirical but nevertheless theoretically informed research model is most apparent (and perhaps most necessary). This specification had perhaps more effect than it was intended to; the vast majority of abstracts received would have been immediately appropriate for this 'special session'. There was therefore no separate session with this thematic focus, rather the entire conference was strongly orientated in this direction. It would appear that there is a wider feeling among linguists that this field is seeing innovation and is therefore interesting.

There was however a rather different distinction between the contributions which became apparent, and which we have applied in the proceedings: the contents of the two volumes are distinguished by whether they chiefly concern the process of linguistic data collection or the linguistic results of doing so. The first of the two volumes, *Process,* contains those papers in which the accent is on empirical approaches and procedures, the second, *Product*, incorporates those whose central point is the linguistic insights accessible with the more data-driven research. It almost goes without saying that this basic division is by no means categorical; many of the papers in the more methodological first part report and discuss important linguistic results, and many of the more results-orientated papers contain comment and reflection on the success, aptness, or weaknesses of the methods employed.

As is traditional at Linguistic Evidence conferences, the papers reflect a wide variety of questions and utilize a similarly broad range of methodological techniques. Nevertheless the common theme of exploring what more data-driven and data-dependent approaches can offer to the field of linguistics is very clear. What is also shared is the ambition to go beyond merely describing the data, and instead or additionally interpret the findings either within current theoretical models or as additions to existing models or analyses, in order to gain insights into linguistic structures and achieve advances in linguistic theory.

Within each volume, thematic sub-divisions can be drawn. In the *Process* volume, we may distinguish three different groups of papers. There are two which take a broader perspective and address meta-methodological questions. Frederick **Newmeyer** addresses the issue of the sorts of evidence which form an appropriate basis for syntactic theory building. His position is that the original autonomy of syntax assumption in generative grammar is being undermined by linguists making use of semantic evidence in arguments for structure. He reminds readers what originally motivated this methodological restriction and shows in several example cases why this limitation is still justified. In each case, he argues forcefully, the loosening of this practice leads to no greater generalization and obstructs the attainment of syntactic descriptive and explanatory aims. Hubert **Haider**'s contribution too is programmatic. He takes a step backward from the practical applications, and discusses three general outstanding issues in empirical approaches to the study of grammar. The first, Wundt's problem, is the status of introspection as valid data. The second, Orwell's problem, concerns the evidential weight to be given to evidence from different languages. The third, Crick's problem, relates to the degree of immediacy that linguists can assume between the data available to them and the contents of the black box of grammar. These two thoughtful contributions to the debate on the role of data and data types in linguistic theory effectively set the scene for the other more applied papers on the collection, processing, and interpretation of linguistic evidence.

Most papers in this volume directly concern the means of gathering data, whether it be information about occurrence or from perceived well-formedness. Thomas **Pilz** and Wolfram **Luther** report their work in developing a fuzzy search engine for orthographically unstandardized electronic documents. This tool is essential if text collections with more liberal spelling conventions, for example from earlier stages of the language, are to be fully accessible as a resource for linguists. The focus is on the automated support of evidence collection, the underlying methods, and their value for linguistic research. The study by Antti **Arppe** applies similar methods and seeks to answer the question how well lexical choice can be accounted for using the standard analytical categories that linguistic theory makes use of, and how this variation can be modelled using statistical methods. The contextual factors addressed include morphology, argument structure, semantic classification of arguments, and wider features such as medium. The results reveal that these contextual factors can go some significant way towards determining lexical choice, but that a degree of unexplained variation in most cases remains. He relates this to work arguing for a probabilistic relationship between linguistic production and the underlying linguistic system. Aurelie **Herbelot** and Ann **Copestake**'s paper is a contribution towards developing automated information extraction from written texts. In this process, keeping track of reference is essential, but in the case of generic use of NPs, often difficult, since the form of specific NPs (*the elephant looked at me*) and generic NPs (*the elephant is the largest land mammal*) is the same. The authors present their work developing and testing a set of guidelines for humans to follow in annotating genericity, which can serve as a basis to be replicated in machine learning.

The paper by Tim **Züwerink** presents a novel design for an experimental study. It makes crucial use of a statistical technique, Conjoint Analysis, which breaks down interacting and cumulative factors affecting linguistic variation. The approach has the advantage of allowing the investigation of a larger number of quite disparate variables at one time, which enables the linguist to distinguish the importance of both narrowly grammatical, more functional or stylistic, and even sociolinguistic factors playing a role in an alternation. James **Myers** presents two tools which automate and greatly simplify the task of gathering and analysing linguistic data. In an example study, MiniCorp was used to analyze the reliability of a proposed analysis of a corpus data set on Mandarin phonotactics. The results were further tested using the MiniJudge package which both implements and statistically analyzes binary judgement tests. These tools offer significant user-friendly support to the linguist wishing to examine hypotheses quantitatively.

The article by Thomas **Weskott** and Gisbert **Fanselow** is a response to the increasing popularity of the Magnitude Estimation method for collecting introspective well-formedness data. The authors present both experimental evidence and linguistic arguments which suggest that gathering judgements on a simple linear scale or even using the frequency distribution of categorical judgements can produce results similar to those of magnitude estimation. The authors therefore call for methodological plurality and tolerance. Sam **Featherston** echoes this theme and discusses the optimal method of gathering well-formedness judgements. He suggests that the Magnitude Estimation methodology, in spite of its advantages over traditional informal methods, can yet be improved upon. His own method, Thermometer Judgements, is designed to avoid these problems, especially when used in combination with standard comparison items.

The final two papers show what can be done with other data types. Oliver **Bott** and Janina **Radó** present the results of their innovative work investigating quantifier scope. They show that altogether three data sources are required in order to determine the final interpretation of scope ambiguous sentences without interfering with the normal process of interpretation. The novel element is the double use of the eye-tracker: first to yield reading times on the linguistic material, and then to show the fixations on the groups of items in the visual world paradigm. The combination of these two with the final interpretation choice allows the effects of the linguistic factors to be isolated. Rather different evidence is presented by Christina **Manouilidou** and Roberto **de Almeida**. Their evidence from pathological language throws light onto the nature of the linguistic impairment suffered by patients with probable Alzheimer's Disease (pAD). They show that such patients have specific problems with verbs with non-canonical argument realization, such as subject-experiencer (eg *fear*) and object-experiencer (eg *frighten*). In a production task, subjects had a low success rate in distinguishing these. They did not however choose distractor items, which demonstrates that the effect is specific to the argument structure. This result provides a new perspective on the mental representation of argument structure.

The second volume, **Product**, contains the papers from Linguistic Evidence 2008 in which the linguistic results, rather than the methods, are at the forefront of attention. To an extent this can be seen as empirical syntax and semantics coming of age: it is no longer necessary to talk about carrying out such studies in order to justify the approach; the case is made, so researchers can get on with the job of using the empirical paradigms to gain new insights. One interesting development is a degree of standardization in the approaches used: eight papers in this second volume make use of some form of judgement or rating study as a part of their evidential base. Five papers report both such experimental data and also frequency information. It would seem that the ease of collection and also robust evidential value of judgement studies are convincing linguists of the value of this data type and gaining general acceptance, especially when the well-formedness judgements are combined with data on occurrence.

Two papers however take a contrasting line and investigate syntax using historical data. Kathrin **Axel** and Angelika **Wöllstein** make interesting use of a combination of data types. These authors are defending an unorthodox hypothesis about German verb-first conditionals, arguing that the conditional clause and consecutive clauses are paratactically rather than syntactically linked. To this end they deliver an impressive array of empirical evidence: firstly, synchronic judgement data and synchronic corpus data, but secondly diachronic findings from texts since the Middle High German period. They argue for the more systematic use of diachronic data in work on current grammar. One other paper takes a similar approach, addressing a synchronic syntactic issue using largely historical data. The topic is the syntax of comparative structures, in particular the analysis of comparative inversion (eg *Venus has won more titles than has her sister*). Remus **Gergel** analyzes clausal comparative structures in a historical corpus but also draws upon lexically extracted data from the Old English text *Beowulf*. The author concludes that both data types are useful, the first giving better coverage of overall developments in comparatives, but the second shedding light on an individual case study.

The range of subjects treated in this volume testifies strongly to the wide applicability of the empirical approach. Lyn **Frazier's** paper is a consideration of two ellipsis structures: verb phrase ellipsis and sluicing. The paper poses the question at what descriptive levels the most adequate accounts of these structures should be located. The paper reports a series of experiments measuring reading times and well-formedness judgements, on the basis of which the author makes some interesting claims about the most appropriate sub-theory. She argues that for phenomena such as ellipsis we must be willing to allow both discourse and syntactic constraints to apply, and that the best theory will make use of both of them. On a similar theme, Andreas **Konietzko** investigates bare argument ellipsis (eg *Peter smokes cigarettes but not cigars*). He provides experimental evidence from judgement studies to support the claim that coordinate ellipsis is subject to a parallelism constraint, which is checked not only at the syntactic level but also at the syntax/information structure interface. Using data on across-the-board extraction he shows that bare argument ellipsis data is judged better if the two conjuncts fulfil the information-structural requirements imposed by the coordinating conjunction.

Questions of ordering and positioning are a classic syntactic concern on which understanding has been recently considerably extended by the use of experimental techniques and frequency studies. The work of Markus **Bader**, Tanja **Schmid** & Jana **Häussler** provides a neat example. Clause-final verbs in German can appear in variant orders apparently optionally. Both the precise distribution of these alternate orders in verb clusters and their syntactic analysis have given rise much discussion and are areas of continuing doubt. This paper rectifies both of these problems, reporting experimental work gathering speeded grammaticality judgements and an analysis in terms of categorial grammar. The study by Molly **Diesing**, Dušica **Filipović Đurđević**, and Draga **Zec** concerns a complex case of clitic placement from Serbian, where 'second place' clitics can apparently occur either after the first word or else after the first phrase. In order to discover the circumstances which determine placement, they carried out a corpus search and two experimental studies: one production task and one measuring reading times. These different data types provided converging evidence that the distribution of clitics is not optional, but clearly determined by the linguistic status of the host clause.

Movement and constraints on movement are also a form of ordering. Long wh-movement in English displays a subject/object asymmetry: subjects are usually harder to extract across a complementizer than objects. The paper by Tanja **Kiziak** investigates whether the same kind of subject/object asymmetry can be found in long extraction in German, where the data is not uncontroversial. A Thermometer Judgement study on different extraction contexts reveals that the asymmetry does in fact exist in German, and that it interacts with a number of independent factors such as the semantic complexity of the complementizer and word order preferences.

One of the advantages of the finer detail available in the experimental approach is that the researcher can often tease apart confounding factors affecting a phenomenon. Ilona **Steiner** also finds non-syntactic factors affecting phenomena traditionally regarded as syntactic. Her paper looks at sentences with conjunctions as subjects and their agreement behaviour. At least marginally, verbal agreement with just one conjunct appears possible in German ('partial agreement'). The author investigates whether processing evidence can play a role in explaining this phenomenon. By examining the issue with different data types (frequency data, incremental judgement data, and reading times), and contrasting their findings, she is able to show that it is best treated as a processing issue rather than as narrowly grammatical. Another paper reveals sensitivity to context. Helga **Gese**, Britta **Stolterfoht**, and Claudia **Maienborn** argue that the term 'adjectival passive' in German (eg *Das Fenster ist geschlossen*, 'The window is closed') is a misnomer, and that 'adjectival resultative' would be more appropriate. They show on the basis of corpus data and rating studies on unaccusatives, firstly, that their recategorization is empirically well-founded, but secondly, that any unaccusative can have an adjectival resultative reading if it is given sufficient contextual support.

Mingya **Liu** and Jan-Philipp **Soehn** address polarity items in German, focusing on those which occur in positive rather than negative contexts. The aim is to identify the set of lexical items which fulfil the conditions for being a member of the group, as a first step towards providing a wider analysis and categorization of the phenomenon. The authors report their multi-stage selection and sorting procedure, consisting first of corpus and internet searches, and then followed up by well-formedness judgement studies and speeded grammaticality judgements. They identify 51 validated examples and provide the tools to distinguish between stronger and weaker cases.

Our final paper concerns the cross-linguistic study of definiteness. Since definiteness in NPs normally presupposes that they have previously been introduced into discourse, 'first-mention definites' represent a problem for standard assumptions. On the basis of corpus studies of Spanish and Catalan, Marta **Recasens**, M. Antònia **Martí**, and Mariona **Taulé** demonstrate that cross-linguistically different degrees of grammaticalization of the article need to be distinguished (the 'definiteness ratio'). They further show that certain head nouns (in fact: noun types) are associated with a definite determiner as a 'unit of usage'. The combination of these two insights is a step towards developing a linguistically well-founded heuristic for use in natural language processing.

As both editors and conference organizers we should like to express our thanks to the members of the *Sonderforschungsbereich 441* 'Linguistic Data Structures' for their help and willing support in making the conference happen, for being good colleagues generous with their time, humour, and patience, but most of all for the many interesting and informed discussions on linguistic and other topics. The conference could never have taken place without the core organizational team of Serge Doitchinov, Doris Penka, Jan-Philipp Soehn, Britta Stolterfoht, Bettina Zeisler, but especially Beate Starke.

The *Sonderforschungsbereich 441* could never have taken place without Marga Reis, whose talents, inter-personal and linguistic, as well as others, have won her so many friends and admirers. The papers in these volume and in their sister publications, the Linguistic Evidence proceedings 2004 and 2006 should be thought of as dedicated to Marga.

We should also like to thank the reviewers, both of the initial conference abstracts but also of the written papers, for their cooperation and expertise, and the proof readers and the index compiler. The Sonderforschungsbereich, the conference series, and the published versions are all generously supported by the Deutsche Forschungsgemeinschaft, the German academic research body.

Sam Featherston and Susanne Winkler

Linguistic choices vs. probabilities – how much and what can linguistic theory explain?

Antti Arppe

1. Introduction and background

A question of general theoretical interest in linguistics is what is the relationship between naturally produced language, evident in e.g. corpora, and the posited underlying language system that governs such usage. This concerns on the one hand the use and choice among lexical and structural alternatives in language, and on the other the underlying explanatory factors, following some theory representing language as a cohesive system. A subsequent subservient methodological challenge is how this can be modeled using appropriate statistical methods. The associated question of general theoretical import is to what extent we can describe the observed usage and the variation it contains in terms of the selected analytical features that conventional linguistic theory incorporates and works upon. The practical purpose of this paper is to present a case study elucidating how multivariate statistical models can be interpreted to shed light on these questions, focusing on a set of near-synonyms as the particular type of linguistic alternation. With multivariate modeling, I mean two distinct things. Firstly, I imply the use of multiple linguistic variables from a range of analytical levels and categories, instead of only one or two, in order to study and explain some linguistic phenomenon. Secondly, I mean with this term the use of multivariate statistical methods such as polytomous logistic regression. In the following introduction, I will first present research demonstrating that one and the same linguistic phenomenon can be associated with, and appear to be explainable in terms of a wide range of different variables from various levels of linguistic analysis. Next, I will note research indicating that satisfactory explanations of such linguistic phenomena requires multivariate (multicausal) models, i.e. the incorporation of all of these variables at the same time in the analysis. This leads us to the final and central question of how much of the phenomena we can in the end account for with the fullest set of explanatory variables available to us in current linguistic analysis.

In the modeling of lexical choice among semantically similar words, specifically near-synonyms, it has been suggested in computational theory that (at least) three levels of representation would be necessary to account for fine-grained meaning differences and the associated usage preferences (Edmonds and Hirst 2002: 117–124). These are 1) a conceptual-semantic level, 2) a subconceptual/stylistic-semantic level, and 3) a syntactic-semantic level, each corresponding to increasingly more detailed representations, i.e. granularity, of (word) meaning. The last, syntactic-semantic level (3) in such a *clustered model of lexical knowledge* concerns the combinatorial preferences of individual words in forming written sentences and spoken utterances. At this level, it has been shown in (mainly) lexicographically motivated corpus-based studies of actual lexical usage that semantically similar words differ significantly as to the different types of context in which are used. This has been observed to concern 1) lexical context (e.g. English adjectives *powerful* vs. *strong* in Church et al. 1991), 2) syntactic argument patterns (e.g. English verbs *begin* vs. *start* in Biber, Conrad and Reppen 1998: 95–100), and 3) the semantic classification of some particular argument (e.g. the subjects/agents of English *shake/quake* verbs in Atkins and Levin 1995), as well as 4) the rather style-associated text types or registers (e.g. English adjectives *big* vs. *large* vs. *great* in Biber, Conrad and Reppen 1998: 43–54). In addition to these studies that have focused on English, with its minimal morphology, it has also been shown for languages with extensive morphology, such as Finnish, that similar differentiation is evident as to 5) the inflectional forms and the associated morphosyntactic features in which synonyms are used (e.g. the Finnish adjectives *tärkeä* and *keskeinen* 'important, central' in Jantunen 2001; and the Finnish verbs *miettiä* and *pohtia* 'think, ponder, reflect, consider' in Arppe 2002, Arppe and Järvikivi 2007). Recently, in their studies of Russian near-synonymous verbs denoting TRY as well as INTEND, Divjak (2006) and Divjak and Gries (2006) have shown that there is often more than one type of these factors in play at the same time. Divjak and Gries' subsequent conclusion is that it is necessary to observe all categories together and in unison rather than separately one by one.

Similar corpus-based work has also been conducted on the syntactic level concerning *constructional alternations* (referred alternatively to as *synonymous structural variants* in Biber, Conrad and Reppen 1998: 76–83), often from starting points which would be considered to be anchored more within theoretical linguistics. Constructional alternations resemble lexical synonymy in that the essential associated meaning is understood to remain for the most part constant regardless of which of the alternative constructions is selected, though they may differ with respect to e.g. some pragmatic aspect such as focus. Relevant studies concerning these phenomena have been conducted by e.g. Gries (2003a) concerning the English verb-particle placement, i.e. [*V P NP*] vs. [*V NP P*], and Gries (2003b) as well as Bresnan et al. (2007) concerning the English dative alternation, i.e. [*GIVE* NP_{DIRECT_OBJECT} $PP_{INDIRECT\_OBJECT}$] vs. [*GIVE* $NP_{INDIRECT\_OBJECT}$ NP_{DIRECT_OBJECT}], to name but just a few.

With the exception of Gries (2003a, 2003b), Bresnan et al. (2007), Divjak (2006), and Divjak and Gries (2006), the aforementioned studies have in practice been monocausal, focusing on only one linguistic category or even a singular feature within a category at a time in the linguistic analysis applied. Though Jantunen (2001, 2004) does set out to cover a broad range of feature categories and notes that a linguistic trait may be evident at several different levels of context at the same time (2004: 150–151), he does not quantitatively evaluate their interactions. Bresnan et al. (2007) have suggested that such a tendency for reductive theories would result from pervasive correlations among the possible explanatory variables in the available data. Indeed, Gries (2003a: 32–36) has criticized this traditional tendency for monocausal explanations and demonstrated convincingly that such individual univariate analyses are insufficient and often even mutually contradictory. As a necessary remedy in order to attain scientific validity in explaining the observed linguistic phenomena, he has argued forcefully for a holistic approach using multifactorial setups covering a representative range of linguistic categories, leading to and requiring the exploitation of multivariate statistical methods. In such an approach, linguistic choices, whether synonyms or alternative constructions, are understood to be determined by a *plurality* of factors, in *interaction* with each other.

Furthermore, as has been pointed out by Divjak and Gries (2006), the majority of the above and other synonym studies appear to focus on word pairs, perhaps due to the methodological simplicity of such setups. The same criticism of limited scope applies also to studies of constructional alternations, including e.g. Gries' (2003a) own study on English particle placement. However, it is clearly evident in lexicographical descriptions such as dictionaries that there are often more than just two members to a synonym group, and this is supported by experimental evidence (Divjak and Gries 2008). Likewise, it is quite easy to come up with examples of constructional alternations with more than two conceivable and fully possible variants, e.g. in word order. This clearly motivates a shift of focus in synonym studies from word pairs to sets of similar lexemes with more than two members; the same naturally applies also to the study of constructional alternations.

Finally, Bresnan (2007) has suggested that the selections of alternatives in a context, i.e. lexical or structural outcomes for some combinations of variables, are generally speaking probabilistic, even though the individual choices in isolation are discrete. In other words, the workings of a linguistic system, represented by the range of variables according to some theory, and its resultant usage would in practice not be categorical, following from exception-less rules, but rather exhibit degrees of potential variation which becomes evident over longer stretches of linguistic usage. This is manifested in the observed proportions of occurrence among the possible alternating structures, given a set of contextual features. Bresnan (2007) uses logistic regression to model and represent these proportions as estimated expected probabilities, producing a continuum of variation between the practically categorical extremes (see Figure 1 in Bresnan 2007: 77, based on results from Bresnan et al. 2007). Moreover, both Gries (2003b) and Bresnan (2007) have shown that there is evidence for such probabilistic character both in natural language use in corpora as well as in language judgements in experiments, and that these two sources of evidence are convergent.

Nevertheless, one may question whether Bresnan's (2007) results entail that an idealization of linguistic system as a whole, as knowledge incorporated in an *ideally complete* theoretical model that describes its workings in its entirety (disregarding if such is in practice attainable at all), with syntax as one constituent level interacting with phonological, prosodic, lexical, semantic, pragmatic and extralinguistic ones, need be fundamentally non-categorical (see e.g. Yang 2008 and references therein). Rather, we may entertain the thought that the syntactic rules and regularities we are able to practically identify and generalize on the basis of actually observed linguistic usage only allow for a probabilistic description of the resultant utterances. In any case, how linguistic probabilities are represented within speakers' minds, how they come about as either individual linguistic judgments, or as proportions in language usage , and how they (inevitably) change over time within a linguistic community, is beyond the scope of this paper.

However, the aforementioned studies by Bresnan and Gries, too, have concerned only dichotomous outcome alternatives. Consequently, my intention is to extend this line of research to a polytomous setting involving the lexical choice among more than two alternatives, using as a case example the most frequent near-synonymous THINK lexemes in Finnish, namely *ajatella*, *miettiä*, *pohtia*, and *harkita* 'think, reflect, ponder, consider'. Furthermore, in line with the aforementioned previous research, I will include in the analysis a broad range of contextual features as explanatory variables. Thus, I will cover 1) the morphological features of both the selected verbs and the verb-chains they may be part of, 2) the entire syntactic argument structure of the verbs, 3) the semantic subclassifications of the individual argument types, 4) the semantic characterizations of the entire verb-chains in which the verbs occur, as well as 5) extralinguistic features such as medium.

2. Research corpus as well as linguistic and statistical analysis methods

As my research corpus, I selected two months worth (January–February 1995) of written text from Helsingin Sanomat (1995), Finland's major daily newspaper, and six months worth (October 2002 – April 2003) of written discussion in the SFNET (2002–2003) Internet discussion forum, namely regarding (personal) relationships (`sfnet.keskustelu.ihmissuhteet`) and politics (`sfnet.keskustelu.politiikka`). The newspaper subcorpus consisted altogether of 3,304,512 words of body text, excluding headers and captions (as well as punctuation tokens), and included 1,750 representatives of the selected THINK verbs. In turn, the Internet subcorpus comprised altogether 1,174,693 words of body text, excluding quotes of previous postings as well as punctuation tokens, adding up to 1,654 representatives of the selected THINK verbs. The individual overall frequencies among the THINK lexemes in the research corpus were 1492 for *ajatella*, 812 for *miettiä*, 713 for *pohtia*, and 387 for *harkita*.

The details of the various stages and levels of linguistic analysis applied to this research corpus are covered at length in Arppe (2008), but I will briefly cover the main points also here. The research corpus was first automatically morphologically and syntactically analyzed using a computational implementation of Functional Dependency Grammar (Tapanainen and Järvinen, 1997, Järvinen and Tapanainen 1997) for Finnish, namely the FI-FDG parser (Connexor 2007). After this automatic analysis, all the instances of the THINK lexemes together with their syntactic arguments were manually validated and corrected, if necessary, and subsequently supplemented with semantic classifications by hand. Each nominal argument (in practice nouns or pronouns) was semantically classified into one of the 25 top-level *unique beginners* for (originally English) nouns in WordNet (Miller 1990). Furthermore, subordinate clauses or other phrasal structures assigned to the PATIENT argument slot were classified following Pajunen (2001) into the traditional types of either participles, infinitives, indirect questions, clause propositions indicated with the subordinate conjunction *että* 'that', or direct quotes with attributions of the speaker using one of the THINK lexemes (e.g. "... " *miettii/pohtii joku* '"... " thinks/ponders somebody'). This covered satisfactorily AGENTS, PATIENTS, SOURCES, GOALS and LOCATIONS among the frequent syntactic argument types as well as INSTRUMENTS and VOCATIVES among the less frequent ones.

However, other syntactic argument types which were also frequent in the context of the THINK lexemes, indicating MANNER, TIME (as a moment or period), DURATION, FREQUENCY and QUANTITY, had a high proportion of adverbs, prepositional/postpositional phrases and subordinate clauses (or their equivalents based on non-finite verb forms). These argument types were semantically classified following the *ad hoc* evidence-driven procedure proposed by Hanks (1996), in which one scrutinizes and groups the individual observed argument lexemes or phrases in a piece-meal fashion. In Hanks' approach, as contextual examples accumulate, one generalizes semantic classes out of them, possibly reanalyzing the emergent classification if need be, without attempting to apply some prior theoretical model. Only in the case of MANNER arguments did several levels of granularity emerge at this stage in the semantic analysis. Even though clause-adverbials (i.e. META-comments such as *myös* 'also', *kuitenkin* 'nevertheless/however' and *ehkä* 'maybe' as well as subordinate clauses initiated with *mutta* 'but' and *vaikka* 'although') were also relatively quite frequent as an argument type, they were excluded from this level of analysis due to their generally parenthetical nature.

Furthermore, as an extension to Arppe (2006) the verb chains which the THINK lexemes form part of were semantically classified with respect to their modality and other related characteristics, following Kangasniemi (1992) and Flint (1980). Likewise, those other verbs which are syntactically in a co-ordinated (and similar) position in relation to the THINK lexemes were also semantically classified, following Pajunen (2001). Moreover, with respect to morphological variables, I chose to supplement analytic features characterizing the entire verb chain of which the THINK lexemes were components of, concerning polarity (i.e. AFFIRMATION in addition to the explicitly marked NEGATION), voice, mood, tense and person/number. Thus, if a non-finite form of the THINK lexemes is an integral part of a verb-chain, which contains constituents that are explicitly marked with respect to person-number or any of the other features normally associated only with finite verb forms, such features will be considered to apply for the non-finite THINK form, too. In addition, the six distinct person/number features (e.g. FIRST PERSON SINGULAR, FIRST PERSON PLURAL, SECOND PERSON SINGULAR, and so on) were decomposed as a matrix of three person features (FIRST VS. SECOND VS. THIRD) and two number features (SINGULAR VS. PLURAL). A representative overview of the entire range of feature categories and individual features applied in the linguistic analysis of the research corpus is presented in Table 1.

As is evident in Table 1, there were in all quite a large number of contextual variables evident with substantial frequency in the research corpus. Of these, only a subset could be included in the multivariate analysis due to recommendations concerning the ratio of explanatory variables and outcome classes (synonyms) to the number of instances in the data (cf. Harrell 2001: 60–71). Consequently, semantic subtypes were included for only the most frequent syntactic argument types, and many feature variables were also lumped together,

Table 1. Overview of the various contextual feature categories and individual features included in the linguistic analysis of the research corpus; features in (parentheses) have been excluded from some models in the multivariate statistical analyses due to their low frequency, e.g. POTENTIAL mood, or high level of association with some other feature, e.g. IMPERATIVE mood (in comparison with SECOND person) on the verb-chain general level, or a complementary or near-complementary distribution, e.g. AFFIRMATION (VS. NEGATION), also on the verb-chain general level; furthermore, some features in {brackets} have been lumped together in some models, e.g. human INDIVIDUALS and GROUPS under syntactic AGENTS are sometimes collapsed together as HUMAN referents.

Node-specific morphological features	
infinitive subtype	FIRST INFINITIVE (*-A-*), SECOND INFINITIVE (*-E-*), THIRD INFINITIVE (*-MA-*), FOURTH INFINITIVE (*-minen*)
participle subtype	FIRST PARTICIPLE (present), SECOND PARTICIPLE (past)
non-finite case	NOMINATIVE, GENITIVE, PARTITIVE, TRANSLATIVE, INESSIVE
non-finite number	SINGULAR, PLURAL
non-finite possessive suffix	THIRD PERSON SINGULAR
polarity	NEGATION
voice	ACTIVE, PASSIVE
mood	INDICATIVE, CONDITIONAL, IMPERATIVE, (POTENTIAL)
simplex tense	PRESENT, PAST
finite person-number	FIRST PERSON SINGULAR, SECOND PERSON SINGULAR, THIRD PERSON SINGULAR, FIRST PERSON PLURAL, SECOND PERSON PLURAL, THIRD PERSON PLURAL
Verb-chain general morphological features	
polarity	(AFFIRMATION), NEGATION
voice	(ACTIVE), PASSIVE
mood	INDICATIVE, CONDITIONAL, (IMPERATIVE)
person (finite+non-finite)	FIRST, SECOND, THIRD
number (finite+non-finite)	(SINGULAR), PLURAL
surface-syntax	CLAUSE-EQUIVALENT form, COVERT subject (implictly manifested agent)
Syntactic argument types	
AGENT, PATIENT, SOURCE, GOAL, MANNER, QUANTITY, LOCATION, TIME (as moment or period), DURATION, FREQUENCY, REASON+PURPOSE, CONDITION, META-ARGUMENT (clause-adverbial), NEGATIVE AUXILIARY, ADJACENT AUXILIARY, NON-ADJACENT NON-NEGATION AUXILIARY, (verb-chain-internal nominal) COMPLEMENT, (CO-ORDINATED CONJUNCTION), CO-ORDINATED VERB	
Semantic and structural subtypes of syntactic arguments and verb-chains	
AGENT	INDIVIDUAL, GROUP
PATIENT	HUMAN ← {INDIVIDUAL, GROUP}, ABSTRACTION ← {NOTION, STATE, ATTRIBUTE, TIME}, ACTIVITY, EVENT, INFINITIVE, PARTICIPLE, INDIRECT QUESTION, DIRECT QUOTE *että* ('that' subordinate clause)
MANNER	GENERIC, FRAME, POSITIVE (external evaluation), NEGATIVE, JOINT (activity), AGREEMENT
QUANTITY	MUCH, LITTLE
LOCATION	LOCATION (physical), GROUP, EVENT
TIME (as moment or period)	DEFINITE, INDEFINITE
DURATION	LONG, SHORT, OPEN, OTHER (fixed temporal reference)
FREQUENCY	OFTEN, AGAIN, OTHER ("non-often")
CO-ORDINATED VERB	MENTAL, ACTION
VERB-CHAIN (general semantic characteristics)	POSSIBILITY ← {POSSIBILITY (POSITIVE), IMPOSSIBILITY}, NECESSITY ← {NECESSITY (OBLIGATION), NONNECESSITY, FUTILITY}, EXTERNAL (cause), VOLITION, TEMPORAL, ACCIDENTAL
Extra-linguistic features	
QUOTATION (within newspaper text)	
MEDIUM: INTERNET newsgroup discussion (VS. NEWSPAPER text)	

when possible and appropriate. The entire variable selection process, building upon univariate and bivariate statistical analyses, is presented in detail in Arppe (2008). In the end, 46 linguistic contextual feature variables were chosen for the "proper" full model (VI in Table 2), of which 10 were morphological, concerning the entire verb chain, 10 simple syntactic arguments (without any semantic subtypes), 20 combinations of syntactic arguments with semantic classifications, and 6 semantic characterizations of the verb chains. This full model will be the "gold standard" (Harrell 2001: 98–99), against which we can then compare simpler models, incorporating different levels of linguistic analysis and their combinations, with varying degrees of overall complexity (i.e. Models I–V, VII–XI in Table 2). Furthermore, I am intrigued by what results might be produced with the entire variable set containing all the semantic and structural subtypes of the syntactic arguments identified in the corpus and satisfying a minimum frequency requirement ($n \geq 24$). Therefore, because the only real cost is computational, I will also try out such an extended model, even at the risk of not setting the best example in the methodological sense. This extended model (VIII), when supplemented with extra-linguistic features (Model IX), largely conforms in its size and composition to the one used in Arppe (2007).

Among various multivariate statistical methods, *polytomous logistic regression* analysis (see e.g. Hosmer and Lemeshow 2000: 260–287) appeared to be the most attractive approach. As a *direct probability model* (Harrell 2001: 217) polytomous as well as binary logistic regression yields probability estimates, corresponding to the expected proportions of occurrences, conditional on the values of the explanatory variables that have been selected for inclusion in the model. This characteristic fits well together with prior linguistic research (e.g., Featherston 2005, Bresnan et al. 2007, Arppe and Järvikivi 2007), from which we know that in practice individual features or sets of features are *not* observed in corpora to be categorically matched with the occurrence (in a corpus) of only one lexeme in some particular synonymous set, or only one constructional variant, and no others. Rather, while one lexeme in a synonymous set, or one constructional alternative among the possible variants, may be by far the most frequent for some particular context, others do also occur, albeit with often a considerably lower relative frequency. Furthermore, with respect to the weighting of individual variables in polytomous logistic regression, the parameters associated with each variable have a natural interpretation in that they reflect the increased (or decreased) *odds* of a particular outcome (i.e. lexeme) occurring, when the particular feature is present in the context (instead of being absent), with all the other explanatory variables being equal. The exact meaning of the odds varies depending on which practical heuristic has been selected, and can concern e.g. a contrast with all the rest or with some baseline category.

Table 2. Composition of the various features sets to be incorporated in the multivariate analysis models as explanatory variables.

Model index	Feature set composition	Overall number of features
I	Only node-specific morphological features	26
II	Verb-chain general morphological features (10) Node-specific features not subsumed by the verb-chain general features (17)	27
III	Syntactic argument types, *without* semantic and structural subclassifications	18
IV	Verb-chain general morphological features (10) Non-subsumed node-specific morphological features (17) Syntactic argument types (17) without their subtypes	44
V	Verb-chain general features (10) Most common semantic classifications of AGENTS and PATIENTS with their less frequent subtypes collapsed together (12) Other syntactic argument types *without* their subtypes (15)	37
VI	*"Proper" full model:* Verb-chain general morphological features (10) Semantic characterizations of verb chains (6) Syntactic argument types alone (10) Syntactic argument types with selected or collapsed subtypes (20)	46
VII	Verb-chain general morphological features (10) Semantic characterizations of verb chains (6) Syntactic argument types alone (10) Syntactic argument types with their subtypes (20) Extra-linguistic features (2)	48
VIII	*Extended full model*: Verb-chain general morphological features (10) Semantic characterizations of verb chains (9) Syntactic argument types alone (5) All subtypes of syntactic arguments exceeding minimum frequency (38)	62
IX	Verb-chain general morphological features (10) Semantic characterizations of verb chains (9) Syntactic argument types (5) All subtypes of syntactic arguments exceeding minimum frequency (38) Extra-linguistic features (2)	64
X	Extra-linguistic features alone (2)	2
XI	Semantic characterizations of verb chains (6) Syntactic argument types alone (10) Selected or collapsed subtypes of syntactic arguments (20) (*excluding* any node-specific or verb-chain general morphological features)	36

There are a number of heuristics for implementing polytomous logistic regression, which are all based on the splitting of the polytomous setting into a set of dichotomous cases, to each of which a corresponding binary logistic regression model can then be applied and fitted either simultaneously or separately. These heuristics are presented and their characteristics discussed from the linguistic perspective in Arppe (2008, see also Frank and Kramer 2004). In order to get both lexeme-specific parameters for the selected contextual features, without having to select one lexeme as a baseline category, and probability estimates for the occurrences of each lexeme, I have found the *one-vs-rest* heuristic (Rifkin and Klautau 2004) as the most appealing of the lot. This methodological choice is facilitated by the observation that its performance does not significantly differ from that of the other heuristics, at least in the case of the studied phenomenon (Arppe 2007, 2008). The necessary statistical calculations were undertaken in the public-domain *R* statistical programming environment (R Core Development Team, 2007), using both ready-made functions (specifically `glm` for binary logistic regression incorporated in *R*'s `base` package) and functions written by myself. The latter were required for implementing the one-vs-rest heuristic, as well as statistic measures for the assessment of model performance, based on Menard (1995).

3. Results

Feature-wise odds for each of the THINK lexemes are already covered at length in Arppe (2007, 2008), so I will not discuss them any further here. I will rather shift the focus to the performance of different types of Models (I–XI), with varying levels of linguistic explanatory features and analytical complexity. Both the fit of the models and their prediction efficiency were evaluated using the entire research corpus as data ($n = 3404$), the same which had been used to train the models, so the performance results should tentatively be considered somewhat optimistic. Nevertheless, validating the full model using 1000-fold simple bootstrap resampling yields only slightly lower performance figures, being mean $R^2_{\mathrm{L}} = 0.287$ with 95% Confidence Interval CI $= (0.264, 0.300)$, overall *Recall*$=$ 63.8% and 95% CI $= (63.1\%, 64.5\%)$, $\lambda_{prediction} = 0.355$ with 95% CI $= (0.343, 0.368)$, and $\tau_{classification} = 0.479$ with 95% CI $=$ $(0.468, 0.489)$ (see Arppe 2008).

Of these four measures, R^2_{L} is an indicator of how well a logistic regression model fits with the actual occurrences in the original data (Hosmer and Lemeshow 2000: 165–166). This is calculated as a comparison of the probabilities predicted by the model for each actually occurring outcome and the associated feature cluster, against the baseline probability for each outcome class, the latter which are simply the lexemes' overall proportions in the entire data. In comparison to the R^2 measure used in ordinary linear regression, R^2_{L} does *not* tell us the proportion of variation in the data that a logistic regression model succeeds in explaining, but R^2_{L} does allow us to compare the overall fit of different models with varying sets of explanatory variables on the same data. The three other measures concern efficiency in prediction (Menard 1995: 28–30). Firstly, *Recall* tells us how often overall a prediction is correct, based in the case of the one-vs-rest heuristic on a prediction rule of selecting per each context the lexeme receiving the highest probability estimate. The *Recall* measures presented here are an aggregate of the lexeme-wise *Recall* values, which in the case of the above full model are quite divergent, favoring *ajatella* with a mean *Recall* of 85.40%, in comparison to the respective values of 45.1% for *miettiä*, 49.5% for *pohtia*, and 46.0% for *harkita*. Secondly, $\lambda_{prediction}$ is a measure for the *proportionate reduction of prediction error*, which tells us how much better the model performs over the baseline strategy of always picking the most frequent outcome class (i.e. the mode, in this case *ajatella*). Thirdly, $\tau_{classification}$ is the measure for *proportionate reduction of classification error*, which on top of instance-wise prediction accuracy considers how well the model is able to replicate the overall distribution of outcome classes in the original data, in this case the relative lexeme frequencies.

As can be seen in Table 3, increasing the number of feature categories and levels in linguistic analysis quite naturally has a positive impact on how much of the occurrences of the selected THINK lexemes can be accounted for. Starting at the simplest end, node-specific morphology (Model I), and somewhat surprisingly even if supplemented with verb-chain general morphological features (Model II), as well as extra-linguistic features alone (Model X), appear to have roughly equal (and low) explanatory power both in terms of fit with the original data as well as their added value in prediction. The *Recall* levels for these three models (I: 47.15%, II: 47.71% and X: 47.21%) do not substantially rise above the proportion of the most frequent THINK lexemes, *ajatella*, in the research corpus, being $1492/3404 = 43.8\%$. This is in fact reflected in the measures concerning the reduction of prediction error with $\lambda_{prediction}$ ranging 0.059–0.060–0.059, which indicate a minimal improvement in the results over always predicting the most frequent outcome class. In contrast, the measures for the reduction of classification error with these models are already clearly higher, with $\tau_{classification}$ ranging at 0.239–0.240–0.247, but among all the models considered here these values rank nevertheless as the lowest.

Syntactic argument types alone (Model III), without any of their semantic and structural subtypes and excluding all morphological features, fare already

Table 3. The descriptive and predictive properties of the various types of Models (I–XI) with different compositions of explanatory variables, based on the single-fit training and testing of each model with the one-vs-rest heuristic on the entire data ($n = 3404$).

Model index	Recall (%)	R^2_L	$\lambda_{prediction}$	$\tau_{classification}$
I	47.15	0.094	0.059	0.239
II	47.71	0.100	0.069	0.247
III	50.18	0.098	0.113	0.282
IV	56.82	0.180	0.231	0.378
V	63.04	0.288	0.342	0.468
VI	64.60	0.313	0.370	0.490
VII	65.57	0.325	0.387	0.504
VIII	65.60	0.325	0.388	0.504
IX	65.80	0.337	0.391	0.507
X	47.21	0.057	0.060	0.240
XI	63.10	0.292	0.343	0.468

slightly better. The fit with the original data is roughly equal to that achieved with the node-specific and verb-chain general morphological features (Models I–II), and almost twice the corresponding value for extralinguistic features (Model X). As *Recall* with Model III increases to above the half-way-mark, the measures of prediction and classification error improve also accordingly, with $\lambda_{prediction}$ almost doubling in value in contrast to Models I–II and X; for $\tau_{classification}$ the absolute improvement is of a similar magnitude but lesser in relative terms. When morphological features concerning the entire verb chain and the node are combined with syntactic argument types (Model IV), the performance overall notches up noticeably. Now, the fit with the original data at $R^2_L = 0.180$ is twice that of the morphological or syntactic arguments types alone (Models I–III), and over three times the level reached with extralinguistic features (Model X). Whereas *Recall* increases moderately to only 56.82%, especially the reduction of prediction error in comparison to syntactic argument types alone (Model III) roughly doubles, and also classification error reduces considerably, with $\lambda_{prediction} = 0.231$ and $\tau_{classification} = 0.378$.

If we further supplement the morphological and syntactic argument features with the semantic and structural classifications of the two most common and important arguments in the case of the THINK lexemes, namely their AGENTS and PATIENTS (Model V), the results in terms of the descriptive fit of the model with the original data or prediction accuracy all improve again visibly. While

Recall increases to 63.04%, the other measures grow less modestly by roughly one-third, as now $R_L^2 = 0.288$, $\lambda_{prediction} = 0.342$ and $\tau_{classification} = 0.468$. In contrast, adding further the subtypes for MANNER and TIME (as a moment or period) arguments as well as the semantic classifications of verb-chains incorporated in the full Model (VI) does not continue the improvement of the performance of the models at the same rate. Now, though descriptive fit has yet grown somewhat to $R_L^2 = 0.313$, on the predictive side *Recall* has increased by only one percent to 64.6%, while the reduction of prediction error is modestly up at $\lambda_{prediction} = 0.370$ and $\tau_{classification} = 0.490$.

The most complex model with the extended semantic classifications (Model VIII, with as many as 16 more semantic subtypes of syntactic arguments in comparison to Model VI) produces but quite minute improvements, with $R_L^2 = 0.325$, *Recall* = 65.6%, $\lambda_{prediction} = 0.388$ and $\tau_{classification} = 0.504$. Thus, it would appear that we are approaching some sort of upper limit, seemingly around a level of two-thirds accuracy in prediction, as to what can be achieved with the types of quite conventional linguistic analysis features applied in this study, concerning morphology, syntax and semantics within the immediate sentential context. A similar conclusion was earlier noted in Arppe (2007) with a slightly differently selected extended variable set. Furthermore, dropping out the proper morphological verb-chain general features altogether but retaining the semantic characterizations of verb-chains and combining these with the syntactic arguments as well as those among their semantic subtypes selected for the full Model (VI), amounting to the feature set in Model XI, results in a surprisingly small drop in performance, as $R_L^2 = 0.292$ with a *Recall* = 63.1%, $\lambda_{prediction} = 0.343$ and $\tau_{classification} = 0.468$. Thus, the linguistic information coded in the morphological features, whether on the node-verb or the associated verb-chain in general, would appear to an essential extent be already incorporated in the syntactic and semantic argument structure. This is supported by the fact that the mean odds for morphological features, when incorporated into a model together with syntactic arguments and their semantic subtypes as well as overall semantic characterizations of verb-chains, are considerably smaller in comparison to those for these other feature categories (Arppe 2008).

As these results are clearly less than the performance levels achieved by Gries (2003b, *Recall* = 88.9%, canonical $R = 0.821$) and Bresnan et al. (2007, *Recall* = 92%), even if achieved in simpler dichotomous settings, one possible avenue for improvement would be to add entirely new linguistic analysis categories such as longer-distance discourse factors, as was done in these prior studies. However, the inclusion of the two extralinguistic features selected in this study, indicating the medium of usage (newspaper vs. Internet newsgroup discussion, and quoted fragments vs. body text), yield only small improvements of around one percent-unit in magnitude for the various performance measures. This is apparent for both Model VII, for which the performance measures are $R_L^2 = 0.325$, *Recall* = 65.57%, $\lambda_{prediction} = 0.387$ and $\tau_{classification} = 0.504$, as well as for Model IX, in which case the corresponding values are $R_L^2 = 0.337$, *Recall* = 65.8%, $\lambda_{prediction} = 0.391$ and $\tau_{classification} = 0.507$. These results correspond in absolute terms to 33 more correctly classified lexeme selections with Model VII in comparison to Model VI, but only 7 with Model IX in comparison to Model VIII.

Furthermore, similar, less than perfect levels of prediction accuracy (54%[1]) have been reached for the even more complex 6-way prediction of synonymous Russian TRY verbs, using the simultaneously fit multinomial heuristic with a baseline category. In this particular case, the explanatory variables have consisted of the semantic properties of their subjects and the following infinitives as well as Tense-Aspect-Mood (TAM) marking on the TRY verbs themselves (personal communications from Dagmar Divjak 4.12.2007, 16.5.2008 and 19.5.2008). This would suggest that the performance levels reached in this study would not at all be exceptionally poor or low. By contrast, Inkpen and Hirst (2006: 25–27, see also Inkpen 2004: 111–112) achieved over 90 percent accuracy in correctly selecting a synonym from several multiple-lexeme sets. This would indicate that the choices can in fact be highly precisely modeled, but this requires explanatory variables indicating 1) "nuances" such as denotational microdistinctions, 2) the speaker's intention to express some attitude, and 3) the sought-after style. These are not necessarily explicitly evident in the immediate sentential context nor easily amenable to accurate automated extraction (Edmonds and Hirst 2002: 128, cf. Hanks 1996: 90, 97).

4. Discussion

The current performance plateau may result from technical restrictions related to the application of the one-vs-rest heuristic in particular, and on the basis of the similarities in the performance of all the heuristics demonstrated in Arppe (2008), of polytomous logistic regression in general, to the more complex, multiple-outcome setting in this study. This may also result to some extent from the exclusion of interaction terms among the explanatory variables included in all the Models I–XI presented above, due to restrictions set by the size of the available data and its outcome frequencies. But this might also reflect genuine synonymy, or at least some extent of interchangeability in at least some contexts, which the current analysis variables cannot (possibly: can never) get an exact hold of (cf. Gries 2003b: 13–16). Even more radically we may interpret such (varying degrees of) interchangeability as evidence rather for inherent variability in language, following Bresnan (2007).

The underlying premises of logistic regression analysis, i.e. assuming relative proportions of occurrence rather than categorical selections, suggest that we should not focus only on the maximum probabilities assigned for each instance (which according to the classification rule for the one-vs-rest heuristic, i.e. $arg_{Lexeme}\{max[P(Lexeme|Context)]\}$, determine the lexeme predicted per each instance). Rather, we should expand our scrutiny to the entire spectrum of probabilities estimated for each outcome (i.e. *Lexeme* $\sim L$) in a particular context ($\sim C$). Indeed, as we can see in Figure 1, the maximum probability assigned (using Model VIII) for any lexeme in any context rarely approaches the theoretical maximum $P(L|C) = 1.0$, and the predictions are practically categorical in only 258 (7.6%) instances for which $P_{max}(L|C) > 0.90$. On the contrary, the mean maximum probability per all instances and contexts is only $\bar{x}(P_{max}[L|C])$ $= 0.636$, while the overall span of maximal values is as broad as (0.28, 1.00), and even the 95% *Confidence Interval* is very wide at $CI = (0.369, 0.966)$. The lower-ranked instance-wise probability estimates have similar overall characteristics of intermediate-level means and broad ranges. The second-highest probability estimates per instances have a mean $\bar{x}(P_{max-1}[L|C]) = 0.244$, with an overall range of (0.000, 0.490) and a 95% $CI = (0.026, 0.415)$, and the third-highest (i.e. second-lowest) probability estimates have a mean $\bar{x}(P_{max-2}[L|C]) = 0.096$, with an overall range of (0.000, 0.307) and a 95% $CI = (0.000, 0.241)$. Even the minimum probability estimates clearly keep some distance from zero as their mean $\bar{x}(P_{min}[L|C]) = 0.043$, even though their overall range is (0.000, 0.212) as well as 95% $CI = (0.000, 0.144)$. Nevertheless, as many as 764 (22.4%) of the minimum estimated probabilities per instance are practically nil with $P_{min}(L|C)$ < 0.01. However, turning this the other way around, for 2640 (77.6%) instances in the entire data the minimum estimated probability $P_{min}(L|C) \geq 0.01$. This latter case represents an expected possibility of occurrence at least once every hundred times or even more often in a similar context for *all four* THINK lexemes.

Looking at the instance-wise estimated probabilities as a whole, in 64 (1.9%) instances all four estimates are $P(L|C) \geq 0.15$, indicating relatively equal values for all lexemes, and in 331 (9.7%) instances all four are $P(L|C) \geq 0.10$. Discarding always the minimum value, in 303 (8.9%) cases the remaining three higher-ranked probability estimates are all $P(L|C) \geq 0.2$, and in as many as 1436 (42.2%) cases $P(L|C) \geq 0.10$. Narrowing our focus only to the two topmost-ranked lexemes per instance, in 961 (26.2%) cases both probability estimates are $P(L|C) \geq 0.3$, and for as many as 150 (4.4%) cases both $P(L|C) \geq 0.4$. The contextual settings associated with these last-mentioned instances would be prime candidates for fully or partially synonymous usage within the selected

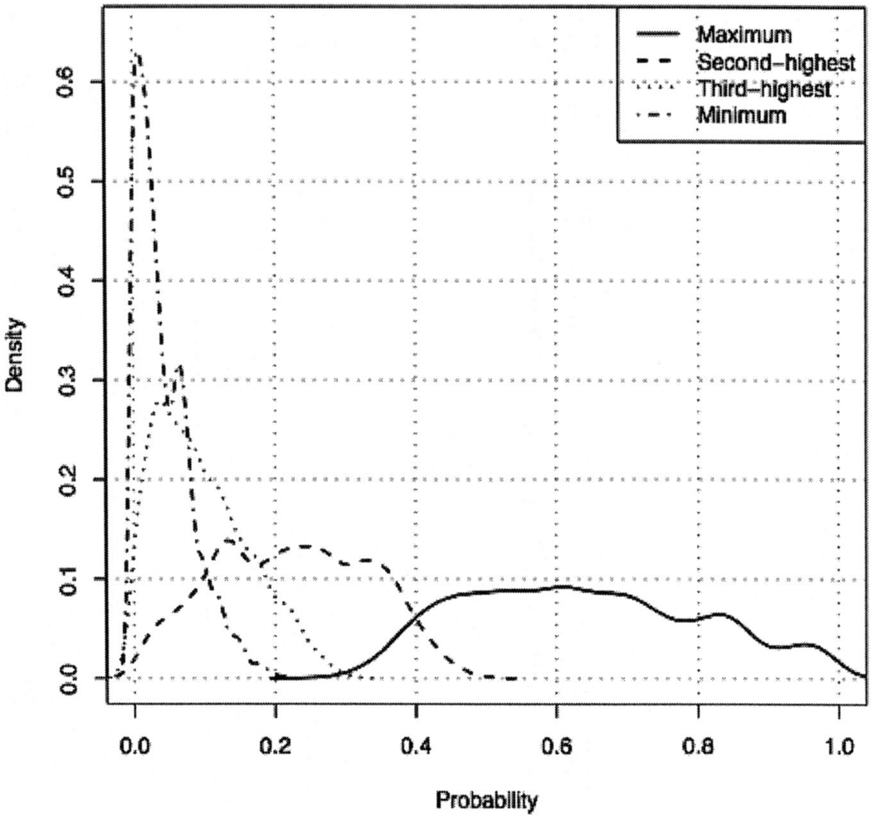

Figure 1. Densities of the distributions of the estimated probabilities by rank order for all instances in the data ($n = 3404$).

set of THINK lexemes, as their joint probabilities would indicate high mutual interchangeability. In sum, these distributions of instance-wise probability estimates for all four THINK lexemes suggest that, to the extent these probabilities even approximately represent the proportions of actual occurrences in given contexts, very few combinations of contextual features are associated with categorical, exception-less outcomes. On the contrary, quite a few of the contexts can realistically have two or even more outcomes, though preferential differences among the lexemes remain to varying extents (cf. Hanks 1996: 79). Lastly, let us assume for the sake of argument that a theory about language consists simply of two parts: 1) the fundamental components of which language is considered to consist and with which language can be comprehensively analyzed, and 2) the rules or regularities concerning how these components interact and are allowed to combine into sequences. If we accept that the contextual features used in this study are good and satisfactory representatives of a theory of language, these results certainly support Bresnan's (2007) probabilistic view of the relationship between language usage and the underlying linguistic system.

Zooming in on individual sentences in the research corpus (Table 3), we can observe various scenarios of how the entire estimated probability space (with $\sum P[L|C] = 1.0$) can be distributed among the THINK lexemes on the basis of the selected features manifested in each context. Firstly, the probability distribution may approach categorical, exception-less choice, so that only one of the lexemes is assigned in practice the maximum possible probability $P(L|C) \approx 1.0$, while the rest receive none (exemplified by sentence #1 in Table 3). However, such a scenario applies to as few as 7.6% of the sentences in the research corpus. Secondly, selectional situations for some contexts may inherently incorporate variation so that one lexeme is clearly preferred in such circumstances, receiving the highest probability, but one or more of the others may also have a real though more occasional chance of occurring to a varying degree (e.g. sentence #2 in Table 3). This can also be observed to result (as a logical consequence of the premises of logistic regression modeling) in individual instances of actual usage for which the originally selected lexeme is not the one which has been assigned the highest probability estimate (e.g. sentence #3 in Table 3). Lastly, we can observe cases in which all four lexemes are estimated to have approximately equal probability with respect to the observable context (e.g. sentence #4 in Table 3). Such instances with close-to-equal estimated probabilities of occurrences could be considered as candidate examples of "genuine" synonymy and full interchangeability in context for the entire selected set of four THINK lexemes. These quite sensible scenarios, identified on the basis of manual inspection of the original data, can in fact be verified by applying statistical techniques such as hierarchical agglomerative clustering (HAC) to systematically arrange and group the entire set of lexeme-wise probability distribution estimates available for all instances ($n = 3404$) in the data (Arppe 2008).

Scrutinizing the actual linguistic contexts in the example sentences in Table 3 with at least some degree of dispersion among the lexeme-wise probability estimates (i.e. #2, #3, and #4, as well as similar cases in the entire research corpus, see Arppe 2008), I find it difficult to identify any additional contextual features or essentially new feature categories, which would allow us to distinguish among the lexemes or select one over the rest. Here, I restrict my consideration to features which pertain to current, conventional models of morphology, syntax and semantics, and which concern the immediate sentential context. Rather, it seems that the semantic differences between using any of the THINK lexemes in these

Table 4. A small selection of sentences from the research corpus with varying distributions of estimated probabilities for the four THINK lexemes; maximum probability in boldface (e.g. **0.5**); probability assigned to actually occurring lexeme under-lined (e.g. $\underline{0.5}$); pertinent feature variables as subscripts next to the appropriate word (or head in the case of a phrase/clause)

#/(Features)	Sentence
#1(7) $P(ajatella \| Context_1)=\underline{\mathbf{1}}$ $P(miettiä \| Context_1)=0$ $P(pohtia \| Context_1)=0$ $P(harkita \| Context_1)=0$	*Miten*$_{\text{MANNER+GENERIC}}$ ***ajattelit***$_{\text{INDICATIVE+SECOND, COVERT, AGENT+INDIVIDUAL}}$ *erota*$_{\text{PATIENT+INFINITIVE}}$ *mitenkään jostain SAKn umpimielisistä luokka-ajattelun kannattajasta?* [3066/politiikka_9967] 'How did you **think** to differ at all from some dense supporter of class-thinking in SAK?'
#2 (7) $P(ajatella \| Context_2)=0.018$ $P(miettiä \| Context_2)=\underline{\mathbf{0.878}}$ $P(pohtia \| Context_2)=0084$ $P(harkita \| Context_2)=0.020$	*Vilkaise*$_{\text{CO-ORDINATED\_VERB(+MENTAL)}}$ *joskus*$_{\text{FREQUENCY(+SOMETIMES)}}$ *valtuuston esityslistaa ja* ***mieti***$_{\text{(IMPERATIVE+)SECOND, COVERT, AGENT+INDIVIDUAL}}$ *monestako*$_{\text{PATIENT+INDIRECT\_QUESTION}}$ *asiasta sinulla on jotain tietoa.* [2815/politiikka_728] 'Glance sometimes at the agenda for the council and **think** on how many issues you have some information.'
#3 (8) $P(ajatella \| Context_3)=0.025$ $P(miettiä \| Context_3)=0.125$ $P(pohtia \| Context_3)=\underline{0.125}$ $P(harkita \| Context_3)=\mathbf{0.725}$	*Tarkastusviraston mielestä*$_{\text{META}}$ *tätä ehdotusta*$_{\text{PATIENT+ACTIVITY}}$ *olisi*$_{\text{CONDITIONAL+THIRD,COVERT}}$ *syytä*$_{\text{VERB\_CHAIN+NECESSITY}}$ ***pohtia*** *tarkemmin*$_{\text{MANNER+POSITIVE}}$. [766/hs95_7542] 'In the opinion of the Revision Office there is reason to **ponder** this proposal more thoroughly.'
#4 (8) $P(ajatella \| Context_4)=\underline{\mathbf{0.301}}$ $P(miettiä \| Context_4)=0.272$ $P(pohtia \| Context_4)=0.215$ $P(harkita \| Context_4)=0.212$	*Aluksi harvemmin, mutta myöhemmin tyttö alkoi viettää öitä T:n luona ja vuoden tapailun päätteeksi P*$_{\text{AGENT+INDIVIDUAL}}$ *sanoi, että voisi*$_{\text{CONDITIONAL+THIRD, VERB-CHAIN+POSSIBILITY, COVERT}}$ ***ajatella*** *asiaa*$_{\text{PATIENT+ABSTRACTION(<NOTION)}}$ *vakavamminkin*$_{\text{MANNER+POSITIVE}}$. *(SFNET)* [50/ihmissuhteet_8319] '... P said that [she] could **think** about the matter more seriously [perhaps]'

example sentences are embedded and manifested in the lexemes themselves. Moreover, these distinctions would appear to be of the kind that do not and would not necessarily have or require an explicit manifestation in the surrounding context and argument structure. That is, the selection of any one of the THINK lexemes in these sentences each emphasizes some possible, though slightly distinct aspect or manner of THINKing. Nonetheless, all such aspects could be mostly fully conceivable and acceptable as far as concerns the constraints set by the surrounding linguistic structure. In this, the relevant discriminatory selective characteristics would concern features outside the traditional linguistic domain, i.e. expressed attitude, emotion and style. These correspond to the "nuances" which Inkpen and Hirst (2006: 1–4) have found accurate in reduplicating which of the various near-synonymous alternative lexemes (with the tested sets comprising more than two synonyms) have actually been used (Inkpen and Hirst 2006: 26–27). Such shades of meaning, which could be considered to incorporate the implications and presuppositions discussed by Hanks (1996), cannot in the most cases be resolved on the basis of the immediate sentence context alone. However, they might be deduced from prior passages in the same text from which the particular sentence is taken, or from previous related texts in the same discussion thread, or on the basis of extra-linguistic knowledge about the context or even concerning the participant persons in the linguistic exchange (cf. Hanks 1996: 90, 97).

5. Conclusions

In conclusion, the observed general upper limit to *Recall* in prediction, at approximately two-thirds, or 64.6–65.6% to be exact, of the instances in the research corpus, as well as an in-depth scrutiny of the sentences with lexemewise dispersion among the estimates of probability, can be viewed to represent the explanatory limits of linguistic analysis which can be reached within the immediate sentential context and applying the conventional descriptive and analytical apparatus based on currently available linguistic theories and models (cf. Gries 2003b: 13–16). Looking from the other angle of the estimated probabilities for lexical outcomes, given a set of contextual features, the results indicate that there exists for the most part substantial and tangible variation with respect to which lexemes can actually occur in the close-to-same contexts. In fact, for 77.6% of the sentences in the research corpus the estimated expected probabilities are for all four lexemes at least $P(Lexeme|Context) > 0.01$. The closer inspection of not only sentences with roughly equal estimates of probability for all four lexemes but also those with non-categorical preferences for one or two of the lexemes would suggest that such variation in context is both common and acceptable. Furthermore, it seems that any distinctive features there may be are not explicitly evident in the immediate sentential context, but rather pertain to stylistic attitudes and intended shades of expression that the speaker/writer writer wishes to convey (belonging to the intermediate stylistic/subconceptual level in the clustered model of lexical choice by Edmonds and Hirst 2002). More generally, these results support a probabilistic notion of the relationship between linguistic usage and the underlying linguistic system, akin to that presented by Bresnan (2007). Few choices are categorical, given the known context (feature cluster) that can be analytically grasped and identified. Rather, most contexts exhibit various degrees of variation as to their outcomes, resulting in proportionate choices on the long run. Nevertheless, these results should be corroborated with other types of linguistic evidence, for instance experimentation, such as e.g. Bresnan (2007) and Gries (2003b) have done.

Acknowledgements. I am grateful for insightful comments and feedback provided to me by Martti Vainio, Lauri Carlson, Dagmar Divjak and Simo Vihjanen with respect to the interpretation of the results, though the burden of accurate representation of all matters in this paper rests solely on myself.

Notes

1. In the validation of this model, the jack-knife estimate was 50.8%. Furthermore, splitting 100 times randomly the entire data sample of 1351 instances into training sets of 1000 instances and testing sets with the remaining 351 instances yielded a mean correct classification rate of 49%, with a standard deviation of 2.45% (Personal communication from Dagmar Divjak 16.5.2008).

Corpora

Helsingin Sanomat

1995 ~22 million words of Finnish newspaper articles published in Helsingin Sanomat during January–December 1995. Compiled by the Research Institute for the Languages of Finland [KOTUS] and CSC – Center for Scientific Computing, Finland. Available on-line at URL: http://www.csc.fi/kielipankki/

SFNET

2002–2003 ~100 million words of Finnish internet newsgroup discussion posted during October 2002–April 2003. Compiled by Tuuli Tuominen and Panu Kalliokoski, Computing Centre, University of Helsinki, and Antti Arppe, Department of General Linguistics, University of Helsinki, and CSC – Center for Scientific Computing, Finland. Available on-line at URL: http://www.csc.fi/kielipankki/

References

Arppe, Antti

2002 The usage patterns and selectional preferences of synonyms in a morphologically rich language. In: Morin, Annie and Pascale Sébillot (eds.), *JADT-2002. 6th International Conference on Textual Data Statistical Analysis*, 13–15.3.2002, Vol. 1, 21–32. Rennes: INRIA.

2006 Complex phenomena deserve complex explanations. *Quantitative Investigations in Theoretical Linguistics* (QITL2) Conference, Osnabrück, Germany, 1–2.6.2006, 8–11. Available on-line at URL: http://www.cogsci.uni-osnabrueck.de/~qitl/

2007 Multivariate methods in corpus-based lexicography. A study of synonymy in Finnish. In: Davies, Matthew, Paul Rayson, Susan Hunston, and Pernilla Danielsson (eds.), *Proceedings from the Corpus Linguistics Conference (CL2007)*, July 28–30, 2007, Birmingham, UK. Available on-line at: URL: http://www.corpus.bham.ac.uk/corplingproceedings07/

2008 Univariate, bivariate and multivariate methods in corpus-based lexicography – a study of synonymy. PhD Dissertation. Publications of the Department of General Linguistics, University of Helsinki, No. 44. URN: http://urn.fi/URN:ISBN:978-952-10-5175-3.

Arppe, Antti and Juhani Järvikivi

2007 Every method counts – Combining corpus-based and experimental evidence in the study of synonymy. *Corpus Linguistics and Linguistic Theory* 3 (2): 131–159.

Atkins, Beryl T. S. and Beth Levin

1995 Building on a Corpus: A linguistic and lexicographical look at some near-synonyms. *International Journal of Lexicography* 8 (2): 85–114.

Bresnan, Joan

2007 Is syntactic knowledge probabilistic? Experiments with the English dative alternation. In: Featherston, Sam and Wolfgang Sternefeld (eds.), *Roots: Linguistics in search of its evidential base*. Series: Studies in Generative Grammar 96. Berlin: Mouton de Gruyter.

Bresnan, Joan, Anna Cueni, Tatiana Nikitina and R. Harald Baayen

2007 Predicting the Dative Alternation. In: Boume, G., Kraemer, I. and J. Zwarts (eds.), *Cognitive Foundations of Interpretation*, 69–94. Amsterdam: Royal Netherlands Academy of Science.

Biber, Douglas, Susan Conrad and Randi Reppen

1998 *Corpus Linguistics: Investigating Language Structure and Use*. Cambridge: Cambridge University Press.

Church, Kenneth, William Gale, Patrick Hanks and Douglas Hindle
1991 Using Statistics in Lexical Analysis. In: Zernik, Uri (ed.), *Lexical Acquisition: Exploiting On-Line Resources to Build a Lexicon*, 115–164. Hillsdale: Lawrence Erlbaum Associates.

Connexor
2007 List of morphological, surface-syntactic and functional syntactic features used in the linguistic analysis. [Web documentation] URL: http://www.connexor.com/demo/doc/fifdg3-tags.html (visited 29.5.2007) and URL: http://www.connexor.com/demo/doc/enfdg3-tags.html (visited 5.6.2007).

Divjak, Dagmar
2006 Ways on Intending. Delineating and Structuring Near-Synonyms. In: Gries, Stefan Th. and Anatol Stefanowitsch (eds.), *Corpora in cognitive linguistics*. Vol. 2: The syntax-lexis interface, 19–56. Berlin: Mouton De Gruyter.

Divjak, Dagmar and Stefan Th. Gries
2006 Ways of trying in Russian: Clustering and comparing behavioral profiles. *Corpus Linguistics and Linguistic Theory* 2 (1): 23–60.
2008 Clusters in the mind? Converging evidence from near-synonymy in Russian. *The Mental Lexicon* 3 (2): 188–213.

Edmonds, Philip and Graeme Hirst
2002 Near-synonymy and Lexical Choice. *Computational Linguistics* 28 (2): 105–144.

Featherston, Sam
2005 The Decathlon Model. In: Kepser and Reis (eds.), *Linguistic Evidence. Empirical, Theoretical and Computational Perspectives*, 187–208. (Studies in Generative Grammar 85.) Berlin/New York: Mouton de Gruyter.

Flint, Aili
1980 *Semantic Structure in the Finnish Lexicon: Verbs of Possibility and Sufficiency.* (SKST 360.) Helsinki: Suomalaisen Kirjallisuuden Seura.

Frank, Eibe and Stefan Kramer
2004 Ensembles of Nested Dichotomies for Multi-Class Problemes. *Proceedings of the 21st International Conference on Machine Learning*, Banff, Canada.

Gries, Stefan Th.
2003a *Multifactorial analysis in corpus linguistics: a study of particle placement*. London: Continuum.
2003b Towards a corpus-based identification of prototypical instances of constructions. *Annual Review of Cognitive Linguistics*, Vol. 1, 1–27

Hanks, Patrick
1996 Contextual Dependency and Lexical Sets. *International Journal of Corpus Linguistics*, 1 (1): 75–98.

Harrell, Frank E.
2001 *Regression Modeling Strategies. With Applications to Linear Models, Logistic Regression and Survival Analysis.* New York: Springer-Verlag.

Hosmer, David W., Jr., and Stanley Lemeshow
2000 *Applied Regression Analysis* (2nd edition). New York: Wiley.

Inkpen, Diana
2004 Building a Lexical Knowledge-Base of Near-Synonym Differences. Ph. D. dissertation, Department of Computer Science, University of Toronto.

Inkpen, Diana and Graeme Hirst
2006 Building and Using a Lexical Knowledge-Base of Near-Synonym Differences. *Computational Linguistics* 32 (2): 223–262.

Jantunen, Jarmo H.
2001 Tärkeä seikka ja keskeinen kysymys. Mitä korpuslingvistinen analyysi paljastaa lähisynonyymeistä? [Important point and central question. What can corpus-linguistic analysis reveal about near-synonyms] *Virittäjä* 105 (2): 170–192.
2004 *Synonymia ja käännössuomi: korpusnäkökulma samamerkityksisyyden kontekstuaalisuuteen ja käännöskielen leksikaalisiin erityispiirteisiin* [Synonymy in translated Finnish. A corpus-based view of contextuality of synonymous expressions and lexical features specific to translated languages]. Ph. D. dissertation. (University of Joensuu Publications in the Humanities 35). Joensuu: University of Joensuu.

Järvinen, Timo and Pasi Tapanainen
1997 *A Dependency Parser for English.* TR-1, Technical Reports of the Department of General Linguistics, University of Helsinki.

Kangasniemi, Heikki
1992 *Modal Expressions in Finnish.* (Studia Fennica, Linguistica 2.) Helsinki: Suomalaisen Kirjallisuuden Seura.

Menard, Scott
1995 Applied Logistic Regression Analysis. (Sage University Paper Series on Quantitative Applications in the Social Sciences 07-106.) Thousand Oaks: Sage Publications.

Miller, George A.
1990 Nouns in WordNet: a lexical inheritance system. (revised August 1993). *International Journal of Lexicography*, 3 (4): 245–264. Available on-line at: ftp://ftp.cogsci.princeton.edu/pub/wordnet/5papers.ps

Pajunen, Anneli
2001 *Argumenttirakenne: Asiaintilojen luokitus ja verbien käyttäytyminen suomen kielessä* [Argument structure: the classification of states-of-affairs and the behavior of verbs in Finnish]. (Suomi 187.) Helsinki: Suomalaisen Kirjallisuuden Seura.

R Development Core Team.
2007 *R: A language and environment for statistical computing*. Vienna: R Foundation for Statistical Computing. ISBN 3-900051-07-0, URL: http://www.R-project.org.

Rifkin, Ryan and Aldebaro Krakatau
2004 In Defense of One-Vs-All Classification. *Journal of Machine Learning Research*, 5 (January): 101–141.

Tapanainen, Pasi and Timo Järvinen
1997 A non-projective dependency parser. In: *Proceedings of the 5th Conference on Applied Natural Language Processing*, Washington, D.C., April 1997, Association of Computational Linguistics, 64–71.

Yang, Charles
2008 The great number crunch. *Journal of Linguistics* 44: 205–228.

How to provide exactly one interpretation for every sentence, or what eye movements reveal about quantifier scope

Oliver Bott and Janina Radó

1. Introduction

A sentence with two quantifiers is potentially scope-ambiguous: the second quantifier may take narrow or wide scope with respect to the first one. Whether both interpretations are discernible, though, depends on factors like the type of the quantifier, its syntactic function, and word order. For instance, *all* tends not to take wide scope. When it appears in the object position, following a subject quantifier, the only perceived reading may be the one corresponding to the linear order of the quantifiers, as in (1a)

(1) a. *Some airline serves all continents.*
  b. *Some airline serves each continent.*

However, replacing *all* with *each* as in (1b) makes a second, inverse scope reading available as well. This is because *each*, which is distributive, demands wide scope.

If our primary interest is to determine what factors influence quantifier scope and how strong these factors are, it may be sufficient to examine the relative preference among the readings of a multiply-quantified sentence. In some cases, though, it is also important to find out how we arrive at those readings. Is a quantified expression interpreted immediately? If it is then we expect the computation of relative scope to begin as soon as the second quantifier is encountered. Alternatively, the interpretation of quantifiers could be delayed until some interpretation domain (e.g. the clause) has been processed completely.

Although both the process of quantifier interpretation and the final preference are highly relevant for semantic and psycholinguistic theories of quantifiers, existing studies examine these questions separately. The offline measures that are used to establish the preferred reading cannot assess when and how the reported reading was computed. The time course of interpretation is investigated in online experiments, typically using reading time measures. These experiments are supposed to reveal whether there is initial commitment to one reading;

if this is the case then a continuation incompatible with that reading should cause measurable difficulty in processing. For this method it is thus necessary to disambiguate the sentences towards one or the other scope interpretation and compare the reading times at the point of disambiguation. A frequently used disambiguation method is shown in (2).

(2) *Every child climbed a tree.*
   a. *The tree was full of apples.*
   b. *The trees were full of apples.*

We have argued elsewhere (Bott and Radó 2007) that this type of disambiguation is not sufficient: The singular continuation in (2a), which is intended to only allow the wide-scope existential reading (all children climbed one and the same tree) is compatible with the wide-scope universal reading as well, roughly as "the tree that the child climbed". What this means is that the reading times for (2a) may include both scope interpretations, or possibly an underspecified representation. Thus a different method of disambiguation is necessary to be able to interpret the results. However, there is also a more general problem with this type of online experiment, namely a possible distortion of the preferences on earlier, ambiguous parts of the sentence. If the disambiguation is successful, we can't tell anymore how big the preference for one reading had been – the indication of difficulty only shows which reading was preferred at the point where the disambiguating material was encountered.

Thus online and offline results contribute different aspects to the picture of quantifier scope interpretation, but the pieces cannot be fitted together easily. Even if the same set of materials is tested both in an offline questionnaire and in a reading-time experiment, it is still not possible to map a set of reading times for a given item to the reported readings for that item. This is a problem not only for psycholinguistic theories but also for semantic analyses of scope: it seems that the only thing we can test is whether the predicted reading is in fact the preferred one – we cannot measure or compare the size of preference in different constructions.

In this paper we propose a method to overcome this problem. We describe a way of measuring reading times and determining the final interpretation without imposing a particular interpretation on the subjects. That way we should be able to tell both which reading is preferred, and when readers converge on that reading. The method we will present here is a version of the visual world paradigm (Tanenhaus et al. 1995). Participants read scope-ambiguous sentences of the sort given in (3)[1]:

(3) a. *Genau ein Tier auf jedem Bild sollst du nennen!*
exactly one animal on each picture should you name
'Name an animal in each field.'

b. *Genau ein Tier auf allen Bildern sollst du nennen!*
exactly one animal on all pictures should you name
'Name an animal in all fields.'

They inspect computer displays in order to provide an answer. The displays are constructed in such a way as to be compatible both with a wide-scope universal and a wide-scope existential reading of the sentence. Eye movements monitored during reading reveal whether there is any difference in the way the constructions with *all* vs. *each* are interpreted; the final answer participants provide shows which interpretation they chose.

2. Experiment

2.1. Inverse linking

The experiment we report here was conducted in German. We tested sentences like (3) above, which exemplify the phenomenon called inverse linking. In inverse linking constructions the quantifier embedded in a PP inside an NP prefers to take wide scope (May and Bale 2006). In our examples this corresponds to a highly salient wide-scope universal interpretation.

This construction was chosen for two reasons: first, the influence of certain scope factors such as distributivity is well-documented in subject-object and double-object configurations (cf. Kurtzman and MacDonald 1993, Tunstall 1998, Filik, Paterson, and Liversedge 2004, for German see Pafel 2005, Bott and Radó 2007), but it has not been investigated in inverse linking constructions. Second, in this construction both quantifiers are contained in an NP preceding the verb. This makes it possible to separate the "pure" effect of the quantifiers from the influence of syntactic position or thematic roles.

2.2. Design

The ambiguous experimental conditions always involved a sentence-initial NP consisting of an existential quantifier and a PP containing a universal quantifier. *Genau ein* (*exactly one*) was chosen as existential quantifier to exclude the possibility of a non-quantificational reading. We compared two types of universal

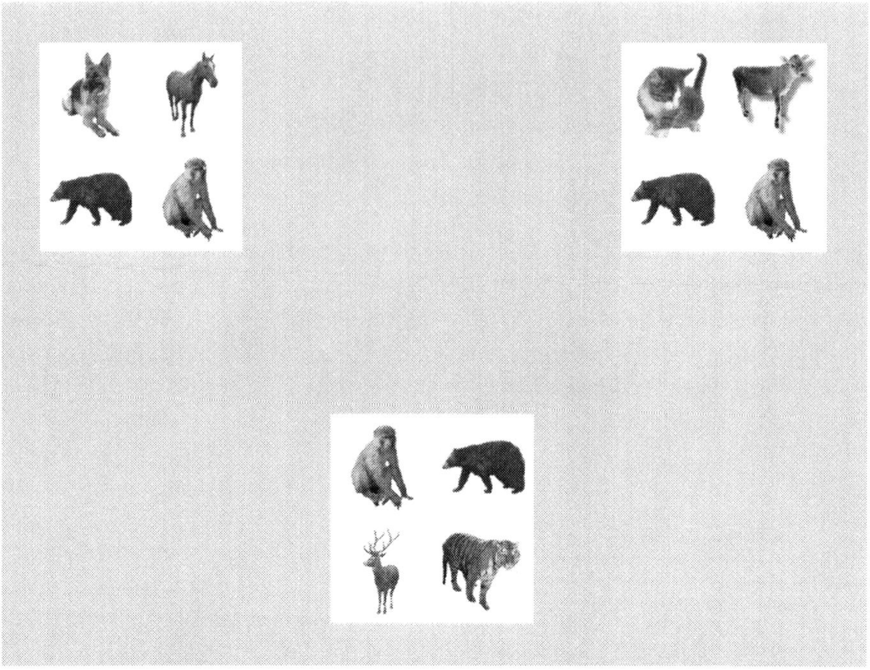

Figure 1. Sample picture used with scope-ambiguous sentences and Control B

quantifiers: *jeder* (*each*) and *alle* (*all*) (cf. (3)). *Jeder* is distributive and has a strong tendency to take wide scope, which should make the inverse scope reading even more salient in (3a). *Alle*, on the other hand, prefers narrow scope, which is expected to conflict with the inverse-scope preference inherent in the construction.

The sentences were paired with displays consisting of three fields with four pictures each (cf. Figure 1). The wide-scope existential interpretation of (3) requires a particular animal in every field. There were two animals in the display (viz. the bear and the monkey) that satisfied this requirement, to make the use of *genau ein* (*exactly one*) felicitous as well[2]. The other two pictures in a field were also animals, but different ones across fields. Thus for a wide-scope universal interpretation subjects could name the dog in field 1, the bear in 2, and the tiger in 3, for instance.

In addition to the ambiguous quantifier conditions we also included two types of control conditions. Control B consisted of unambiguous sentences containing two quantifiers, such as those in (4).

(4) Control B:

a. *Von jedem Bild sollst du irgendein Tier nennen!*
of each picture should you some animal name
'From each field name an animal.'

b. *Ein Tier, das sich auf allen Bildern befindet, sollst du nennen!*
an animal that self in all pictures locates should you name
'Name an animal that is to be found in all fields.'

These constructions used similar quantifiers (∀ and ∃) as the ambiguous quantifier conditions in (3). However, the particular syntactic configuration only allows a linear scope reading. The sentences in Control B were paired with the same displays as the items in (3). Their purpose was to check whether subjects do indeed compute the necessary reading.

Another set of control conditions (Control A) was needed in order to interpret the reading times on the doubly-quantified sentences. In Control A the existential quantifier was replaced with a definite NP. Definite NPs are typically considered non-quantificational (e.g. Strawson 1950, Heim 1991, Glanzberg forthcoming, but see Russell 1905, Neale 1990), thus we did not expect any scope interaction with the universal quantifier in these conditions. That means that any reading time difference between (5a) and (5b) must reflect pure lexical differences between *jeder* and *alle*, which must be taken into account in comparing (3a) and (3b). At the same time the answers provided to (5a) and (5b) may be informative concerning the debate about the status of definite NPs (see the references above).

(5) Control A

a. *Das Tier auf jedem Bild sollst du nennen!*
the animal on each picture should you name
'Name the animal in each field.'

b. *Das Tier auf allen Bildern sollst du nennen!*
the animal on all pictures should you name
'Name the animal in all fields.'

To satisfy the uniqueness presupposition introduced by the definite NP, the displays that appeared with Control A only included one picture corresponding to the NP in the sentence. This picture (in this case, the deer) was the same in all three fields. All other pictures belonged to a different category (cf. Figure 2).

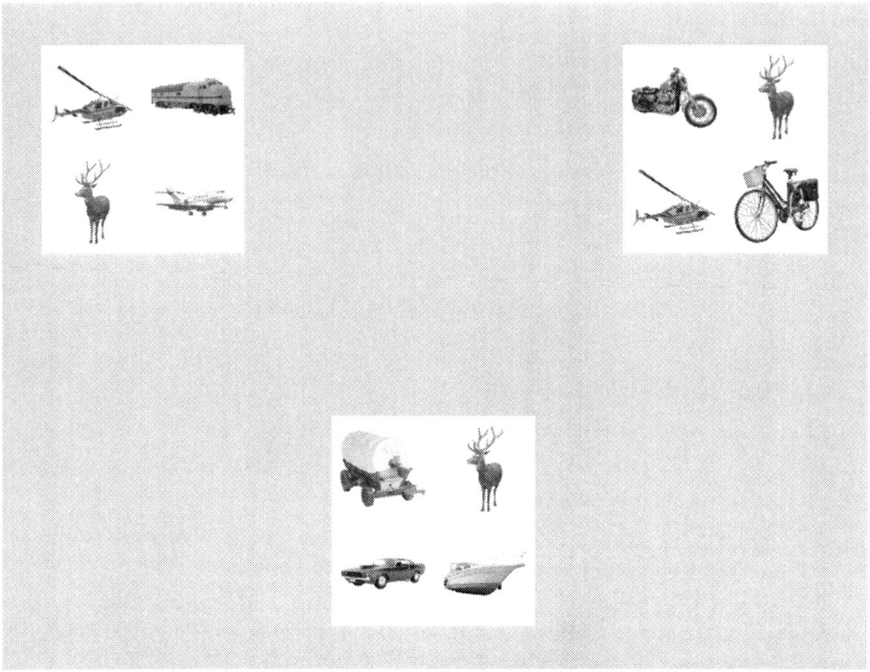

Figure 2. Sample picture used with Control A

To summarize, the sentence materials included the following six conditions:

(6) a. *two quantifiers, 'each', ambiguous*
b. *two quantifiers, 'all', ambiguous*
c. *definite NP, 'each'*
d. *definite NP, 'all'*
e. *Control B: ∀∃ only*
f. *Control B: ∃∀ only*

An experimental trial consisted of the subject reading a sentence, then inspecting the corresponding display, and finally providing an answer. We expected condition (6a) to be easy to process since the inverse scope bias that is inherent in the inverse-linking construction fits well with *jeder*'s need to take wide scope. Further, the resulting wide-scope universal interpretation should be reflected in a large proportion of wide-scope universal responses. In (6b), however, there should be a conflict between the inverse scope imposed by the construction, and *alle*'s resistance to take wide scope. This should lead to processing difficulty at the point where the conflict becomes apparent (presumably at the second quantifier). Moreover, at least in some cases the conflict should be resolved in favor of the linear scope reading, thus a greater proportion of wide-scope existential responses is expected than in (6a).

2.3. Materials and subjects

72 items were written in six conditions each. Each item was paired with two displays: one used with the quantifier conditions and with Control B, the other used with Control A. The displays prepared for half of the items included pictures (photographs or drawings), the other half consisted of words (e.g. names), letters, or numbers. In addition, 70 fillers were constructed. They included other numerals (*two* or *three*) or other quantifiers (*both cars*, *only one animal*) instead of *exactly one*, or other kinds of displays.

Six presentation lists were created according to a Latin square design. Two pseudo-random orders were generated, making sure that adjacent experimental items belonged to different conditions. A filler was inserted between any two items. The same pseudo-random orders were used in all presentation lists. Twelve subjects were tested with the first order and eighteen with the second.

Thirty subjects participated in the experiment for a payment of 10 euros. They were all native German speakers and had normal or corrected vision. Eight additional participants had to be excluded from the analysis due to calibration problems (N = 3) or error rates higher than 20% (N = 5).

2.4. Apparatus

A tower-mounted Eyelink 1000 eyetracker monitored the gaze location of participants' right eyes. The eyetracker has a spatial resolution of 0.01 degrees of visual angle and samples gaze location every millisecond. Participants viewed the stimuli binocularly on a 19 inch monitor 70 cm from their eyes. A head rest minimized head movements. The experiment was implemented using the SR Research Experiment Builder software and eyetracking data were exported with the SR Research Data Viewer.

2.5. Procedure

Subjects were tested individually. The tracker was calibrated using a 3x3 grid guaranteeing that all fixations were less than 0.5 degrees apart from the calibration stimuli. After calibration was completed, participants read the experimental instructions on the screen. This was followed by a practice session of 10 items. In the experiment, each trial started with a calibration check. The tracker was recalibrated as necessary. Eye movements were recorded both during reading and while inspecting the displays. The displays were presented in a way that it was impossible for the participants to inspect the whole screen at once. To get information about what's in a field, they had to fixate on it.

Figure 3 summarizes subsequent steps in a trial. The trial began with the presentation of a screen which served as calibration check with a little black dot in the position where the center of the first word would appear. If no fixation was registered within five seconds, recalibration was enforced. Otherwise a sentence appeared in the center of a white screen. It was printed in black letters with 14 point font size. Four characters corresponded approximately to one degree of visual angle. After reading the sentence participants had to move their eyes to an asterisk in the lower right corner. Fixating the asterisk triggered the presentation of a black screen with a white fixation cross which appeared in central position for 250 ms. This was done to guarantee that subjects were looking at the center of the screen when the display appeared. Then the display was presented and

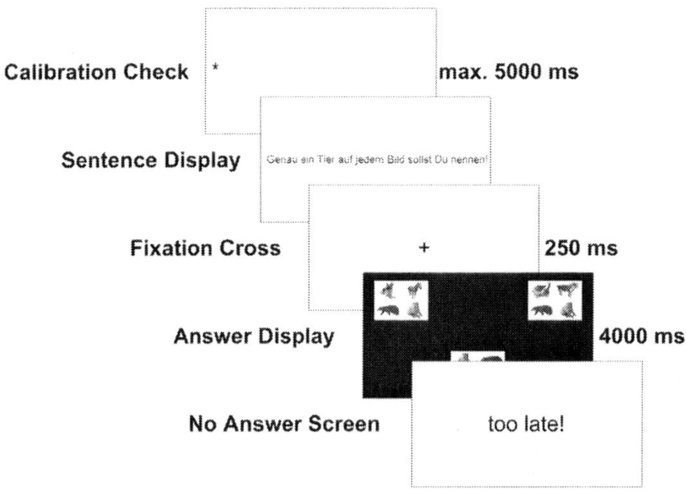

Figure 3. A sample trial in the experiment

the timer was started. Answers had to be provided orally within four seconds, measured with a voice key. If the participant started answering within the time limit the display remained visible until the end of the trial. If no answer was provided the trial was automatically aborted and a 'too late' message appeared on the screen. Participants started the next trial by pressing a button on a joy-pad.

The answers that the subject provided were recorded by the experimenter on a prepared score sheet. They were categorized as corresponding to the wide-scope existential reading, the wide-scope universal reading, or neither. The experiment lasted 35–60 minutes.

2.6. Results

Comprehension rates were high. On the filler trials, participants provided a correct answer 92.7% (SD 26.0) of the time. All participants scored higher than 80%.

2.6.1. Scope interpretation

The chosen scope interpretation was determined on the basis of the inspection-answer pattern. A trial was categorized as having received a wide-scope existential reading if the participant inspected all three fields and provided a single answer. The reading was coded wide-scope universal if the subject responded field-by-field, that is, provided a multiple answer that started before all fields had been inspected. This coding procedure can be applied to scope-ambiguous sentences and the unambiguous sentences in Control B as well as to the definite descriptions in Control A. According to these criteria, 18% of all cases couldn't be categorized and were excluded from the analysis.

Figure 4 shows the percentage of wide-scope universal readings in all six conditions. In Control B the reported readings matched the scope of the disambiguated sentences. The ∀∃-condition received 97.2% wide-scope universal interpretations, the ∃∀-condition 2.2% wide-scope universal interpretations.

The scope data of the ambiguous conditions and the definite descriptions in Control A were subjected to 2 × 2 repeated measures analyses of variance (ANOVAs) with the within factors NP-type (quantifier vs. definite NP) and distributivity (*all* vs. *each*) using participants (F_1) and items (F_2) as random factors[3].

In the scope-ambiguous quantifier sentences, the proportions of wide-scope universal readings differed between *each* and *all*. The ∀∃ interpretation was more preferred for *each* (83.4%) than for *all* (59.6%). One sample t-tests (one tailed) revealed that the latter was significantly above 50% ($t_1(29) = 1.70$;

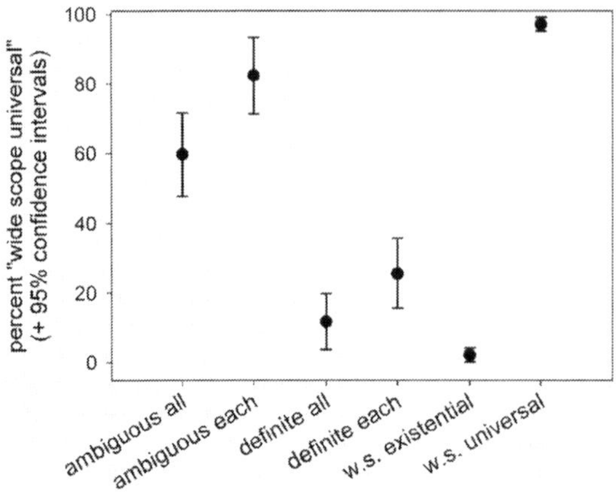

Figure 4. Mean percent wide-scope universal readings in all six conditions. Error bars indicate 95% confidence intervals.

$p < .05$; $t_2(71) = 3.45$; $p < .01$). The definite NPs (Control A) showed a similar contrast: A ∀∃ interpretation was more frequent in constructions with *each* (24.1%) than with *all* (11.4%). ANOVAs revealed a significant main effect of NP-type ($F_1(1,29) = 87.05$; $p < .01$; $F_2(1,71) = 682.01$; $p < .01$) as well as of distributivity ($F_1(1,29) = 42.89$; $p < .01$; $F_2(1,71) = 51.50$; $p < .01$). The former reflects more inverse scope readings in the ambiguous conditions than in Control A. The latter comes from *each* taking wide scope more frequently than *all*. The interaction between NP-type and distributivity was significant by items ($F_1(1,29) = 3.71$; $p = .07$; $F_2(1,72) = 6.49$; $p < .05$). It is due to a somewhat bigger contrast between *all* and *each* in the quantifier conditions than in the definite NP conditions. Nevertheless, the difference between *all* and *each* in control A was significant, as a pairwise t-test shows ($t_1(29) = 3.79$; $p < .01$; $t_2(71) = 3.54$; $p < .01$).

2.6.2. Reading Times

Three regions of interest were defined for the purposes of the analysis. The pre-target region consisted of the first DP (*genau ein Tier* vs. *das Tier*). The post-target region contained the last three words of the sentence (*sollst du nennen*). 98.4% of all regions were fixated during the first pass. Fixations shorter than 80 ms were eliminated from the data set. This excluded less than 0.5% of the data.

Four standard eye-movement measures were computed for all three regions. We will define them as follows: First pass reading time is the sum of all fixations from first entering a region until leaving it. Total reading time is the sum of all fixations on a region. Regressions-out is the proportion of times a regression was launched from a region. Finally, regressions-in is the proportion of times a regression was made back into the region. While first-pass reading time and regression out are taken to reflect immediate processing, total time and regression in are taken to reflect late processes like reanalysis.

Reading time data were subjected to 2 × 2 repeated measures ANOVAs with the within factors NP-type and distributivity. In addition, we analyzed reading times contingent on the reported reading using linear mixed effects models (for an introduction see Baayen, Davidson, and Bates (2008) and the references therein).

Table 1 summarizes the reading time data of the quantifier and definite NP conditions for all three regions. Total and first pass reading times are depicted in Figure 5.

In the pretarget region, the only difference among conditions was that the much shorter definite descriptions were read faster than quantifying expressions. This difference was reflected by a significant main effect of NP-type both in total times ($F_1(1,29) = 49.59$; $p < .01$; $F_2(1,71) = 115.45$; $p < .01$) and in first pass times ($F_1(1,29) = 156.05$; $p < .01$; $F_2(1,71) = 168.89$; $p < .01$). The *all* and *each* conditions didn't differ either in total times ($F_{1/2} < 1$) or in first pass times ($F_{1/2} < 1$). Moreover, the interaction between NP-type and distributivity wasn't reliable either in total times ($F_{1/2} < 1.2$) or in first pass

Table 1. Reading time data reporting means (+ SDs)

Condition	Measure	Pretarget Region	Target Region	Posttarget Region
Q-All	First-Pass	725 ms (349)	514 ms (262)	476 ms (361)
	Total	1194 ms (843)	964 ms (793)	708 ms (671)
	Regression Out		9.2% (15.1)	29.0% (27.4)
	Regression In	14.6% (15.0)	9.9% (15.2)	
Q-Each	First-Pass	754 ms (400)	446 ms (202)	461 ms (318)
	Total	1142 ms (855)	743 ms (629)	652 ms (526)
	Regression Out		9.6% (16.9)	25.3% (27.1)
	Regression In	12.1% (14.1)	11.6% (18.1)	
Def-All	First-Pass	524 ms (291)	488 ms (220)	475 ms (322)
	Total	785 ms (503)	809 ms (523)	654 ms (573)
	Regression Out		8.7% (13.2)	27.4% (26.8)
	Regression In	17.5% (19.7)	12.9% (17.5)	
Def-Each	First-Pass	510 ms (330)	497 ms (215)	495 ms (363)
	Total	811 ms (614)	824 ms (558)	698 ms (533)
	Regression Out		7.5% (12.9)	25.8% (25.5)
	Regression In	17.3% (19.2)	11.2% (15.9)	

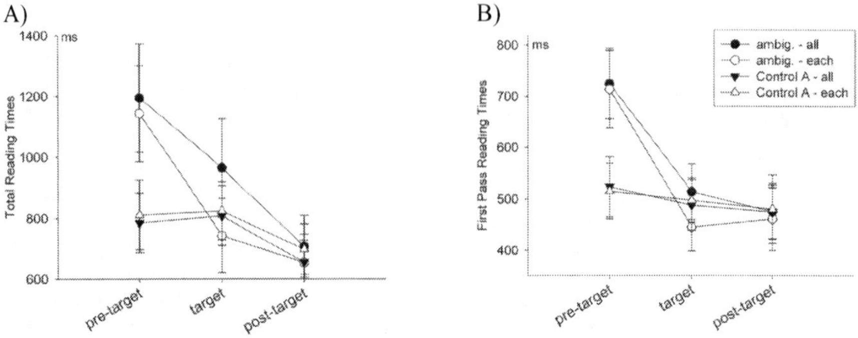

Figure 5. Panel A depicts total reading times for all three regions. Panel B shows first pass reading times. Error bars indicate 95% confidence intervals.

times ($F_{1/2} < 1.7$). ANOVAs on regressions-in revealed a significant main effect of NP-type ($F_1(1,29) = 13.17$; $p < .01$; $F_2(1,71) = 26.07$; $p < .01$). This isn't surprising because the much shorter definite NPs were fixated less often than quantifying NPs resulting in an apparently higher proportion of regressions. No other effects reached significance ($F_1 < 3.6$; $F_2 < 2.6$).

In the target region, in the quantifier conditions *all* was read slower than *each*. However, the definite NP conditions show the opposite pattern: at least numerically, *all* was faster than *each*. Statistically, this was reflected in a significant main effect both in total times ($F_1(1,29) = 8.84$; $p < .01$; $F_2(1,71) = 8.53$; $p < .01$) and in first pass times ($F_1(1,29) = 5.71$; $p < .05$; $F_2(1,71) = 6.25$; $p < .05$) and a significant interaction between NP-type and distributivity both in total times ($F_1(1,29) = 19.75$; $p < .01$; $F_2(1,71) = 12.75$; $p < .01$) and in first pass times ($F_1(1,29) = 14.79$; $p < .01$; $F_2(1,71) = 12.67$; $p < .01$). The main effect of NP-type didn't reach significance (total times: $F_{1/2} < 2$; first pass times: $F_{1/2} < 2$). ANOVAs performed on regressions-in and regressions-out didn't reveal any significant differences.

At the posttarget region,- out, we analyzed the difference between the quantifier conditions with a paired t-test. The *all* condition lead to a higher proportion of regressions-out which was marginal by subjects and significant by items ($t_1(29) = 1.92$; $p = .065$; $t_2(71) = 2.03$; $p < .05$).

2.6.3. *Contingent Reading Times*

Total and first pass reading times contingent on the reported reading are depicted in Figure 6.

The graph shows that the quantifier *all* condition was read more slowly than the quantifier *each* condition irrespective of the reading. But there was

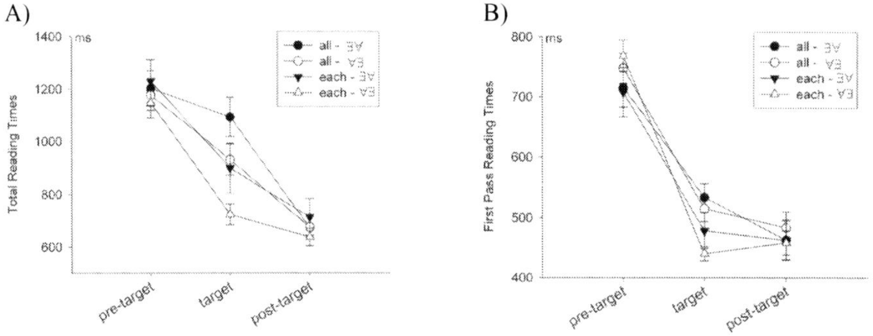

Figure 6. Panel A depicts total reading times contingent on the scope reading for the scope ambiguous conditions. Panel B shows contingent first pass reading times. Error bars indicate standard errors of the mean.

also a contrast among the two readings of the quantifier *all* condition in the total times[4]. *All* was read more slowly when a linear scope interpretation was computed than under inverse scope. For statistical analyses, we used linear mixed effect models to analyze reading times on the target region. Linear mixed effects models incorporate both fixed and random effects and provide a flexible method to deal with missing data. Participants and items were treated as random effects while quantifier, scope and length of the second quantifier measured in number of characters[5] were treated as fixed effects. We computed the following four models only including reading times from trials for which the reading could be determined according to the criteria mentioned above. Each model was computed separately for total reading times and first pass times.

Model A) Analyzing the complete set of ambiguous conditions:

$$\mathrm{y_{ij}} = \mu + \mathrm{Scope_{ij}} * \beta_1 + \mathrm{Quantifier_{ij}} * \beta_2 + \mathrm{Length_{ij}} * \beta_3 + \mathrm{S} * \mathrm{s_i} + \mathrm{W} * \mathrm{w_j} + \varepsilon_{\mathrm{ij}}$$

Model B) Analyzing the two scope readings separately in the ambiguous 'all' condition:

$$\mathrm{y_{ij}} = \mu + \mathrm{Scope_{ij}} * \beta_1 + \mathrm{S} * \mathrm{s_i} + \mathrm{W} * \mathrm{w_j} + \varepsilon_{\mathrm{ij}}$$

Model C) Comparing the ambiguous 'all' and 'each' condition only under inverse scope:

$$\mathrm{y_{ij}} = \mu + \mathrm{Quantifier_{ij}} * \beta_2 + \mathrm{Length_{ij}} * \beta_3 + \mathrm{S} * \mathrm{s_i} + \mathrm{W} * \mathrm{w_j} + \varepsilon_{\mathrm{ij}}$$

Model D) Control comparison of DefQ conditions only analyzing linear scope:

$$\mathrm{y_{ij}} = \mu + \mathrm{Quantifier_{ij}} * \beta_2 + \mathrm{Length_{ij}} * \beta_3 + \mathrm{S} * \mathrm{s_i} + \mathrm{W} * \mathrm{w_j} + \varepsilon_{\mathrm{ij}}$$

The logic behind this analysis is similar to the one used in computing ordinary ANOVA and paired t-tests. After computing the global analysis (Model A), we systematically conducted simple comparisons (Models B and C). Finally, we compared the effects of Model C with the definites of Control A in their preferred scope interpretation (Model D).

Consider the global analysis in Model A. The vector y_{ij} represents the reading time of subject i for item j and is modeled by the sum of a constant term μ, the fixed effect of scope modeled by the coefficient β_1, the fixed effect of quantifier β_2, the fixed effect of length β_3 and the random effects of subject, where s_i is a random intercept for each subject and the random effect of item, where w_j is a random intercept for each item. Finally, ε_{ij} is the vector of residual errors and models the per-observation noise. When a mixed-effects model is fitted to the data, its set of estimated parameters includes the coefficients for the fixed effects. For these, we computed t-statistics and estimated p-values based on Markov chain Monte Carlo sampling from the posterior distribution of the parameters (running 10000 simulations for each model) as suggested by Baayen et al. (2008). Linear mixed effects models were computed using the lme4 library and the MCMC package of R.

In our analysis we started with the global Model A and then analyzed the contrasts in Models B and C using only the relevant "conditions", that is subsets of the data used in model A. The results are summarized in Table 2. Applying

Table 2. Results of linear fixed effects models modelling contingent reading times

Model	**Fixed Effect**	**Est. Coefficient**	**t-value**	**p-value**
A (total)	Scope	243.0 ms	3.31	0.001**
	Quantifier	161.9 ms	2.66	0.008**
	Length	12.1 ms	0.95	0.343
A (first pass)	Scope	40.8 ms	1.74	0.082
	Quantifier	57.3 ms	2.97	0.003**
	Length	4.4 ms	1.09	0.276
B (total)	Scope	234.6 ms	2.42	0.016*
B (first pass)	Scope	43.4 ms	1.35	0.178
C (total)	Quantifier	170.4 ms	2.44	0.015*
	Length	16.6 ms	1.07	0.283
C (first pass)	Quantifier	63.52 ms	2.78	0.006**
	Length	5.40 ms	1.08	0.281
D (total)	Quantifier	97.1 ms	1.72	0.087
	Length	37.2 ms	3.15	0.002**
D (first pass)	Quantifier	33.3 ms	1.59	0.112
	Length	10.1 ms	2.23	0.026*

Model A to total reading times, the fixed effects of both scope and quantifier turned out to be significant. Processing *all* was more difficult than processing *each* and computing a linear reading was more difficult than computing an inverse reading. There was no significant effect of length. In Model A using first pass times as the dependent variable, the fixed effect of quantifier was significant but there was no effect of either scope or length. In total times, both of the contrasts investigated with Models B and C turned out to be significant. In Model B, the significant effect of scope shows that linear scope was processed more slowly than inverse scope. In Model C, which keeps the scope reading constant (inverse scope), *all* was processed more slowly than *each*. In first pass times only the contrast in model C was significant.

To examine the lexical differences between *all* and *each* we also analyzed reading times of Control A keeping the reading constant. In these conditions, participants overwhelmingly chose linear scope, so we compared *all* vs. *each* with linear scope. Descriptive statistics revealed that the definite *all* condition was faster in total reading times than the definite *each* condition (852 vs. 877 ms), which is the opposite of the contrast found in the quantifier conditions. In first pass reading times the definite *all* condition (496 ms) was numerically also faster than the *each* condition (511 ms). The fixed effect of quantifier was not significant in Model D either in the total times or in the first pass analysis. Only length turned out to be a reliable predictor.

2.7. Discussion

As expected, there was an overwhelming preference for inverse scope in the quantifier conditions. This preference was modulated by the type of quantifier: the condition with *all* resulted in inverse scope readings significantly less often than quantifier-*each*. This is consistent with reports in the literature of *all* having less of a tendency to take wide scope than *each*. The novelty of our results lies in demonstrating the effect of quantifier type in inverse linking constructions as well. Furthermore, our results make it apparent that the effect of the construction is stronger than scope preferences of the quantifiers: reading times on ambiguous quantifier-*all* sentences that received a linear scope interpretation were still slower than in those trials where the ambiguous quantifier-*all* sentences were interpreted with inverse scope, as the results of the analyses in model B show.

Moreover, the reading time results indicate that scope relations were computed immediately: the differences were already present in the first pass reading times, and they did not carry over to the next region. As there was no pressure in the experiment to disambiguate the sentences during reading, this finding suggests that quantifier scope is immediately and fully specified during comprehension. However, a word of caution is in order: Although the sentences themselves required no disambiguation, the task of naming an object or objects did. This task was fully predictable and had to be completed within a limited amount of time. It is thus possible that participants performed some disambiguation during reading that would have been delayed otherwise. Another potential cause for worry could be the fact that the instructions had a highly predictable structure, and in particular, that the final segment was always identical (*sollst du nennen*/*should you name*). This may have led to subjects effectively skipping this segment and performing end-of-sentence interpretation as soon as they had read the second quantifier. We do not consider this a serious objection since the effect was already present in first-pass reading times. Furthermore, the differences in the regressions-out measure between *all* and *each* in the final region strongly indicate that processing wasn't completed as soon as the second quantifier had been encountered. Thus we contend that the consistent early disambiguation of quantifier scope in our experiment was not an artefact, but reflects immediate interpretation of quantifier constructions during normal processing.

Our results suggest the following picture of quantifier scope interpretation in inverse linking: The first quantifier is interpreted immediately. When the second quantifier is encountered, it is given wide scope, determined by the properties of the construction. In the case of *jeder*, this interpretation fits well with the quantifier's need for wide scope, thus the resulting reading is overwhelmingly $\forall\exists$. When the universal quantifier is *alle*, however, then there is a conflict between the construction and the scope preferences of the quantifier. As the construction is the stronger factor of the two, it is still easier to settle on an inverse-scope reading for the sentence. This is reflected both in faster reading times for *alle* with inverse scope, and a higher percent of $\forall\exists$ interpretations in this condition. Still, *alle*'s reluctance to take wide scope is strong enough to result in an $\exists\forall$ interpretation roughly 40% of the time.

This view of scope interpretation raises the question what happens when the first NP is a definite NP rather than a quantifier. The analysis in May and Bale (2005) would suggest, for instance, that the quantifier in the PP would still resist an in-situ interpretation and would try to obtain wider scope. Is there evidence for a wide-scope interpretation of the quantifier inside the PP in these cases? We will now take a closer look at the conditions in Control A to answer this question.

3. Definite NPs

The definite NPs were originally included in the study to serve as controls in interpreting the reading time results. However, as briefly mentioned before, they were also interesting in their own right: a comparison of scope preferences in the two conditions in Control A makes it possible to address the question whether definite NPs should be considered quantificational or not. The lack of reading time differences in the definite NP conditions (section 2.6, especially Model D) suggest that there is no scope interaction between the definite NP and the universal quantifier. This is consistent with analysing definite NPs as effectively scopeless (e.g. Glanzberg forthcoming). Alternatively, the definite NP could receive widest scope the same way topic elements are claimed to have scope over the rest of the sentence (e.g. Beghelli and Stowell 1997, Endriss 2002). Either of these possibilities is compatible with the embedded quantifier getting wider scope than its surface position would allow, since it still remains within the scope of the definite NP.

The interpretation of the reported readings reveals another picture. The definite descriptions differed in their scopal behaviour when interacting with *alle* as compared to *jeder*. First let us consider what it means to distinguish two readings in the conditions with definite NPs. The reading where the universal quantifier has narrow scope with respect to the definite NP can be paraphrased as "Name an animal that is in each/all field(s)". The wide-scope universal reading would be "From each field/From all fields, name an animal". Both of these readings are compatible with the displays we used with Control A, which included only one object corresponding to the definite NP in the sentence, and that object was present in all fields. What distinguishes the two answers is thus not the NP named, but the eye-movement behavior of the participants: The linear scope interpretation requires the inspection of all fields first to make sure that the NP corresponding to the sentence is present in all of them. In case of a wide-scope universal interpretation, however, participants can start answering before all fields have been inspected. In addition to the eye-movement patterns, the latter interpretation was sometimes also suggested by answers naming the same object three times ("deer, deer, deer").

Although there was a very strong overall preference for linear scope in the NP-conditions, *each* resulted in more wide-scope universal interpretations than *all*. The difference was somewhat smaller than in the quantifier conditions; nevertheless, it was fully significant. Thus it appears that definite NPs do have scope properties: although they have very wide scope it is still possible to outscope them. This is compatible with a view where they take scope from a position that is higher than the one where the universal quantifier is interpreted in the ambiguous quantifier conditions. Consequently the "ordinary" wide scope interpretation of the universal quantifier still results in narrow scope with respect to the definite NP. However, there must be a second position available for universal quantifiers as well, and it must be higher than the position where the definite NP is interpreted. The low percentage of wide-scope universal interpretations in the definite NP conditions suggest that this position can only be filled under special circumstances.

If obtaining a wide-scope universal interpretation over a definite NP is so difficult, why didn't this difficulty show up in the reading time data? We can only speculate here. Perhaps with definite NPs the interpretation of the universal quantifier requires two steps to result in an inverse-scope reading. The immediate interpretation of the universal quantifier would then involve assigning it the same scope it has in the ambiguous quantifier conditions as well. This is sufficient to satisfy the scope requirements of the construction. A second step would be needed for the universal quantifier to outscope the definite NP. This step may be related to the need for special "support" for this interpretation, and thus may come relatively late in the interpretation of the quantifier, possibly after the whole sentence has been read.

What is left to explain now is the lack of a reading time difference between *each* and *all* during the first step of raising the universal quantifier to the (lower) scope position. Recall that in the corresponding ambiguous quantifier conditions *each* was read significantly faster than *all*. We attributed this effect to *all*'s resistance to move to the scope position. If that were the full story, however, then there should be a similar effect in the definite NP conditions as well. We want to propose that the lack of a difference is related to the way (existential) quantifiers (such as *genau ein*) versus definite NPs are interpreted. Suppose the structure of the whole preverbal NP in our sentences is the following:

(7)

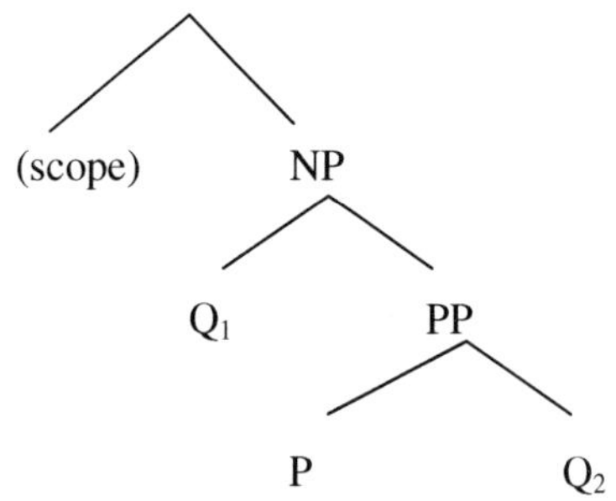

We assume that *genau ein* is interpreted in situ, that is, in Q_1. However, the universal quantifier (Q_2) cannot remain inside the PP and should raise to the position marked as 'scope'. This is relatively easy for *jeder*, leading to short reading times and a large percentage of inverse scope readings in the quantifier-*jeder* condition. *Alle* cannot get past *genau ein* quite so easily, so inverse scope readings are less frequent; when it does reach the scope position, though, interpretation proceeds relatively smoothly. The reading time difference between *each* and *all* comes from those cases where *alle* does not manage to reach the scope position, and has to find some other position below Q_1 where it can be interpreted. As Q_2 by assumption does not allow scope interpretation, the position where *alle* ends up in these cases must be just above the PP node.

When Q_1 is occupied by a definite NP the situation is different: the definite NP needs very wide scope so it must move to some position higher than the scope position in (7). As Q_1 is empty (it only contains a trace), nothing blocks movement of the universal quantifier to the scope position. The resulting interpretation is still one with linear scope, though, since this scope position is lower than the one the definite NP occupies.

Under this modified account, *alle* does not resist wide scope; in fact, it moves to a scope position whenever possible. The apparent preference for narrow scope comes from *alle* being relatively "weak": the scope interpretation it receives is largely determined by other scope-bearing elements within the same sentence. *Jeder* is "stronger", so it can assert its scope needs more easily. Relative scope in a construction is thus the result of the interplay of a number of different factors (Pafel 2005). For instance it should be possible to find some quantifier Q_1 that is interpreted in situ the same way we assume for *genau ein*, but that allows movement of *alle* to the scope position more easily. Testing such predictions is beyond the scope of the present paper.

4. Conclusions

We have proposed a method of combining in a single experiment online measures of difficulty during interpretation with offline indications of the resulting interpretation. Individual components of the method have already been used successfully to investigate a number of phenomena in psycholinguistic experimentation. What is novel here is the use of the visual world paradigm to investigate quantifier scope, and its combination with more traditional reading time measures. As the results show, the eye-movement data together with the answers participants provide are sufficient to determine the final reading of a scope-ambiguous quantified sentence. This means that no overt disambiguation is necessary to investigate the unfolding interpretation of an ambiguous sentence. The new method thus makes it possible to avoid the unwanted consequences of overt disambiguation of quantifier scope (see section 1) and study quantifier interpretation in a paradigm that is maximally similar to normal interpretation.

Notes

1. We think that *jeder* is more strongly distributive than English *every*. This is intended to be reflected in translating it as *each*.
2. This becomes clear when a sentence with *exactly one*, for instance, *you may choose exactly one item* is uttered in a situation only containing a single item. In such a situation, the utterance seems to be infelicitous to us.
3. Control B was not included in the analyses of variance, as the impact of the near-perfect answers in the scope-disambiguated conditions was likely to distort the pattern of data in the potentially ambiguous conditions.
4. The *each* condition under inverse scope was left out of the analysis, since there were only very few data points in this condition (N = 56).
5. The *all* conditions were approximately 1.6 characters longer than the *each* conditions.

References

Baayen, Harald, Doug J. Davidson and Douglas M. Bates
2008 Mixed-effects modeling with crossed random effects for subjects and items. To appear in *Journal of Memory and Language*, special issue on Emerging Data Analysis Techniques.

Beghelli, Filippo and Tim Stowell
1997 Distributivity and negation: The syntax of *each* and *every*. In: Anna Szabolcsi (ed.), *Ways of scope taking*. Dordrecht: Kluwer.

Bott, Oliver and Janina Radó
2007 Quantifying quantifier scope: a cross-methodological comparison. In: S. Featherston and W. Sternefeld (eds.), *Roots – linguistics in search of its evidential base* (Studies in Generative Grammar 96). Berlin/New York: Mouton de Gruyter.

Endriss, Cornelia
2002 The Double Scope of Quantifier Phrases. Linguistics in Potsdam. University of Potsdam.

Filik, Ruth, Kevin B. Paterson and Simon P. Liversedge
2004 Processing doubly quantified sentences: evidence from eye-movements. *Psychonomic Bulletin & Review* 11 (5): 953–59.

Glanzberg, Michael
Forthcoming Definite descriptions and quantifier scope: some Mates cases reconsidered. Forthcoming in the *European Journal of Analytic Philosophy* special issue on descriptions.

Heim, Irene
1991 Artikel und Definitheit. In: Arnim von Stechow and Dieter Wunderlich (eds.), *Semantik/Semantics. Ein internationales Handbuch der zeitgenössischen Forschung*. Berlin/New York: Walter de Gruyter.

Kurtzman, Howard S. and Maryellen C. MacDonald
1993 Resolution of quantifier scope ambiguities. *Cognition* 8: 243–79.

May, Robert and Alan Bale
2006 Inverse linking. In: M. Everaert and H. van Riemsdijk (eds.), *Blackwell Companion to Syntax*. Oxford: Blackwell.

Neale, Stephen
1990 *Descriptions*. Cambridge, MA: MIT Press.

Pafel, Jürgen
2005 *Quantifier scope in German. An investigation into the relation between syntax and semantics*. Amsterdam: Benjamins.

Russell, Bertrand
1905 On Denoting. *Mind, New Series* 14 (56): 479–93.

Strawson, Peter F.
1950 On Referring. *Mind, New Series* 59, (235): 320–44.

Tanenhaus, Michael K., Michael J. Spivey-Knowlton, Kathleen M. Eberhard and Julie C. Sedivy
1995 Integration of visual and linguistic information in spoken language comprehension. *Science* 268 (5217): 1632–34.

Tunstall, Susanne L.
1998 The interpretation of quantifiers: semantics and processing. PhD Diss., University of Massachusetts, Amherst.

A scale for measuring well-formedness: Why syntax needs boiling and freezing points*

Sam Featherston

This article is a response to a tendency which is apparent in the literature, namely to treat the methodology of magnitude estimation, especially in the specific variant described in Bard et al (1996), as the standard experimental method of gathering judgements. The specificity of this methodology is that it assumes that informants will and should provide introspective judgements on a ratio scale. I will suggest that this assumption is false and that magnitude estimation should not be adopted in linguistics as the standard method. Instead I will argue that the advantages of magnitude estimation and those of the traditional seven-point category scale can be largely combined in our own *thermometer judgements*.

Magnitude estimation, introduced to the linguistic world by Bard et al (1996), derives from the field of psychophysics, specifically from the school strongly associated with the renowned psychophysicist Stanley Stevens (for review Stevens 1975). This tradition interprets informants' numerical judgements of stimulus strength as a direct reflection of the magnitude of the sensation perceived. These sensations are held to to be a power function of the stimulus magnitudes which triggered them. This result has been replicated over very many stimulus types (visual, auditory, taste, smell) and in many laboratories across the world (Gescheider 1997).

The situation in linguistics is fundamentally different. This finding cannot be replicated in well-formedness judgements, for the simple reason that there is no objectively measurable stimulus to compare the subjective reports of sensations to. While linguists can carry out studies which reveal that the methodology can produce interesting results, they are to an extent dependent upon work done within psychophysics for evidence about the validity of magnitude estimation. This paper adopts this approach, and blends insights from the psychophysical literature with our own specifically linguistic findings on the issue of the collection and evidential value of introspective well-formedness judgements.

Stevens' school of psychophysics claimed to measure *sensation*, which was seen as the mental representation of a stimulus. For linguists, the stimulus is the language structure, and it is this which is the object of research. Psychophysicists, incidentally, regard this approach as valid; the use of judgements in linguistics is just one use among many in which responses to stimuli are gathered for which there is no direct physical measurement, most commonly social attitudes, or none accessible, such as pain. I would see linguistic intuitions of well-formedness as being similar to this latter, but we shall not discuss the issue further here. The key point is that psychophysicists consider this use of judgements to be unproblematic and indeed regard its success as evidence of the robustness of the method (eg Gescheider 1997, 322f).

While the psychophysics literature provides support for the use of judgements, there are still a range of ways of gathering them. We shall discuss some of the findings from psychophysics which relate to magnitude estimation as a methodology, which has been controversial in academic psychology for a substantial period of time. The first question we shall seek to answer is whether the method is sufficiently empirically well-supported in the psychophysical literature to be a candidate as a standard method in linguistics. We further explore, basing our discussion on our own use of the method, whether precisely the variant described in Bard et al (1996) is the ideal procedure. We shall argue for negative answers on both these points. This conclusion does not however weaken the case for using judgements in linguistics, quite the contrary. Newer perspectives in psychophysics dismiss the concept of 'sensation' as a mental construct, but state instead that judgements should be regarded as a function of the magnitude of the stimulus (eg Laming 1997). This newer insight would thus suggest that judgements are a very relevant approach for linguists, whose object of study is the precisely the linguistic stimulus.

In the second part of the paper, we shall sketch our own preferred methodology for gathering judgements, motivating the choices we make. We believe this method to be much more suitable as a standard method, but note that not every question to be addressed with introspective judgements requires exactly the same experimental treatment (see also Weskott and Fanselow, this volume). In the last part of this paper, we shall touch upon a closely related question, namely the issue of the reporting of well-formedness judgements. Here we shall introduce our approach to the difficulty of communicating a subjective response such as introspective judgements, namely a standard scale. This has another advantage, since it is established among psychophysicists that the existence of a familiar scale allows more consistent and accurate estimates of a variable to be given. We thus present our attempt at a standard scale of perceived well-formedness.

Magnitude estimation

In the *magnitude estimation* procedure, the subject makes numerical estimates of the apparent relative magnitudes of stimuli. The procedure starts with a practice stage to introduce the task. This gives them the chance to learn how to assign magnitude values on some fairly simple variable, such as line length. They are first shown a reference line and instructed to give it a value. All following lines are to be assigned values relative to the value of the reference item. This is fairly undemanding for a parameter such as line length which can have multiples and fractions. Next the informant is given the same task but told to judge the acceptability (or some such term) of linguistic examples, starting, as before, with a reference item. This too is practised before the experiment proper begins.

The method thus has much in common with the traditional method of gathering grammaticality judgements on a five-point or seven-point scale: informants report their intuitions in numerical form. But a fixed scale has disadvantages due to its inflexibility. First, only the number of distinctions can be made that the scale has points. Our own experiments demonstrate that subjects are able to distinguish far more shades of difference. Second, informants can easily find themselves squeezed at one end of the scale or another, since they cannot know in advance how much better or worse later examples will be. This is particularly problematic since linguistic well-formedness does not have any clear anchor points which would help subjects distribute their judgements ideally and avoid stretching and squashing.

Magnitude estimation, since it has no scale ends and no minimum division, does not suffer from these problems. Individual informants can suit their own subjective preferences and effectively create for themselves the scale that they feel most comfortable with. The magnitude estimation method thus allows informants to express all and only the differences that they perceive with minimum interference from the scale.

This methodology works well. It permits the collection of finely graded linguistic intuitions and has become rapidly more popular as its advantages have become better known (see for example several papers in this volume). It has thus become something like an unofficial 'standard method' for gathering relative judgements, especially for researchers who are seeking to compare experimentally obtained judgements with other data types or methodologies. Since the Bard et al (1996) paper is always cited as the source, the particular choices in terms of data manipulation made there have also become more or less standard. This paper seeks to examine the appropriateness of this.

Practical problems with magnitude estimation

While the positive aspects of magnitude estimation (in the following *MagEst*) are clear, there are some downsides which do not appear to be widely recognized (1).

(1) a. No magnitude pattern in results
b. Preference for integers near zero
c. Logarithmic conversions unmotivated
d. Reference item too variable as basis for normalization

The first problem relates to MagEst generically and is by far the most serious. The last two problems concern only the procedure followed Bard et al (1996). We shall discuss each in turn.

The first issue concerns the data pattern. MagEst assumes that subjects give ratio judgements; thus if the reference item is 10, an example twice as good will be 20, one half as good will be a 5. Raw MagEst results should yield an upwardly concave pattern on a graph. But when informants give judgements in a MagEst experiment, they do not in fact give magnitude judgements. In fact, it is both theoretically and practically impossible for them to do so. In the light of the extensive literature using MagEst, this claim may initially sound surprising, but the evidence is unequivocal. Consider the clearest theoretical reason first: informants cannot give judgements of magnitudes because these require the existence of a known zero point (Poulton 1989: xv). Linguistic well-formedness has no such zero point and so the statement that example A is twice as good as example B is meaningless. It is perhaps helpful to compare this situation with temperature measurement: Anders Celsius developed the temperature scale with 100 degrees between boiling and freezing point in 1742. But while this scale could be used to express temperature differences, it could not be used to express temperature ratios because it had no absolute zero temperature. Only with the calculation of a figure for absolute zero (Lord Kelvin, 1848) did any statement about proportions become possible.

This would have been no surprise to Stevens. He made a distinction between *prothetic* variables and *metathetic* variables: the first are quantitative sensory continua and associated with additive neural processes, they thus obey the power law; the second group (eg social and attitudinal variables) are associated with substitutive neural processes and do not (Stevens and Gallanter 1957). Whether linguistic well-formedness is of the first or of the second type depends upon whether one sees judgements of well-formedness as reports of a social variable or of processing load.

If we deny that MagEst produces a magnitude scale, what sort of results pattern does it produce? There can be no simple answer. It is hard to answer conclusively because we have, as we noted above, no fixed scale of stimulus values against which to test results. We can thus cause informants to produce any result pattern we choose by selecting the set of stimuli. For example, if we put many 'bad' examples and a few 'good' examples into an experiment design, we will get an upwardly concave results pattern (1, 2, 4, 8, 16 ...). If we put many 'good' and few 'bad' examples in, we will get a upwardly convex pattern (1, 4, 6, 7 ...). Since we have no independently motivated way of obtaining a evenly distributed range of stimulus values, we cannot gain a clear view of the output pattern of a evenly distributed input patten.

Keller (2001) is a respectable attempt to show otherwise. He claims that linguistic judgements produce a function in line with Stevens' Power Law (1975), if mapped against the number of violations. He looks at the effects of three constraints on word order in the German mittelfeld, which we give and paraphrase in (2). He uses MagEst to gather judgements of examples containing zero, one, or two of these, sometimes multiple violations of the same type, and finds a power function in the results.

(2) a. *VERB: X < V[-MC]*
In a subordinate clause, the verb comes last.
b. *NOM: [+NOM] < [-NOM]*
A nominative precedes non-nominatives.
c. *PRO: [+PRO] < [-PRO]*
A pronoun precedes non-pronominals.

But Keller's argument makes use of questionable assumptions and neglects known confounding effects. First, he assumes that the number of violations in a violating structure can be objectively ascertained, and that informants will interpret violating structures in just this way. Neither of these holds up on closer consideration. For example, if an accusative NP linearly precedes a nominative (in violation of NOM), will informants perceive this as two violations, since both accusative and nominative are in the 'wrong' places (the incremental processing view)? Or will they only see one violation as Keller assumes (the whole-string representational view)? Can we assume, as Keller does, that the positions of dative and accusative NPs are only regulated by their position relative to nominatives, but not relative to each other? If not, his informants will be responding to rule violations which he is not counting.

Keller himself notes that the NOM constraint is treated as a single constraint by one author (Müller 1999) and as two separate constraints by another (Uszkoreit 1987). The fact that we can come to very different conclusions about the number of violations involved with only the most natural of assumptions is an example of just how questionable it is whether this construct can have a usable definition. We therefore have very serious reservations whether number of constraint violations as in Keller's study can constitute a stimulus continuum and thus a valid test of output pattern.

Keller also assumes that multiple occurrences of a single violation type in a single example will produce an exactly cumulative effect. Now violation costs are generally cumulative (Keller 2000), but the extension of this to multiple infringements of the same constraint is questionable, in part because the violations are not independent of each other. Let us consider variants of the noun phrase *the old car*. In *old the car* the article is one place away from its canonical location, in *old car the* it is two. Would we want to describe the second example as containing two violations? And would we expect it to be twice as bad for that reason?

We can also advance an alternative reason why Keller's results might show a upwardly concave pattern: the floor effect. The examples with mislocated verbs in particular are, as he himself writes, "seriously unacceptable". It is unsurprising that such impossible examples do not become much worse with the addition of a fairly mild word order dispreference. This will cause flattening at the bottom, distorting the data towards a more concave pattern.

In the light of these doubts about Keller's study, we shall conclude that his claim is not sufficiently well supported for it to be accepted.

Let us reiterate: since linguistic well-formedness can offer us no clear stimulus scale, we can make no strong claim about the relation of stimulus and result patterns in MagEst in any one study. However, we can observe what the data looks like in general. In fact, whenever we can assume that no independent factor is affecting the results, we most frequently see simple cumulativity on an apparently linear background. It would therefore appear that informants, not being able to produce judgements on a magnitude scale in spite of their instructions, usually just judge differences directly, and thus produce a linear scale (see also Sprouse 2007). This is in line with the findings of psychophysicists too (eg Birnbaum 1980, Poulton 1989, Anderson 1989, McBride 1993).

To illustrate this we shall present the results of a typical magnitude estimation experiment on a subject closely related to Keller's (2001). It will be necessary to describe the experiment in some detail, because the reader cannot otherwise judge for themself that the factors affecting the result pattern have not been chosen to produce a particular effect. This requires an excursus into the linguistic basis of the experiment.

We investigated the effects of noun phrase *heaviness* and the relative order of accusative and dative case in 18 conditions. Each complement NP appeared in one of three forms: heavy NP (HNP), light NP (LNP), or pronoun (Prn). Light NPs consisted of an article and a noun, heavy NPs additionally had a two-syllable adjective. We presented all nine combinations of two NPs (HNP HNP, HNP LNP, HNP Prn, LNP HNP, LNP LNP, LNP Prn, Prn HNP, Prn LNP, Prn Prn). These nine NP heaviness conditions were presented in both dative > accusative and accusative > dative order, making a total of eigh-

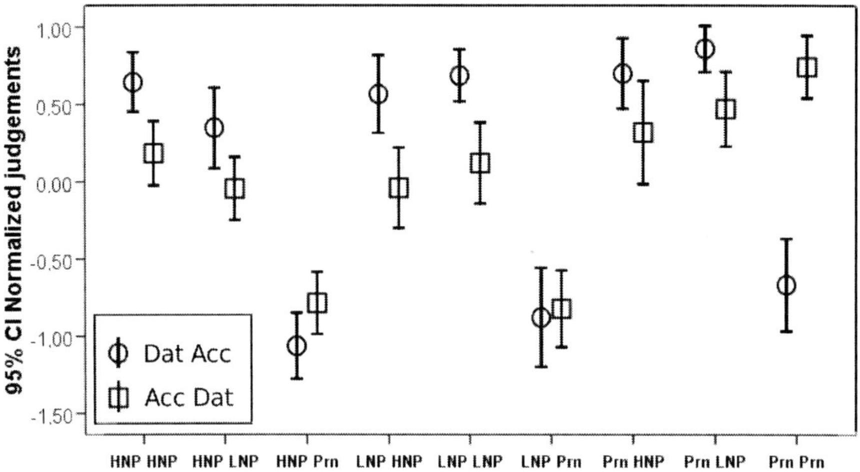

Figure 1. Results of experiment on the effects of NP heaviness and case order on preferred complement order in the German mittelfeld.

teen conditions. We illustrate the first three conditions here; the rest should be reconstructible.[1]

(3) a. HNP HNP Dat > Acc
Der Agent hat dem alten Feind den ganzen Plan verraten.
the agent has to.the old enemy the whole plan betrayed
"The agent has betrayed the whole plan to the old enemy."

b. HNP LNP Dat > Acc
Der Agent hat dem alten Feind den Plan verraten.

c. HNP Prn Dat > Acc
Der Agent hat dem alten Feind ihn (='it') verraten.

The results are shown in Figure 1. The nine NP heaviness conditions are shown across the horizontal axis, each distinguished by case order. The error bars show mean values and 95% confidence intervals for the normalized judgements given by the informants. Note that these are *relative* judgements: there is no cut-off point between well-formed and ill-formed.

The results illustrate several effects that linguists are familiar with (eg Lenerz 1977, Uszkoreit 1987, Jacobs 1988).[2] Of the five clearly worst conditions, four are examples with pronouns following full NPs, in violation of the Law of Increasing Members (Behagel 1909). The fifth one is a sequence of two pronouns, the dative preceding the accusative, which is not the canonical order. More generally, we can see a consistent preference for datives to precede accusatives, unless both are pronouns (compare circles and squares), and for heavy NPs not to precede lighter ones. This effect is complicated by a simultaneous preference for globally lighter example sentences.[3] We shall finish our excursus by noting two phenomena visible in this data which I think are new. First, a dative pronoun following a full NP is judged better than an accusative one in the same non-canonical position (see also Featherston 2002). Intuitively we might relate this to the greater ability of the dative pronoun *ihm* to bear focus than the accusative pronoun *ihn*. The second phenomenon is the continuation of the dative before accusative preference, even when the first of the pair is a pronoun. It might normally be expected that the preference for pronouns to linearly precede full NPs would override the case order preference, effectively cancelling it, so that all Pronoun > NP strings would be equally good. This result shows this expectation to be erroneous; the two effects operate simultaneously and cumulatively.[4]

Our excursus into German word order in the mittelfeld aimed to provide us with a data set to observe the data pattern which MagEst yields. The linguistic description of the study was necessary to demonstrate that the syntactic conditions were not chosen to produce a particular data pattern, rather they were motivated by linguistic factors. Figure 1 showed the results by experimental condition, figure 2 shows the data set ordered by score values. The numbers on the x-axis in figure 2 indicate the order of conditions in the figure 1; so the lowest score in figure 2 is the fifth condition from left in figure 1 (HNP Prn, DatAcc).

The issue to consider is whether the data in figure 3 resembles a ratio scale of judgements or another scale type. If subjects used a ratio scale, as instructed, and reported their intuitions of well-formedness in multiples, then we should expect to see some sign of an upwardly concave result pattern (recall: twice as good as 10 is 20, but half as good as 10 is 5).

In fact the result pattern shows no sign at all of a concave pattern: we detect two groups of values, each apparently linear, the larger group corresponding to the more acceptable word order variants, the smaller one consisting of the group of conditions which violate the more rigid constraints. Neither group shows any sign of a concave pattern of results; neither seem to be made on a ratio scale, using multiples.

Now this single study is of course only weak evidence about the data pattern, since the result pattern, as we have noted, is heavily dependent on the choice of syntactic conditions, but we can advance two arguments which make a stronger case. First, MagEst data *always* delivers this sort of basically linear pattern. Effects are broadly stable, whether they occur among fairly good examples or

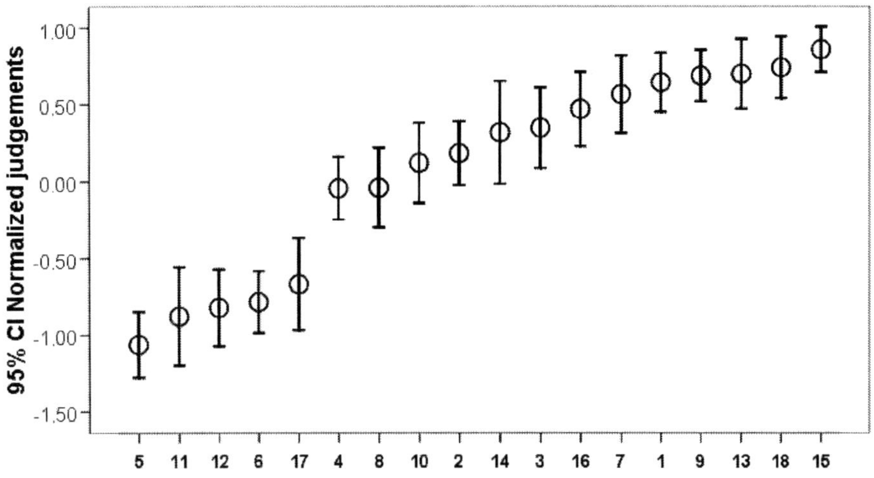

Figure 2. NP heaviness and case experiment results ordered by scores. The condition numbers relate to the order of conditions in the previous figure.

fairly bad ones, in contradiction to the assumptions of MagEst. Effects are also simply additive (eg Featherston 2002). We may find some squashing at the upper and lower margins, but this is due to the quite independent ceiling and floor effects. The consistent appearance of a broadly linear pattern offers a weight of evidence that no single study can. Second, any native speaker, performing a MagEst experiment, can recognize in their own consciousness the tendency to produce a sets of judgements based on difference, and thus on a linear scale, not a ratio scale. On the basis of this evidence we consider the assumption that humans naturally produce ratio scale judgements of linguistic stimuli to be falsified. In fact we claim more: subject are not able to produce ratio judgements. Since they cannot, they shift to what they can produce, namely a linear scale based upon *differences*, not ratios.

This might seem to fundamentally undermine MagEst as a methodology, but in fact the mismatch between the assumptions behind MagEst and its result pattern do not *in practice* matter too much. It still produces interesting and revealing results, because the informants adapt the task to their abilities in a systematic maner, but it is nevertheless intellectually unsatisfying to be instructing informants to do something that we know they cannot. We now turn to the other problems with MagEst.

Problems with the specifics of procedure in Bard et al (1996)

While the previous section concerned a fundamental aspect of MagEst, the following three issues are related to the way that MagEst is standardly used in linguistics, following the choices made in Bard et al (1996). While experimenters are not forced to adopt these, and we in our own work have not done so, their appearance in the reference work has led them to be adopted as standard practice. We wish to point out the alternatives here.

Informants who choose a very low value for the reference item often show distortion near zero. The effect of this problem is limited, but it is a known source of distortion. It is in part due to the general preference for integers, which often leads to bunching of judgements and a reduction in differentiation when fractions would be required. While it is intuitively advantageous to allow informants to choose their own reference value and scale amplitude and standardize these by normalization, it should not be overlooked that these steps have costs, both because some informants choose their reference value too close to zero, and because normalization can cause distortion, particularly in assigning execessive weight to outliers.

This effect is related to another point. The log transformation of result scores recommended by Bard et al (1996) is in practice neither necessary nor desirable (Featherston 2005a, Sprouse 2007). The original reason given for it was to correct the data from its assumed skewedness produced by the magnitude scale and the zero scale-end effect (see Sprouse 2007 for discussion), but since informants do not in practice produce ratio judgements, it has no role in producing normality of distribution for statistical purposes. In the study reported above, we tested the normality of distribution of scores by condition on the untransformed data and after conversion to $\log_{10}$ (base 10) and $\log_e$ (natural log). Neither transformation changed the normality of distribution in any meaningful way.[5] In practice, judgement scores are reasonably normally distributed about the mean and have a reasonable homogeneity of variance (eg Featherston 2005a). Since there is no clear reason for this transformation, and the less we manipulate data the better, we would advise against it.

Our final critique of the procedure laid out in Bard et al (1996) concerns the procedure for the normalization of scores. Using just one reference item as an anchor and giving informants a free choice of its value means that each informant effectively develops their own scale, with an individual location and range. To unify these scales and provide them with a common anchor point and common amplitude, it is necessary to normalize each individual's data. They suggest using the value of the reference item as the basis for this normalization, and this seems to have become the standard method.

Table 1. The effects on the statistical analysis of the normalization employed. Data normalized to z-scores provides larger F-values.

Effect F-values	Normalized to z-scores		Normalized by reference	
	by subjs.	by items	by subjs.	by items
NP1 heaviness	28.1**	26.3**	28.3**	8.1**
NP2 heaviness	134.6**	89.2**	86.1**	6.4**
Case order	4.1*	1.8	1.0	0.03
NP1 × NP2	8.4**	7.3**	6.2**	0.7
NP1 × CaseOrd	6.7**	5.2*	7.4**	0.6
NP2 × CaseOrd	46.7**	28.7**	27.9**	4.6 *
NP1 × NP2 × CaseOrd	5.9**	5.2**	2.6*	0.3

* p-value < 0.05, ** p-value <0.01 (Huynh-Feldt correction applied)

However, the value of the reference item is just one value, and as we have shown in past work, single judgements are subject to considerable random variation (Featherston 2007). This noise factor feeds into the normalized values and makes them less consistent over subjects than they might otherwise be. We have therefore used the subject's own mean score as the basis for normalization, thus producing *standard scores*, or *z-scores*. The reduction in variation offered by z-scores compared to Bard et al's suggested procedure is directly visible in greater precision in the statistics; for example, in our study, of the fourteen main effects and interactions, the z-score F values were larger, often much larger, in twelve cases, and about the same in the two others. Table 1 shows the results of repeated measures anovas by subjects and by items for the three main effects NP1 heaviness, NP2 heaviness, and Case Order (Dat Acc, Acc Dat), and the interactions of these, all given for z-scores and for the data normalized on the basis of the reference score. Normalization to z-scores produces more finely differentiated results than the method outlined in Bard et al (1996).

Psychophysical validation of magnitude estimation

We have reported our own findings using MagEst above. The claims we have made are in direct contradiction to those of Stevens' school of psychophysics, which inspired Bard et al (1996). The question must be raised whether we are justified in discarding a method which has been tried and tested over decades, especially since we have ourselves noted that linguistics cannot easily carry out its own validation of the method, as it lacks stimulus variables with independently measurably values on a known scale. We believe the answer to be positive, since the method is much more controversial than its supporters seem to allow.

Stevens was a major figure in psychophysics: head of the Havard psycho-acoustic laboratory and originator of the scale type distinctions nominal, ordinal, interval, and ratio. He was the developer of magnitude estimation and argued that the method was validated by the consistency of the results (1975, Gescheider 1997 Ch.13, cf Anderson 1992 also for partition scales). But even during his lifetime, doubts were cast on the approach. Savage (1970) argues that his data does not really 'measure' anything at all, arguing that for 'measurement', the mere assignment of numbers is not enough, a scale of units must be used. She therefore concludes of Stevens "his methods of psychophysical measurement [...] are spurious" and his psychophysics "conceptually confused".

She is not a lone opponent. Birbaum (eg 1980) worked upon a similar range of phenomena to Stevens but came to the conclusion that the "psychological primitive" is stimulus difference, and that ratios are only derived from them. Shepard (1981) argues that Stevens is wrong to associate the response directly with the 'sensation', a variable internal to the mind. We need additionally to take the response function into account. So Stevens' power law is "invalid". Since the validity of the methodology is held to be shown by the consistency of the results, this questioning of the findings undermines the methodology too. Anderson, in a series of papers (for summary 1992) argues that a linear scale is more appropriate.

The most trenchant criticism comes from E.C. Poulton. He worked at Stevens' laboratory early in his career and even published a joint paper with him on these issues (Stevens & Poulton 1956). After Stevens' death he wrote an entire book entitled *Bias in Quantifying Judgements* (1989), in which he laid out in detail what effects cause the upwardly concave data pattern which Stevens generalized to the power law. His critique is therefore well-informed and particularly biting: "Once most of Stevens' power functions are rejected because they are produced by a logarithmic response bias, there is no need to dwell on their other inadequacies", "... inadequacies in the design or conduct of the investigations." (1989, xvii). He concludes that "ratio judgements are biased and invalid" (1989, 1), and explains how Stevens came to think otherwise. Having developed the power law, Stevens ignored counter-evidence and selected just the data that confirmed it: "Chapter 10 describes how investigators can use these and other techniques to obtain the results that they predict." (1989, xvii).

These are harsh words and serious criticisms, so it is important to note that they are not merely the result of a personal feud. Many other researchers have come to the same conclusions. Laming (1997) demonstrates that Stevens' instructions and recommendations to other researchers contain systematic bias towards obtaining ratio data, quoting from Stevens (1956). First, the instructions to the subjects emphasize that they are to use a ratio scale, eg "[...] if the standard is called 10 what would you call the variable? [...] if the variable sounds 7 times as loud as the standard, say 70. If it sounds one fifth as loud, say 2; if a twentieth as loud, say 0.5, etc.", "Try to make the ratios between the numbers you assign to the different tones correspond to the ratios of the loudnesses between the tones." With such explicitly stated instructions, it certainly cannot be argued that subjects produced ratio judgements of their own accord.

In fact it becomes clear that Stevens had to coerce his subjects into doing so. In his discussion of the methodology Stevens writes "[...] let me say that the success of the foregoing experiment was achieved only after much trial and error in the course of which we learnt at least some of the things not to do." For example, he tells experimenters: "Call the standard by a number, like 10, that is easily multiplied and divided" and warns: "If E [the experimenter] assigns numbers to more than one stimulus, he introduces constraints of the sort that force O [the observer] to make judgements on an interval rather than on a ratio scale." It is easy to concur with Laming's (1997) comment: "Reading between these lines of Stevens' advice, it is evident that even he found it easy to fail to get good power law data"; "[...] that result seems to be the very opposite of robust."

Figure 3. "How do you expect us to make progess if you make judgements like that?" A view of Stevens' attitude to subjects, by a student (From 'Bias in Quantifying Judgements', E.C. Poulton, © 1989 Lawrence Erlbaum. Reproduced by permission of Taylor & Francis Books UK.).

Indeed Stevens more or less tells us this himself: "Another problem we encounter is due to the fact that some Os [observers] seem to make their estimates on an interval-scale, or even an ordinal scale, instead of on the ratio-scale we are trying to get them to use" (Stevens 1956). Figure 3 (from Poulton 1989) shows how one of Stevens students viewed him at the time. It also goes some way to explaining why, given that there has been so much criticism of Stevens' judgement gathering method, it is still represented positively in parts of the literature (eg Gescheider 1997). Poulton notes "Stevens is such a strong and eloquent advocate of ratio judgements, that no investigator firmly articulates the reason for the discrepancy. [...] The invalid ratio judgements will be very difficult, if not impossible, to get rid of" (1989, 14). How true.

Increasingly, at last, researchers are becoming more aware of the downsides of magnitude estimation and the advantages of the alternatives (see for example the papers in the volume *Psychophysics beyond Sensation*, Kaernbach et al 2004), a process which are hoping to contribute to in this paper. There are alternatives, and we shall discuss them in a later section. But let us finish this section by answering our main question about magnitude estimation: Is it suitable to be the 'standard method' of collecting judgements in linguistics? We have seen that our own data does not support the underlying assumptions of the approach, that there are solid theoretical reasons why it cannot possibly work as intended, and that there are many voices from psychophysics who criticize it. Our answer will thus be clear: it is no.

Using judgements 'beyond sensation'

The doubts we have cast on MagEst as a methodology should not lead us to question the value of linguistic judgements, however. In fact the very psychophysics work which leads us to doubt MagEst supports the value of judgements more generally. To see this we must review developments in perspectives in psychophysics about what is being measured.

Stevens' school of psychophysics claimed to measure *sensation*, which was seen as the mental representation of a stimulus. The function from stimulus to sensation was the focus of research, while the response was assumed to be a direct representation of sensation. Stevens' power law thus relates just two variables: stimulus and sensation. More recently, the whole idea of sensation as a unitary independent variable, whose amplitude could be meaningfully measured, has been questioned. Laming (1997) argues that there is no intervening variable between stimulus and response, so that judgements directly reflect the stimulus, modulated by the processing and perception factors. Anderson (1992) focuses on the integration of the multiple perceptual aspects of the stimulus into a single appreciation and judgement of it. The idea that we can "measure sensation" has thus been more or less discarded (eg Kaernbach et al 2004).

It is worth linguists noting this change in perspective in psychophysics, since it has implications for our own work. First, because it means that linguists have clear justification in assuming that judgement data is primarily evidence about the nature of the stimulus, and not just about the processing of the stimulus. This is an important point, since linguists often have clear ideas whether they are chiefly interested in language structure or language processing, and this insight from psychophysics would confirm that introspective judgements constitute a fairly direct source of evidence about language structure modulated by processing effects, not just about processing. Second, because it shows that linguists can use insights from psychophysics to control for the intervening processing factors, thus reducing the number of variables. We can do this because psychophysicists do the work of pinning down these processing factors. Thus Anderson (1992) argues that the perception factors involved in judging a stimulus are accessible to psychophysics, because both stimulus and response can be measured or manipulated. They are therefore dealing with two known variables and one unknown variable, the cognitive functions relating the two, which is the object of their research. For linguists, the stimulus is the language structure, and it is this (for many linguists) which is the object of research and thus the unknown variable. But since the cognitive functions are the subject of intense research in psychophysics, we linguists can also to an extent work with two known variables and only one unknown variable, as long as we pay attention to the findings of psychophysics on how stimuli are judged. We can use psychophysicists' findings about their academic focus, the judgement process, to turn their dependent variable in our controlled factor, thus allowing us more leverage on the structure of the linguistic stimulus.

We might finally mention *integration psychophysics* (Anderson 1981, 1989; McBride 1993), which describes how the component parts of complex stimuli affect the integrated response in simple ways, typically additively. Since perceived well-formedness must be a summary value for the various grammatical and other aspects of a structure, and the well-formedness of its component parts. This psychophysical work supports linguistic judgements as a promising and valid approach to examining linguistic structures, since we can assume that the full range of features in the stimulus example remain represented in the final single response.

Gathering judgements: a new start

We have seen good reasons to reject MagEst, but also good reasons to think judgements a valid approach in linguistics. How then should we gather them? MagEst has considerable advantages as a method, but fortunately, there are alternative methods which have more or less all these advantages, but do not have the disadvantages that we have identified. Here too we can rely upon work done in psychophysics; in particular the work of Anderson, whose paradigm of *functional measurement*, developed over thirty years (1962–1992) is relevant to many of the specific concerns of linguistics.

We shall therefore lay out the parameters which we can vary and indicate what choices can be made. We wish to obtain a task which, like magnitude estimation, imposes the minimum of constraints upon subjects, but which should at the same time be easy for informants to use. Here is our menu of parameters for a judgement elicitation methodology:

(4) a. instructions: ratios or differences?
b. anchors: where? how many? labels or reference examples?
c. end points: closed or open?
d. scale type: continuous or category?
e. scale numbers: location? range?

The choice of instructions is simple. Since we have grave doubts whether subjects can produce ratio linguistic judgements, we shall simply ask them to express differences, this being anyway the neutral choice (cf Birnbaum 1980, Poulton 1989, Anderson 1992, Laming 1997). If subjects want to express magnitudes, this phrasing allows them to do so. Instead of *how many times better A is than B*, we ask *how much better A is than B*.

The remaining questions concern the scale, that is, the range of numbers made available to the subjects to express their intuitions. First of all, the anchors of the scale: MagEst uses a single anchor, the reference item, but there is evidence that more anchor points are useful, since subjects give more accurate judgements relative to a fixed point if the fixed point is closer to the value to be judged (Laming 1997). We can minimize this distance by the use of two anchor points, located not at the ends of the scale but each at a point half-way between an end and the mid-point of the range of numbers we expect to be used (corresponding to the 25 and 75 points on a 100 point scale).

These points can be given reference values either by descriptive labels, such as *fully acceptable*, or else by reference examples which illustrate the value. We prefer to use reference examples to fix these points, just as MagEst does.

The studies reported in Schütze (1996) show how problematic it is to find metalinguistic descriptions of degrees of well-formedness which will be reliably understood by subjects: the practice of using reference items, on the other hand, has proven itself very effective in MagEst and elsewhere (eg Heller 1985). This choice reinforces our preference for the anchor points not to be located at the scale ends, since it is very difficult to find good 'bad' reference items. A bottom end of scale reference item should be absolutely ill-formed, but still clearly *ill-formed* rather than being *un-formed* or simply incomprehensible; gobbledygook is not a good basis for comparison of syntactic well-formedness. We therefore prefer to use a poorly acceptable, but not drastically unacceptable, reference item to mark the lower reference point, and a slightly unnatural but not infeasible item to mark the upper reference point.

Similar considerations motivate our choice to have our scale of responses open-ended. This too has worked well in MagEst, allowing subjects always to add a new better or worse score and thus eliminating scale-end squeezing (Stevens 1956, Poulton 1989, Gescheider 1997). Researchers testing stimuli which can be objectively measured can avoid this by simply locating the end of the scale beyond the range of sensations to be tested. This is not really possible when measuring linguistic well-formedness, since unreachable end points are difficult to exemplify.

We would like to conserve one further aspect of MagEst, namely the continuous scale. Some researchers regard category scales, those with a fixed number of integer scale points, typically five or seven, as simpler for subjects to use. They may be relatively simpler, but in our own experience subjects have had no difficulty using the continuous scale, and there are two good reasons for it. First, an interval scale is an assumption of inferential statistics, (but see Weskott and Fanselow this volume who point out that it is not in fact a prerequisite). Second, as Anderson (1992) puts it: a continuous scale contains *more* information. If subjects can give us extra detail about the question we are asking them with little or no extra effort, why should we prevent them doing so? Even if, for certain purposes, the full differentiation that informants are able to give us is not necessary, the standard methodology for gathering judgements must be one which maximizes the information collected. In fact the advantages of both scale types can be gained by using a scale with so many points that all the differentiation perceptible to the subject can be expressed with just integers. Here the difference between the continuous scale and the category scale is blurred. The subject is not prevented from making any differences that they perceive, but they can do it using only integers. Our own experience ties in with that of Anderson (1992) and suggests that a twenty-point scale will be large enough to have these characteristics.

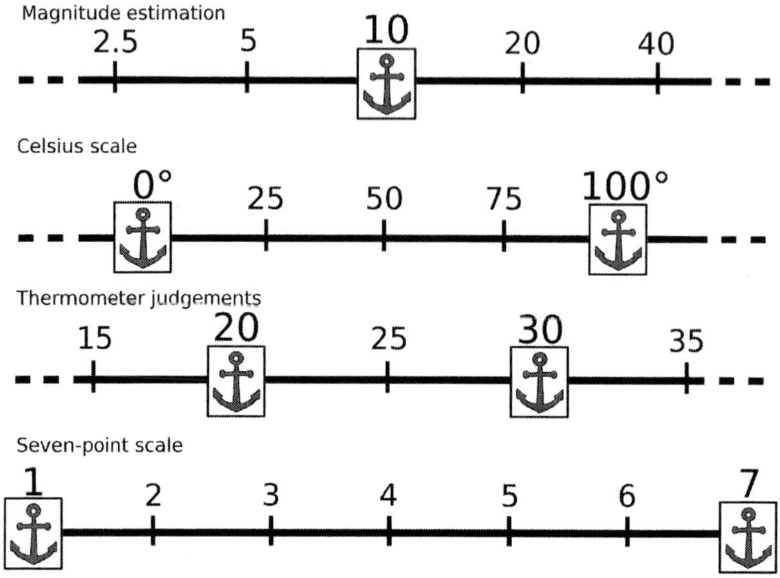

Figure 4. The anchor points and location on the number series of the scales discussed in this article.

The last point to decide is where on the number scale we locate our anchor points. To avoid the distortion near zero apparent in magnitude estimation we have chosen to locate our lower reference item, with a poorly acceptable reference item, at the number 20, and our upper reference item, with a fairly acceptable reference item, at the number 30. We therefore expect the vast majority of judgements to occupy the scale space between 15 and 35. This gives subjects plenty of space and simultaneously avoids the zero point distortion, since extra space above and below is available.

Since we use two essentially arbitrary reference anchors, just like the Celsius scale, which uses boiling and freezing points as anchors, but allow values above and below the anchors and between the integer values, our well-formedness scale rather resembles a thermometer scale. We have therefore labelled this judgement collection method *thermometer judgements*. This is the judgement elicitation method which we now use (eg Featherston 2008). We do not log transform scores and we use the z-score procedure for normalization.

We illustrate the thermometer judgements scale, the Celsius scale, the standard seven-point linguistic scale and the MagEst scale in figure 4 in order to contrast their characteristics. It will be apparent that our own thermometer judgements scale, while it maintains the advantages of magnitude estimation, is also closely related to the traditional seven-point scale used for gathering judgements. The only differences are that our scale is open-ended, to prevent ceiling and floor effects, has no minimum division, to gather all the distinctions subjects are able to make, and occupies a longer number series, to avoid forcing subjects to use fractions.

Cardinal well-formedness values

The thermometer judgements scale has two anchor points, but there is good reason to believe that there are advantages in having more than this for the representation of well-formedness judgements. We have therefore developed a standard scale of five well-formedness values. Each point on the scale should be thought of as an arbitrary standard value, rather like the cardinal vowels, whose phonetic values serve to anchor the wide range of vowel qualities possible. For each cardinal well-formedness value we have developed sets of example sentences, and it is these which anchor the values, not a metalinguistic description. A set of one exemplar of each cardinal well-formedness value can thus act as a comparison set, forming a grounded scale of well-formedness.

There are advantages from both the psychophysical and linguistic perspectives for using a standard comparison set of linguistic examples when gathering judgements. The first relates to the fact that a comparison set forms a de facto scale. Laming (1997) amongst others argues that judgements are always *relative* to given standards; in default of any other comparison point, relative to the previous judgement. This explains why our estimates of a variable with a familiar scale (temperature, length, etc) are more accurate than those of variables without a familiar scale. This increased sensitivity on a scale with familiar points is easy to illustrate: most of us would have difficulty deciding whether a bowl of water is 60 °C or 70 °C, but would have no trouble deciding whether the air temperature is 10 °C or 20 °C. We have no anchor points for the first choice, unlike the second, which is a judgement we make every day before leaving the house: the first means coat and the second shirt sleeves. It follows that a scale consisting of five standard examples which illustrate well-formedness values could sharpen our intuitions, in the same way that known points on the temperature scale can do so. Let us note too that a familiar scale would also make introspective judgements more like objective phenomena, because they would be related to a scale of inter-subjective values.

There are also linguistic reasons for the use of such a standard set. A frequent question about experimentally gathered judgements is their status in terms of grammaticality, often thought of as a binary division. Even methods which of-

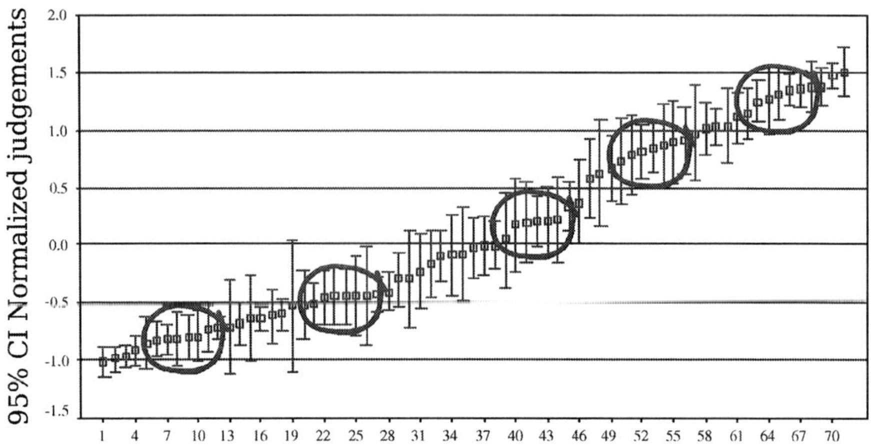

Figure 5. The 72 examples tested formed a continuum of perceived well-formedness. We divided this scale into five arbitrary divisions.

fer the subject only a binary choice face this, since the frequency of choice of two values recreates the continuum of well-formedness offered in methods using a multi-point scale. A standard set of linguistic examples which exemplify a range of values could help here too. The grammaticality/ungrammaticality contrast is itself a scale, though a rather coarse-grained one. Linguists find this scale helpful, because the two values are familiar, and they can associate exemplars with them. Our standard set of five items offers a more finely grained scale of well-formedness, which allows more and finer distinctions to be made.

To select our cardinal well-formedness set we used the experimental methods discussed in this paper to gather judgements of a wide variety of example sentences with many different structures over the full range of well-formedness values. We divided the continuum that we obtained in this way into five roughly equal parts and selected example sentences from the middle of each group as exemplars. Figure 5 shows the full range of 72 items and the location of the five values. In a second step, we tested whether the examples chosen would be reliably associated with their well-formedness value. Subjects were shown examples of the five well-formedness values and asked to assign further items to the groups. All the examples selected were assigned to their group or an adjacent group more the 95% of the time. We list some German exemplars in an endnote.[6]

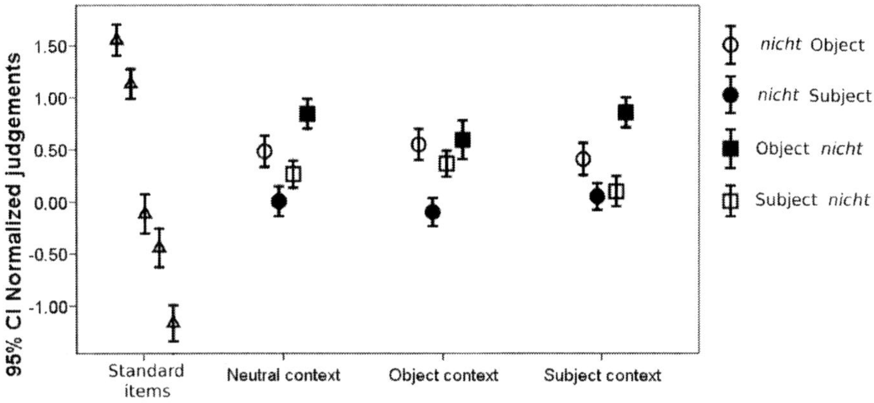

Figure 6. Results of a study of contrastive tags, eg: *Elena strikt sich Pullover, aber nicht Sophie/Socken* ('Elena knits herself jumpers, but not Sophie/socks'). The standard items on the left show that the differences are modest in absolute terms.

We have argued for the utility of the use of a standard scale to sharpen intuitive judgements and provide more grounded values. We shall finish by illustrating the value of including them in experimental studies. The first example is illustrated in figure 6. This data shows the differences between contrastive tags in German, with three parameters of conditions: the discourse context, the position of the negative *nicht* (before NP, after NP), and the grammatical function of the tag (subject, object) (for more detail see Featherston 2007). The point we wish to focus on here is the range of perceived well-formedness in these twelve experimental conditions. The five standard comparison items are on the left of the graph. None of our contrastive tag conditions is better than the second comparison item, and none is worse than the third comparison item. What this tells us is that, while the differences between the conditions show significant effects (Featherston 2007), they are in absolute terms fairly small, not large enough to cause some of them to be grammatical and others ungrammatical, in traditional terms. The standard comparison set thus allows us to make statements about how good or bad structures and contrasts between structures are, in a degree of detail and with a fineness of differentiation that would otherwise not be possible.

Our second example study is from a study of German relative clauses (also Featherston 2007). The eight experimental conditions are relative clauses varying according to the case of their heads (nominative, accusative), the case of their antecedents (nominative, accusative), and whether the relative pronouns

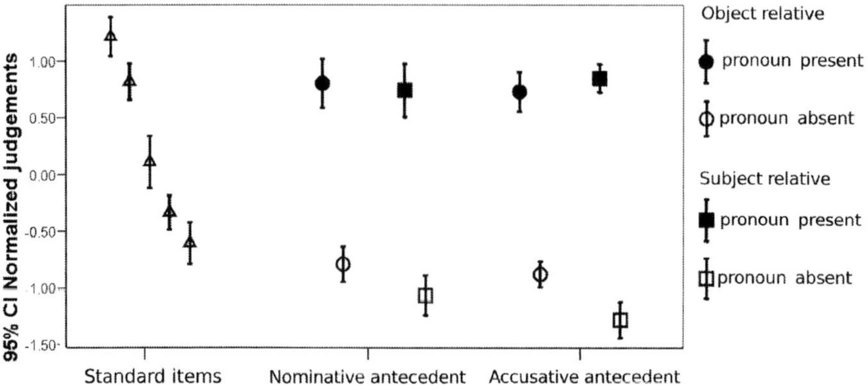

Figure 7. Relative clauses without relative pronouns are judged worse than our worst standard comparison item, but still exhibit a clear subject/object asymmetry.

are overt or covert, as is possible in English, for instance *That is the girl Ø I saw in the bus.* Now the omission of a relative pronoun is quite impossible in German, as this study confirmed: the conditions with absent relative pronouns are judged to be worse even than our lowest standard item (see figure 7). But the graph shows one more thing too: the subject/object asymmetry found in relative pronoun omission in English is visible in the German data too, even though these structures quite are impossible in German. This is an important finding, for it tells us something about the nature of well-formedness and ultimately the architecture of the grammar, perhaps about Universal Grammar. But this observation is dependent upon us having a measure of ungrammaticality, such as our standard comparison items. If we had not included these in the study, the relative ill-formedness of the German relative clauses would have been less clear. In both of these experimental studies therefore the inclusion of the comparison set sharpens the findings.

Conclusion

In this paper we have made three main points. We first argued from theoretical evidence, from our own studies, and from the psychophysical literature, that magnitude estimation, in spite of its advantages, is not an appropriate standard reference method for the collection of introspective judgements. Many psychophysicists have expressed strong reservations about the correctness of its underlying assumptions, and our own empirical work has tended to confirm this for linguistic data too. Since all the evidence suggests that subjects cannot in fact judge magnitudes, this methodology must be regarded as fundamentally undermined.

What subjects can do, and do do even if instructed to judge magnitudes, is give judgements of differences. Since the interval scale can contain all the information that subjects are able to give us, and it allows us to use parametric statistics, there seems little reason to try to encourage them to produce any other scale type, such as a ratio scale. Judgement data of this type can be gathered on a category scale, such as the traditional linguistic seven-point scale with descriptive labels as anchors at each end. Experience with the magnitude estimation scale has taught us an important lesson however, that more finely-grained and less distorted data can be gathered on a scale with open ends and no minimum division, a finding which is robustly backed up in the psychophysical literature. We therefore presented our thermometer judgements scale, which succeeds in unifying most of the advantages of the category scale and of magnitude estimation, and which has proven itself to be easy to use and efficient (eg Featherston 2006, 2007). We sympathize with Weskott and Fanselow, this volume, who argue that for many purposes the simple category scale is adequate, but we should like to suggest our own method as the method of reference for the gathering of judgements of perceived well-formedness.

Our final point was to recommend the use of standard comparison examples to provide a de facto well-formedness scale. This can contribute to the quality of both informal and experimentally gathered judgement data by providing closer familiar reference values, and allows statements to be made about the absolute distribution of judgement scores which would not otherwise be possible, since experimental judgements are relative. If the use of such a well-formedness comparison set were to become generalized in linguistics in the same way that the cardinal vowels are, linguists would have a powerful additional tool to make well-formedness judgements, even a single individual's judgements, more objective, more consistent, more transferable, and more easily communicated.

We shall conclude by highlighting an important conclusion that we may draw from the psychophysical literature about the use of judgements in linguistics. Psychophysicists do not doubt the legitimacy of using judgements to investigate language structure in the way that some linguists do. On the contrary, they regard this practice as an entirely valid extension of their methods. Additionally, recent work regards judgements as primarily related to the stimulus variable, the judgement response being modulated only by the action of perception factors. Since these are the subject of intense psychophysical research, linguists who take account of these findings can utilize judgements as a powerful psychophysically validated tool for the investigation of language structure.

Notes

* This work took place within the project *Suboptimal Syntactic Structures* of the *SFB441* and was supported by the Deutsche Forschungsgemeinschaft. Thanks are due to Wolfgang Sternefeld, project leader, as well as to Tanja Kiziak and other members of the SFB441 in Tübingen. All remaining weakesses are my own.

1. Indirect object NPs were animate, direct objects were inanimate, these being the canonical values in these positions. The pronoun system does not permit the distinction of animacy, but in previous unpublished work we have tested the independent effects of case and animacy in the mittelfeld and found only a very weak effect of animacy independent of case. Complements were matched for length (4–6 letters). Adjectives had 4–6 letters and two syllables.
2. We report the *F*-values of the main effects and interactions below in Table 1. The error bars representing 95% confidence intervals of the mean in figures 1 and 2 give a good idea of the significance of differences.
3. To see the dispreference for heavy NPs to precede light NPs, and the preference for lighter structures generally, look at the first four error bars at the top on the left-hand side. The second pair (HNP LNP) are clearly worse than the first pair (HNP HNP). The second pair violate the 'heavy last' preference, and thus are judged worse.
   Now look at the second group of four error bars at the top (LNP HNP and LNP LNP). These pairs show the opposite pattern: the second pair is judged better. There is no 'heavy last' effect here, but the LNP LNP is lighter as a whole than the LNP HNP, and it is thus judged better.
   Finally, reconsider the first set of four error bars (HNP HNP and HNP LNP). We now realise that the 'heavy last' effect we saw here is net of an overall lightness effect, since the 'worse' pair (HNP LNP) are lighter. Cumulativity of effects requires careful analysis of judgement data sets.
4. In fact this is a nice example of the non-identity of well-formedness and optimality, the first relating to constraint violations and the second to occurrence. Accusative pronouns can occur before full dative NPs because this ordering is optimal, much better than the reverse order with full dative NP before accusative pronoun. But this structure is nevertheless perceived by informants to be less than fully well-formed. The dative before accusative can be seen to have just about the same negative effect on judgements as in the other equivalent strings with two full NPs. We must thus distinguish acceptability relative to a comparison set (= best-of-the-bunch optimality) from inherent well-formedness, independent of a comparison set. It is this construct which our subjects are distinguishing with their judgements.
   It is for this reason that we hold linguistic formalisms making use of optimality to be usable for modelling data based on occurrence, such as corpus frequencies, but quite inadequate for the modelling of grammatical well-formedness, as instantiated here in introspective judgements. The former may describe what structures occur in a language, but the latter allows us to identify the grammatical formants which account for *why* they occur.

5. Using the Shapiro-Wilk procedure we tested the normality of distribution of scores of our eighteen conditions. The untransformed scores were normal in ten conditions, significantly non-normal in eight. Both $\log_{10}$ and $\log_e$ transformed scores were normally distributed in nine conditions and non-normal in nine.
   Let us note here that the non-normality is caused by a few outliers. Excluding just seven data points out of a total of 576 results in fifteen out of eighteen conditions being not significantly different from normal distribution. Given the strength of the effects (see table 1) we regard this as negligible.
6. **Cardinal well-formedness examples from German**

Group A:	In der Mensa essen viele Studenten zu Mittag.
	Nur sehr selten hört man den leisen, krächzenden Ruf eines Schwans
Group B:	Welche Zahnpasta hat der Zahnarzt welchem Patienten empfohlen?
	Sie hofft, das Finanzamt hat den Betrüger überlistet.
Group C:	Was ich wissen will, ist wen wer in dieser Affäre betrügt.
	Ich habe dem Kunden sich selbst im Spiegel gezeigt.
Group D:	Der Komponist hat dem neuen Tenor es zugemutet.
	Welches Zimmer weißt du nicht wo sich befindet?
Group E:	Der Waffenhändler glaubt er, dass den Politiker bestochen hat.
	Wen fragst du dich, ob Maria nicht kennenlernen sollte?

References

Anderson, Norman
1981 *Foundations of Information Integration Theory*. New York: Academic press.
1989 Integration psychophysics. *Behavioral Brain Science* 12: 268–269.
1992 Integration psychophysics and cognition. In: Daniel Algom (ed) *Psychophysical Approaches to Cognition*, 13-113. Amsterdam: North Holland.

Bard, Ellen, Dan Robertson, and Antonella Sorace
1996 Magnitude estimation of linguistic acceptability. *Language* 72(1): 32–68.

Behaghel, Otto
1909 Beziehungen zwischen Umfang und Reihenfolge von Satzgliedern. *Indogermanische Forschungen* 25: 110–142.

Birnbaum, Michael
1980 Comparison of two theories of 'difference' and 'ratio' judgments. *Journal of Experimental Psychology: General* 109: 304–319.

Featherston, Sam
2002 Coreferential objects in German: Experimental evidence on reflexivity. *Linguistische Berichte* 192: 457–484.

2005 Magnitude estimation and what it can do for your syntax: Some wh-constraints in German. *Lingua* 115(11): 1525–1550.

2006 Three types of exceptions – and all of them rule-based. To appear in: Simon H. and Wiese H. (eds), *Auf alles gefasst sein – Ausnahmen in der Grammatik*, Berlin: de Gruyter.

2007 Data in generative grammar: The stick and the carrot. *Theoretical Linguistics* 33(3): 269–318.

2008 Thermometer judgements as linguistic evidence. In: Claudia Riehl, Astrid Rothe (eds) *Was ist linguistische Evidenz?* Aachen: Shaker.

Gescheider, George
1997 *Psychophysics: The fundamentals* (third edition). Mahwah, New Jersey: Lawrence Erlbaum.

Heller, Otto
1985 Hörfeldaudimetrie mit dem Verfahren der Kategorienunterteilung (KU). *Psychologische Beiträge* 27: 478–493.

Jacobs, Joachim
1988 Probleme der freien Wortstellung im Deutschen. In: Inger Rosengren (ed) *Sprache und Pragmatik* 5: 5–37.

Kaernbach, Christian, Erich Schröger, and Hermann Müller (eds)
2004 *Psychophysics beyond Sensation: Laws and Invariants of Human Cognition.* Mahwah, New Jersey: Lawrence Erlbaum.

Keller, Frank
2000 Gradience in grammar: Experimental and computational aspects of degrees of grammaticality. PhD Thesis, University of Edinburgh

Keller, Frank, Martin Corley, Steffan Corley, Lars Konieczny and Amalia Todirascu
1998 WebExp: A Java Toolbox for Web-Based Psychological Experiments. Technical Report HCRC/TR-99, Human Communication Research Centre, University of Edinburgh.

Laming, Donald
1977 *The Measurement of Sensation.* Oxford: OUP.

Lenerz, Jürgen
1977 *Zur Abfolge nominaler Satzglieder im Deutschen.* Tübingen: Narr.

McBride, Robert
1993 Integration psychophysics: the use of functional measurement in the study of mixtures. *Chemical Senses* 18: 83–92.

Müller, Gereon
1999 Optimality, markedness, and word order in German. *Linguistics* 37(5): 777–818.

Poulton, Eustace Christopher
1989 *Bias in Quantifying Judgements.* Hove: Erlbaum.

Savage, C. Wade
1970 *The Measurement of Sensation.* Berkeley: Univ. of California Press.

Schütze, Carson
1996 *The Empirical Base of Linguistics: Grammaticality Judgements and Linguistic Methodology.* Chicago: University of Chicago Press.

Shepard, Roger
1981 Psychological relations and psychophysical scales. *Journal of Mathematical Psychology* 24: 21–57.

Stevens, Stanley
1956 The direct estimation of sensory magnitudes – loudness. *Americal Journal of Psychology* 69: 1–25.
1975 *Psychophysics: Introduction to its Perceptual, Neural and Social Prospects*. New York, John Wiley.

Stevens, Stanley and Eustace Christopher Poulton
1956 The estimation of loudness by unpracticed observers. *Journal of Experimental Psychology* 51: 71–78.

Stevens, Stanley and Eugene Galanter
1957 Ratio scales and category scales for a dozen perceptual continua. *Journal of Experimental Psychology* 54: 377–411.

Uszkoreit, Hans
1987 *Word Order and Constituent Structure in German*. CLSI Lecture notes no.8, Stanford: CSLI.

Weskott, Thomas and Gisbert Fanselow
2009 Scaling issues in the measurement of linguistic acceptability. In: Sam Featherston and Susanne Winkler (eds), *The Fruits of Empirical Linguistics. Volume 1: Process*, 229–245. Berlin: de Gruyter.

The thin line between facts and fiction

Hubert Haider

Abstract. This paper discusses three areas of interest for the topic under discussion, named after three prominent historical figures, an aspect of whose work serves as the appropriate headline for the respective sections. The problems to be discussed are Wundt's, Orwells's, and Crick's problem. Wundt, a founding father of modern psychology, has been the foremost advocate of a rigorous experiment-based paradigm in cognitive research. Orwell is the authoring mind of a well-known slogan that is not only applicable to the diversity of an animal society but also to the modelling of the diversity of languages. Crick provides a quote on the indeterminacy of the relation between theoretic modelling and the reality of a singularly structured black box, if there is no direct access to the details of the complex interior structure of the black box.

1. Wundt's problem – How to deal with introspection

The proper way of dealing with introspectively accessed evidence is not a specific problem of linguistics. It has been a central problem of the emerging discipline of psychology in Wundt's (1832–1920) days. For the (late) 19th century psychology, introspection was considered to be the main approach road to insights about the mind. It was Wilhelm Wundt who argued that *introspection* needs to be controlled and integrated into a *systematic program of psychological experimentation*. As for introspection, he makes a point for the importance of differentiating between two conceptions of introspection, namely 'Selbstbeobachtung' (self-observation) and 'Innere Wahrnehmung' (inner perception). In the English understanding of the concept, the two readings are covered equivocally by the term 'introspection'. Newmeyer (1983: 48) makes a similar difference. He distinguishes 'introspective data' as the result of self-informant work on the one hand, and 'introspective data' as metalinguistic judgements by informants (including the self-informant).

The introspectionist [in the sense of *self-observation*], Wundt contemptuously likens to Baron Münchhausen, who is famous in the German speaking world for his exaggerations and in particular, for his claim of having pulled himself out of the bog by his own pigtail. On the other hand, Wundt emphasized introspection [in the sense of *internal perception*, that is, *Innere Wahrnehmung*] as the foundation of an empirical psychology (Wundt 1888).

As for the known drawbacks of the method of gathering data from internal perception, he emphasizes that

> "*it is totally in the hands of the psychologists to take care that these defects disappear more and more. The only thing they have to do is to seize the experimental method.*"[1]

He admits that for the time being he sees obstacles for a ready change in the following two properties.

> "*One property is arrogance. There are still some people who consider experimenting a philistine art, which one should not deal with, if one does not want to risk loosing the privilege of residing in the pure ether of thoughts.*'[2] '*The other property is mistaken modesty. Every art usually tends to appear to be more difficult than it really is to those who do not understand it.*"[3]

However, Wundt does not overestimate the role of the methodology. For him, it is evident that

> "*experimental psychology is not different from other sciences. The answers that you get are not only dependent on the technical aids you dispose of, but also on the questions you ask. Who asks no questions or only mistaken ones must not be surprised if he receives only irrelevant or useless answers*" (Wundt 1888: 308).[4]

What is the situation in present day grammar theory? First, it is an accepted premise that a satisfactory model of the human language faculty, and in particular, of the grammatical properties of human languages, ultimately has to be a model of how grammar is represented and operative in the human mind. Second, present-day grammar theory, especially in the family of generative grammars, produces highly complex hypotheses on the organisation of a human grammar.

Given this state of affair, one would expect a linguist to proceed like any other scientist in a comparable situation would do and devise suitable experiments for testing the various hypotheses thoroughly. Interestingly, though, modern grammar theory has not been significantly influenced by findings from psycholinguistic experiments on language processing or by acquisition data or data from language pathology. The nearly exclusive source of evidence, it seems, still is the native speaker's intuition of the researcher on the linguistic material (s)he analyses, or in Wundt's terminology, her/his internal perception reports and the (partial)[5] consent of the research community.

Wasow and Arnold (2005:1484) emphasized this point as follows:

> "*For reasons that have never been made explicit, many generative grammarians appear to regard primary intuitions as more direct evidence of linguistic competence than other types of data. But there is no basis for this belief. Since knowledge*

> *of language is not directly observable, linguists should use every type of evidence available to help us infer what is in speakers' minds.*"

It still is an exception if a syntactician adds an appendix to a paper and documents the results of, for instance, a simple questionnaire study on the acceptability judgements for the data discussed in the paper.

The grammar competence apparently is robust enough and, in particular, invariant across individuals to such an extent that this questionable methodology has proven successful over decades of linguistic research and has produced a huge amount of tightly interconnected generalizations on grammatical properties and stable insights into aspects of the architecture of human grammars. Imagine, however, a psychologist investigating, for instance, the cognitive capacity for number processing, submitting a paper to a major journal that is based entirely on his private intuitions (inner perception) sampled from various number processing tasks performed by himself. The chances are very high that the paper will be returned simply because of the basic methodological flaw of not having tested the hypotheses on a sufficiently large group of experimental subjects.

Why is linguistics different? After all, its focus is a cognitive domain, so the canon of scientific methods for empirical work should be mandatory for linguistics just as it is mandatory for any other discipline of cognitive science. An essential difference seems to be this: language data are, unlike data from other capacities, as for instance vision, *discrete* and *bi-directionally* accessible, that is, accessible from both the side of production and the side of perception. The inherently discrete structure that allows to readily observe fine-grained data contrasts plus the high degree of interindividual uniformity is a property of languages. It is this property that gave linguists the chance to produce an extensive set of generalizations in spite of the questionable acquisition of their body of evidence. (Self) informant data are the *easiest* to obtain (Newmeyer 1983:50) and the paradigm has proven *productive* to a large extent. But even if this (lack of a rigorous) approach sufficed to produce satisfactory results, this does not prove that it will be successful indefinitely, for the following reason.

Grammar theory had to start from scratch in the past century and it is rightly identified above all with Noam Chomsky who formulated a cognitive science research program. Descriptive grammars were not concerned with the precise formulation of principles and constraints of grammar. In this pioneering phase, it was enough to rely on working principles like the 'clear case method': if you cannot decide on the basis of the given evidence, find clear cases. If you fail to find clear cases, do not base strong claims on this body of evidence.

Today, the 'clear case method' has covered an extensive territory of grammatical phenomena and is likely to reach its 'territorial' limits. Presently, and of course also in the time before, theoreticians are faced with the situation that major competing hypotheses cover the clear cases equally well, and that the differentiating predictions that follow from each of the competing hypotheses are not always 'clear cases'. It is this situation that calls for a controlled and methodologically rigorous management of the crucial evidence.

Already thirty years ago, researchers in psycholinguistics (Levelt et als. 1977) emphasized a growing but methodologically unsound practice in linguistics:

> "*More and more subtle theory is now being constructed on less and less clear cases. In such a situation one would expect linguistics to turn to appropriate behavioural methods of data gathering and (statistical) analysis. Nothing of the sort occurs, however.*"

Subtle theories normally come as a family, with a common body of clear cases that is covered satisfactorily by each of the family members. So, in order to find out empirical differences between the theory variants, more marginal areas are visited in order to recruit differentiating data. These are too often 'less clear cases'

Usually, the 'unclear cases' are a matter of dispute. They are either recruited as grammatical in support of a given hypothesis, or as ungrammatical, in arguments against a given hypothesis. In the case of defence, alleged counterevidence may be 'explained' away as ungrammatical although it is not. This is the case of '*falsely negative*'. The specific examples used in the argument may indeed be ungrammatical or merely degraded by intervening factors that are irrelevant. In the latter case, they are wrongly dismissed.

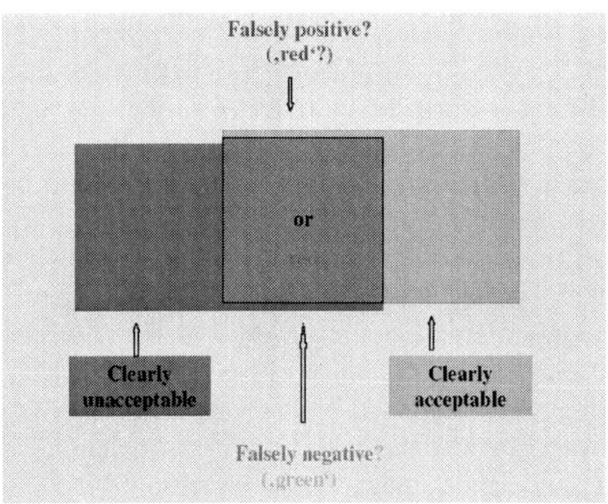

Figure 1.

On the other hand, the evidence that is raised against a given hypothesis may be indeed irrelevant or mistaken as grammatical and judged *falsely positive*. Obviously, in both cases, the evidence needs to be assessed independently.

Figure 1 illustrates the situation. The evidence that is used can be partitioned into three sets, namely the clearly acceptable one, the clearly unacceptable one, and the unclear cases. It is this set, that may be used ambiguously in the argumentations. Does this happen in reality?

Here is a linguistic illustration for the described situation. Figure 2 is a display of the results of a questionnaire inquiry conducted by Gisbert Fanselow and provoked by a preliminary version of Haider (2004). There, it is claimed that the subject-object asymmetry found with in-situ wh-elements in English is a VO property and absent in OV languages. Therefore, Fanselow sent a questionnaire to native Dutch linguists asking for their ratings of a sample of relevant data. The results turned out to be highly puzzling, as the following figure illustrates. *Figure 2*:

	1	5	6	4	3	9	7	2	8	10
	ik weet niet wie wat gekocht heeft	ik weet niet, wie wat an wie gegeven heeft	ik weet wie wat gekocht heeft	ik weet niet wat wie aan wie gegeven heeft	ik weet niet wat welke leraar ge-kocht heeft	wie weet wat wie gekocht heeft voor zijn zusje	wie weet wat wie gekocht heeft	ik weet niet wat wie gekocht heeft	ik weet niet wat wie ge-kocht heeft voor zijn zusje	wie weten al welke boeken deze studenten hebben gekocht, maar wij weten nog niet, wat wie precies heeft gekocht
1	+	+	+	+	+	+	+	+	+	+
2	+	+	+	+	+	+	+	+	+	-
3	+	+	+	+	+	+	+	+	+	+
4	+	+	+	+	+	+	+	+	+	+
5	+	+	+	+	+	0	+	+	-	0
6	+	+	+	+	0	+	+	-	0	-
7	+	+	+	+	0	+	+	0	0	-
8	+	+	+	+	+	+	0	0	0	0
9	+	+	+	+	+	0	0	0	-	-
10	+	+	+	+	+	-	-	0	0	+
11	+	+	+	+	+	-	-	-	-	0
12	+	+	+	+	-	+	-	-	-	-
13	+	+	+	0	+	-	+	-	-	-
14	+	+	+	0	0	0	0	0	-	0
15	+	+	+	0	-	0	0	0	-	-
16	+	+	+	0	0	-	-	0	-	+
17	+	+	+	0	-	-	-	-	-	-
18	+	+	+	0	0	-	-	-	-	0
19	+	+	+	0	0	-	-	-	-	-
20	+	+	+	0	-	-	-	-	-	0
21	+	+	+	-	-	-	-	-	-	-
22	+	+	+	-	-	-	-	-	-	-

Figure 2.

Three of the 22 raters judge all examples as acceptable. On the other hand, there are five, who rate at least 50% of the sentences as deviant. There are clear cases, namely the sentences of the first three rows, but there is no clearly deviant sentence since there is no item ruled out by all raters.

The crucial data for the controversy are 4–10, since in these sentences, the object precedes an in-situ wh-subject, like in (1). Exactly for these sentences the ratings are heterogeneous. Would I be right if I base my claims on the raters who vote positively or should I consider them as mistaken and follow the 'thumbs-down' ratings with the risk that they are wrong?

This situation is a good illustration of an 'unclear data' situation that needs to be clarified. Although this very area of data has been the favourite target of intensive modelling in grammar theory for at least two decades, starting in 1977 with Chomsky's 'On wh-movement', there does not exist a single controlled study on wh-movement asymmetries for English or for any other Germanic language from this time. It is Featherston (2001), who presented the first in-depth experimental study on wh-movement, and this study is worth being replicated and extended for double-checking its basic claims.

In English, a wh-*subject* must not remain in-situ (1b), but it has to be fronted. In German, however, both orders are perfectly acceptable (1c,d). This is uncontroversial, at least for embedded wh-clauses. Why should Dutch be controversial in this respect?

(1) a. *It is unclear what shocked whom*
b. **It is unclear whom what shocked*
c. *Es ist unklar, was wen schockierte* (= 1a)
d. *Es ist unklar, wen was schockierte* (= 1b)

A heterogeneous pattern of acceptance/rejection as in figure (2) is an appropriate illustration of the problem characterized abstractly in figure (1). In this case, it would surely help to have a standardized method of assessing the validity of the evidence. In addition, a standardized method would improve the cross-linguistic validity. How else could I weigh the rejection of (1b) in English in comparison to the rejection of the Dutch counterpart by some informants?

Since Wundt's time, psychology has continuously developed a canon of standards for empirical work. The minimal measures to be observed are to guarantee data collection and data evaluation under controlled circumstances. This presupposes a large enough *number* of experimental subjects, subjects *ignorant* of the test hypotheses, a *randomized* presentation of stimuli, and a *representative* set of stimuli, in a test design with distractor stimuli.

Acceptability judgements, that is, intuitions of informants on the acceptability of stimuli, are a legitimate class of evidence for linguistic hypotheses but they should be treated as what they are, namely experimental data whose quality is dependent on experimental standards.[6] But, even if data are highly accurate in terms of discrimination between acceptable and unacceptable, they are not imprinted with their appropriate interpretation relative to a test hypothesis. Here is an illustration. For details see Fanselow (1991: 330), Müller (1995: 323f.), and Haider (2004).

(2)	a.		*Who(m) did you instruct to get what?*	
	b.		**What did you instruct who(m) to get?*	
	c.		**Who(m) did you instruct who(m) to inform?*	
	d.		*Wen hast du beauftragt was zu besorgen?*	(=2a)
	e.	(?)	*Was hast du wen beauftragt zu besorgen?*	(=2b)
	f.		**Wen hast du wen beauftragt zu informieren?*	(=2c)
	g.	(?)	*Was hat dich wer beauftragt, für uns zu besorgen* *what has you-ACC who-NOM instructed for us to get*	

In the literature, (2b, c) are considered to be clear cases of a superiority restriction (or its present day renderings in terms of a minimal link condition). The German counterpart of (2b), however, is representative for a pattern that is generally judged as acceptable by informants. It is expected, of course, that (2e) is felt to be more difficult to process than (2d), since the antecedent-gap computation is complicated by the intervening wh-item. (2f), however, is strongly deviant in German, too, although its structure is identical with the structure of (2e). Therefore, the crucial difference between (2e) and (2f) is not the structure but the non-distinctness of the two wh-items in (2f). It is this property that seems to be an intolerable processing impediment. Incidentally, Müller (1995: 324) claims that the in-situ subject (2g) in comparison to an in-situ object (2e) is more marginal because of a grammaticality violation. This is a judgement that I feel unable to share and therefore would like to see being tested.

Here is the point announced above: even if we take the acceptability ratings in (2) for granted, this does not tell us whether its causality is to be sought in grammar or in processing. The German contrasts point to processing restrictions. As long as the wh-items are morphologically distinct, crossing does not principally reduce its acceptability. It makes the structure more complicated to process but not ungrammatical.

As for English, the contrast between (2a) and (2b, c) has been taken as a 'clear' case of a grammatical causality, namely a superiority violation. What is needed under these circumstances is a systematic and controlled experimental check that is sensitive for the crucial variable (gradient processing difficulties vs. categorical grammar constraint) of the competing hypotheses.[7]

The pattern of acceptance/rejection in figure 2 is a good illustration for the fact that professional training does not guarantee uniform judgements. This relativises Gleitman and Gleitman's (1970) opinion that

> *"for an in-depth syntactic investigation, native command of the given language is indispensable: Only the most sophisticated speakers can supply the exquisite judgements required for writing a grammar"*

and confirms Labov's (1978) statement that

> *"good practice in the more advanced sciences distrusts most of all the memory and impressions of the investigator himself."*

A simple account for the diverging patterns in figure two would be the (hard to produce) verification that in this case, some raters are likely to have superimposed their theoretical convictions on their own native speaker's judgement. If this was the true cause, the situation is an illustration of the problem to be discussed in the following section.

2. Orwell's problem – all languages are equal, but some are more equal than others

Presently, the majority of languages covered by Generative Grammar come from a single language family (Indo-European: Germanic and Romance subfamilies), and a single type, namely strictly head-initial languages. A single, highly exceptional[8] language of the Germanic family serves as the model language and grammar theoretical 'fruit fly' ('drosophila grammatica'). The modelling of this type of language has resulted in a grammar theory appropriate for this type of languages. It is understandable that a grammar architecture that has proven successful for the modelling of a number of (VO) languages is adopted as the frame of reference for the integration of non-VO languages, too. It is less understandable, though, if empirical discrepancies are explained away as if they were merely accidental deviations rather than analyzed in an empirically adequate model.[9]

It is a legitimate working hypothesis to start with that well-established principles of grammars are considered as valid and that they are therefore immunized and shielded against conflicting evidence by introducing auxiliary hypothesis, for some time. This is legitimate as long as the auxiliary hypotheses are taken as hypotheses that have to be checked and justified with independent evidence. It is not legitimate if the argument runs like this: here is a set of data from language L whose crucial property should follow from hypothesis Y, but it does not. However, if we assume hypothesis X, the properties follow from Y. Therefore, X is part of the grammar of L. It is this conclusion that needs to be checked independently since it this proposition that protects Y, and we have to make sure that the assumption of X is justified, otherwise we would have to give up or at least modify Y. It is this requirement of producing independent evidence that is neglected too often in grammar theoretical argumentation.

Let us return once more to the examples in (1b, d): German does not display the so-called superiority contrasts in the way English does.[10] This challenges the assumption that in German, a nominative DP is confined to the same functional spec-position that an English subject is. In Haider (1986, 2004), it is argued that the lack of an English-like contrast follows from the fact that in German, the subject remains in its VP-internal position and there is no obligatory functional subject position in the German clause structure, and that this follows ultimately from a basic OV/VO difference. In this case, hypothesis Y is the premise that universally, the surface subject position is a functional spec-position (EPP hypothesis: every clause has an obligatory functional subject position). Hypothesis X is produced in order to protect the EPP against these facts. It could run like this:

Wiltschko's (1997: 123f.) suggests the following auxiliary hypothesis: German permits scrambling and scrambling is supposed to produce d-linking and d-linking cancels superiority (Pesetsky 1987). Hence, wh-subjects that stay in situ, stay in a scrambled position and not in their base position. For example, superiority would apply only to the structure (3b), but not to the scrambled variant (3c). Therefore, the acceptability of (3a) is hypothetically guaranteed if it is assigned the structure (3c).

(3) a. *Wen hat was schockiert?*
what has what shocked

b. *Wen$_j$ hat [$_{VP}$ *was e$_j$ schockiert]?* — hypothesis: not scrambled

c. *Wen$_j$ hat [was$_i$ [$_{VP}$ e$_i$ e$_j$ schockiert]?* — hypothesis: 'd-linked' subject

d. *Wen$_j$ hat [e$_j$ [was$_i$ [$_{VP}$ e$_i$ e$_j$ schockiert]?* — hypothesis: scrambled object

Richards (1997: 90) tries to arrive at the same result in a more direct way. He assumes, like Wiltschko, that wh-elements can be scrambled in German. Scrambling has the effect of bringing a 'lower' wh-phrase closer to the target Spec-CP position prior to wh-movement. So the position from where wh-movement of the object in (3d) starts is higher than the subject position and therefore superiority gets pre-empted. However, what both seem to be unaware of is the fact that a scrambled variant of a multiple wh-clause is unacceptable (see also Müller and Sternefeld 1993):

(4) a. **Wann hat was$_i$ denn wer e$_i$ gesehen?*
when has what PRT who seen

Moreover, Richards does not honour the crucial factor for the contrast in (1a,b), namely the fact that the in-situ wh-element must not be a wh-element in the functional *subject* position. A scrambling account as in (3d) would not solve this problem, since the in-situ wh-element would continue to be a subject in a subject position.[11]

In this situation, it is necessary to check data in contexts that do not involve scrambling or d-linking. Here, Dutch comes into play because Dutch does not allow the scrambling of DPs. For Dutch, data as in figure (2) and in (5) are immediately relevant.

(5) a. *Ik kan mij niet herinneren wat aan wie toebehoorde*
I can myself not remember *what to whom* belonged

b. *Ik kan mij niet herinneren aan wie wat toebehoorde*
I can myself not remember *to whom what* belonged

(5b) should be as unacceptable as its English counterpart, if the Dutch sentence structure is identical with the English one, in the relevant aspect. But, informants tell me that they would not at all reject (5b) as unacceptable; some even prefer it over (5a).

If d-linking is invoked, the relevant contrasts for d-linking would have to be checked carefully. DPs with a wh-modifier like 'how many' cannot be d-linked since this is a quantifier ranging over cardinalities of sets and not over individuals. So, if d-linking matters, there should be a contrast between d-linkable wh-items and those that cannot be d-linked. But there is no contrast, it seems.

(6) a. *Wen haben wieviele/welche Zeugen wiedererkannt?*
whom have how-many/which witnesses re-identified

b. *Welchen Briefträger haben wieviele/wessen Hunde gebissen?*
which postman have how-many/whose dogs bitten

I would expect, given my own judgements and a small number of collected ones that a systematic survey would substantiate the claim that there is no relevant acceptability contrast for the examples in (6) that would support the d-linking hypothesis.

Each of these cases illustrates the need of a broad enough investigation into the acceptability properties of the (apparent) evidence and (apparent) counter-evidence for the controversy between a VO-based approach that claims the EPP property for both VO and OV sentence structures and an approach that takes the headedness difference between OV and VO as a crucial difference that is relevant for a set of contrasts that comprise at least the following OV/VO 'mismatches' (Haider 2005):

- EPP property for clause structures of the SVO type only
- VP-shells in VO only
- compactness of head-initial structures only
- edge effect for adjunction to a head-initial structure
- V-clustering in head-final structures

The EPP property is a direct consequence of the SVO property. In SVO languages, the VP is head-initial with respect to the objects, but the VP-internal subject position precedes the verbal head. On the hypothesis that merged elements need a licensing head in the canonical direction, the VP-internal subject is not canonically licensed, unless there is a functional head preceding and licensing the position, and the subject moves to the spec position if case-linking requires this. In OV, the arguments of the verb are all canonically licensed in their VP-internal position, since the direction of merger is identical with the direction of canonical licensing.

(7) a. $[_{FP}$ Spec $[_{F'}$ $F^{\circ\rightarrow}$ $[_{VP}$ *DP* $[_{V'}$ $V^{\circ\rightarrow}$ ...]]]] SVO
b. ... $[_{VP}$DP $^{\leftarrow}$ [... $^{\leftarrow}V^{\circ}$]] SOV

The compactness property (8a) is an immediate consequence of the VP shell structure of head-initial VPs which in itself is a consequence of implementing a head-initial structure in a system with the universal property that merging applies to the left hand side of a phrase only. Since the head must canonically license a complement, the only way to license a complement preceding the original head position, that is $complement_1$ in (8a), is re-merging the head to the left of the higher complement. The result is a VP-shell structure. For OV there is no need for a shell structure since any complement precedes the head.

(8) a. [head (*XP) complement]
b. $[head_i{}^{\rightarrow}$ $[complement_1$ $[e_i{}^{\rightarrow}$ $complement_2]]]$
c. $[head_i{}^{\rightarrow}$ $[(*XP_1)$ $complement_1$ $[(*XP_2)$ $[e_i{}^{\rightarrow}$ $complement_2$]]]]

Compactness follows from the licensing principle: the (extended) head and the licensed position minimally, mutually c-command in the canonical licensing direction. In (8b), $complement_1$ is minimally and canonically c-commanded by the preceding head in the shell structure, and this head is minimally and canonically c-commanded by virtue of the chain relation in the shell structure: the $complement_1$ c-commands the trace of the raised head. In OV, there is in each case a sister relation between the merged phrase and the head V^oor the extended head V′ in the canonical direction:

(9) $[_{VP}$ complement$_1$ $\leftarrow$ $[_{V'}$ complement$_2$ $\leftarrow$ V°]]

An intervening XP, as for instance an adjunct or a scrambled argument, in (8c) destroys the minimality requirement of licensing. The XP_1 prevents the head from minimally c-commanding its compement$_1$, and XP_2 would destroy the minimal c-command relation between complement$_1$ and the trace of the head.

German, like Dutch, is a language with mixed directionality. The VP is head-final and the NP is head-initial. In German and Dutch, an infinitive can be recategorised as a noun. This allows to check the contrast in compactness between the head-final VP and the head-initial NP:

(10) a. *[analyze (*with care) the data]*$_{VP}$
b. *[die Daten (mit Sorgfalt) analysieren*$_{V°}$*]*$_{VP}$
the data-ACC (with care) analyze
c. *das [Analysieren*$_{N°}$ *(*mit Sorgfalt) der Daten/von Daten]*$_{NP}$
the analyz(ing) (with care) the data-GEN/of data

Since scrambling is another source of producing interveners, head-initial structures do not allow scrambling and are characterized by a rigid word order.

The edge effect (Haider 2000) is characteristic of head-initial phrases. An adjunct merged to a head initial phrases behaves as if it selects the phrase as a quasi-complement. The head of the adjunct and the target phrase are immediately adjacent:

(11) a. *He has [(much more) often (*than anyone else) [*$_{VP}$ *participated in this contest]]*$_{VP}$
b. *Er hat [an dem Wettbewerb (sehr viel) öfter (als jemand anderer) teilgenommen]*$_{VP}$
he has in the competition (much more) often /than anyone else) participated
c. *A [bigger (*than John)] [man]]*$_{NP}$
d. *ein [größerer *(als Hans)] [Mann]]*$_{NP}$
a bigger (than Hans) man

The English VP and the English and German NP are head-initial. The head effect for these phrases is illustrated in (11a), (11c) and (11d), respectively. The German VP is head-final and there is no edge effect.

Finally, V clustering is an OV property. It is not found in VO. Straightforward evidence for the existence of V-clustering is the nominalization of clusters. Nominalization is a word formation process and word formation is restricted to the lexical category level. A verbal cluster is a head-to-head adjunction structure (Haider 2003) and therefore a structure of category V°. Hence a cluster is eligible for a word formation process.

(12) Example: nominalized V° cluster[12] in German

a. *[Deadlines [verstreichen lassen]]*$_{VP}$
deadlines expire let

b. *das Verstreichenlassen*$_{N°}$ *der/von Deadlines*
the letting expire the-GEN/of deadlines

c. *[Deadlines [verstreichen lassen müssen]]*$_{VP}$
deadlines expire let must

d. *das Verstreichenlassenmüssen*$_{N°}$ *der/von Deadlines*
the expire-let-must the-GEN/of deadlines
'the having to let the deadlines expire'

e. **the let(ting) (of) deadlines expire

What is the role of evidence for Orwell's problem? While Wundt's problem concerns the level of observational adequacy, Orwell's problem is a problem on the level of descriptive adequacy. Its focus is the empirically adequate formulation of the generalizations covering the data. A generalization is a hypothetical grammatical law for covering properties and correlations of data.

Empirical adequacy at this level is not a matter of data accuracy but of data representativity. Generalizations are generalizations based on partionings of the set of data according to the properties of the subsets. The problem at this level is not a misrepresentation of a datum, but a mispartitioning of the data set. The two main sources for mispartitioning are the following.

One source is the strict adherence to a theoretical premise that requires a particular partitioning. Here is an example. The VO-based model predicts a set of structural subject-object asymmetries in syntax. OV languages do not show the same partitioning. But, there are of course subject-object differences. After all, it is the subject that agrees in finite clauses, and in transitive constructions, the subject precedes the object. So, it is expected that there are subject-object asymmetries. For instance, it is obvious that there is a difference between (13a) and (13b) for multiple wh-constructions. After all, in (13a), a wh-item is fronted across a preceding wh-item. In processing (13a), the working memory is confronted with two wh-items simultaneously. In (13b), the fronted wh-item can be linked to its base position already when the second item is met. In (13a), the fronted wh-item has to be kept on store when the in-situ wh-item has been parsed.

(13) a. *Wen$_i$ hat wer e$_i$ zuerst bemerkt?*
whom has who first noticed

b. *Wer$_i$ hat e$_i$ wen zuerst bemerkt?*
who has what zuerst notices

c. *??Whom has who e$_i$ noticed first?*

But, and this is crucial, the difference is not the kind of structural difference that leads to a grammaticality violation in a VO sentence structure. If there is a difference between (13a,b), it is a processing difference, and it should not be equivocated with the difference in English, with (13c) as the deviant order. The source of the deviance for (13c) in English is the in-situ wh-subject in the functional subject position, and this source is absent in OV.

A second source of getting astray is the reliance on a selective and thereby not fully representative data basis. There are two different ways of committing this mistake. The obvious one is the reliance on too narrow a set of data, neglecting crucial positive data that bear on the issue. A good illustration provides Reinhart's (1983) analysis of extraposition (see below).

A less easy to control, second way is the failure to systematically check the given hypothesis for overgeneration: does a given hypothesis admit data that actually should be excluded? An illustration of this problem can be found in the discussion of the verb clustering phenomenon.

As for extraposition, the following set of data has been taken to be indicative of different adjunction sites by Reinhart (1983) and Culicover and Rochemont (1990). The rule for disjoint reference, that is, Principle C of the binding system, seems to differentiate between extraposed *argument* clauses on the one hand and extraposed *relative* clauses on the other. A referential expression in an extraposed relative clause does not trigger a principle C violation. As a consequence, relative clauses were supposed to be adjoined higher than the object position. Being adjoined to a higher position, they are not in the c-command domain of a VP internal potential binder of the matrix clause.

(14) a. *I sent her^i many gifts last year [that Mary^i did not like]*$_{\text{Relative clause}}$
(C&R 1990: 29)

b. *It bothered her^i [that Rosa^{*i} had failed]*$_{\text{Argument clause}}$
(Reinhart 1983: 49)

If the examples in (14) are assumed to reflect *structurally* conditioned binding effects, this effect is captured if the extraposed clause is in a position c-commanded by the object pronoun of the matrix clause in (14b) but outside the c-command domain of the object in (14a). This is the case if the relative clause is adjoined to a position higher than the VP. The extraposed subject clause (14b) must be in a lower position, namely one that is c-commanded by the indirect object. It is a necessary and unavoidable consequence then that the relative clause must follow the argument clause, if both are extraposed, since the relative clause ends up in a position higher than the extraposed argument clause. Curiously, the authors did not test this consequence. If they had, they would have realized that the prediction is contradicted by the facts (Haider 1997). The correct order (15a) is different from the predicted one (15b), and the binding differences nevertheless hold (15c).

(15) a. *It bothered everyone considerably who knows her that she had failed the exam*

b. **It bothered everyone considerably that she had failed the exam who knows her*

c. *Someone has told her*^{i} *[who Mary*^{i} *had not met before] [that Mary**^{i} *is in danger]*

Incidentally, the order pattern among extraposed clauses still is unaccounted for in the literature. However, it is clear that the original assumption in terms of extraposition sites at different depths of embeddings for relative versus argument clauses cannot be correct.

Brody (2004:151) objects to my conclusion that principle C binding is an unreliable source of evidence and writes

> "*that there are a number of analyses compatible with the observation in (15c) and a c-command dependent principle C.*"[13]

He suggests a Right Node Raising derivation for the complement clause and illustrates it with the following structure assignment.

(16) Someone has told [her$_{x}$ (~~that *Mary$_{x}$ will ...~~)] [who Mary met] [that Mary will prevail]

What this amounts to is binding under reconstruction. In his words,

> "*since principle C is sensitive to elements in A'-trace positions [...], disjointness [...] can be determined in the trace position and the extraposed complement clause could be stacked higher than and on the right of V and its complements.*"

However, what this suggestion completely ignores is the anti-reconstruction property of CPs in A'-position.

It is well-known (see van Riemsdijk and Williams (1981), on anti-crossover) that in principle C contexts, uncontroversially A'-moved *clauses* are *not* reconstructed. (17a) is an A'-moved clause, and it contrasts with the extraposed clause (17b) with respect to disjoint reference. Therefore, it is far from evident, that the disjoint reference effect with extraposed clauses can be attributed to reconstruction.

(17) a. *[Dass Michas*^{i} *Position unhaltbar sei]*$_{j}$ *hat ihm*^{i} *keiner* e_j *gesagt*
[that Micha's position untenable is] has him nobody told

b. *Keiner hat ihm*^{i} (e_j) *gesagt, [dass Michas*^{*i} *Position unhaltbar sei]*$_{j}$
nobody has him told [that Micha's position untenable is]

Let us turn now to the second road to a miss, namely an overlooked over-generation. Investigations of the verb clustering properties in German and the Germanic OV languages usually start with the VO model of stacked verbal projections (18a) as the base structure (18b):

(18) a. $[V_1° [V_2° [V_3° \ldots]_{VP}]_{VP}]_{VP}$ OV: stacked verbal projections
b. $[[[\ldots V_3°]_{VP} V_2°]_{VP} V_1°]_{VP}$ VO: stacked verbal projections ?
– or
c. $[\ldots [[[V_3°] V_2°] V_1°]_{V°}]_{VP}$ verbal cluster ?

An obvious difference between (18a) and (18b) is easy to read off the bracketing. (18b) is a centre-embedding structure. The clustering structure (18c) eliminates the centre-embedded VPs and confines recursion to the local domain of the verbal cluster. It is still a controversial issue in the literature as to whether there exists a genuine cluster as in (18b). The alternative to this assumption is the removal of all the material in the VP of V_3 in (18b), except the verbal head. As a consequence, the resulting subtree would consist only of verbs, but it is still a stacked VP structure. What is neglected (Wurmbrand 2001) or left unexplained (Koopman and Szabolcsi 2001) is a consequence of this analysis that turns out to be negative. It is the following property that is not taken into consideration: the verbal cluster is compact; VPs, however, allow extraposition to their right edge:

(19) a. *dass sie das Problem erkannt haben (*das hier auftritt) müssten*
that they the problem recognized have, that here arises, must

b. *[Das Problem erkannt haben, das hier auftritt]*$_{VP}$ *müssten sie aber*
[the problem recognized have that here arises] must they well

The ungrammaticality of the pattern (19a) is also counterevidence for the still wide-spread assumption that the finite verb in German and Dutch moves to a clause final functional head. In this case, extraposition could target the right edge of the VP and produce the positive evidence for a separate verb position outside of, and to the right of, the VP. The evidence is negative, however.

Let us turn to the general issue of this subsection again. Orwell's problem is not a problem of sloppy data. It is a problem of (mostly unintended) sloppy data management. An affirmative action approach – "here is my hypothesis, there are the data that support it" – does not guarantee success in science if this amounts to disregarding substantive counterevidence that resists integration into the presently favored model. It is well known that there is no logically valid method of verification, but there is a logically valid method of falsification. Hence, counterevidence has primacy over merely supportive evidence.

3. Crick's problem – a black box is a black box

Crick's problem is as follows:

> "The difficulty of the method of the black box is this. If the interior of the box does not have a very simple structure, the method soon will reach a stage in which different theories cover all observable results sufficiently well. Attempts to decide between the theories fail because new experiments only produce new complexities. One has no other choice than groping one's way into the box" (Crick 1979: 148).[14]

The method of collecting native speaker judgements is a black-box-method. The competence of the native speaker is a black-box faculty of mind. The judgements are elicited output data of the black box. The method is an attempt to learn about the structure of the black box by systematically studying input-triggered reactions on potential output qualities. In other words, the native informant is required to judge whether a given expression is a possible acceptable output of his own black box.

The undeniable success of the introspective method in linguistics in the past half century must not be misinterpreted. Sure enough, the method has been sufficient for uncovering a substantive body of intricate grammatical properties, both within a given language as well as cross-linguistically. But, and this is the crucial point, the method is not sufficient for uncovering the structure of the mental system of grammar processing that is the ultimate source of these set of properties. This is the point of Crick's claim. The black box method is a method that is not suited for producing *reliable* insights into the internal make up of the system. All you can do is testing your hypotheses on the level of weakly equivalent systems. The acceptance/rejection reactions of an informant are, as far as the *grammar*-based qualities are concerned, reactions on impenetrable qualia of linguistic expressions produced by the black box.

You might object that this is a situation that scientists are confronted with in other areas of science as well. But this objection would be inappropriate, because the parallel fails in an essential respect. If, for example, a scientist wants to test a hypothesis on what is going on in the interior of the sun, (s)he of course is unable to run an experiment on or within the sun. But, and this is the crucial difference, the scientist has a model at his disposal whose components have been tested and experimentally established in close contact and under immediate supervision in the lab. Branches of cognitive science may use animal models for testing hypothesis on neurocognition. The situation in linguistics is unique in so far as linguistics investigates a mental capacity of a single species, members of which cannot be used as subjects for systematic experimental studies of the kind carried out with primates, for instance. Linguistics lacks an animal model and linguistics lacks a well-understood background theory of the neurophysiologic processes that subserve the specific mental capacity, notwithstanding the significant headway that has been made in the past two decades (Poeppel and Embick 2005). In the present situation, the degree of freedom in the space of explanatory models is vast. In practice, it is impossible to narrow them down to a level where each degree of freedom could be tested separately. This is what Crick seems to have in mind when he remarks that "the theories fail because new experiments only produce new complexities".

How could one grope one's way into the black-box? The answer is obvious. There is no privileged access road. The available way is the way paved by psycho- and neurolinguistics. Given this situation, it is telling that on the one hand, grammar theory claims to model a mental capacity, but on the other hand, the results of psycholinguistic investigations into this mental capacity have no direct influence at all on grammar theory. No theoretical claim has ever been given up for the sole reason that it is in conflict with psycholinguistic findings. Linguistics is in the curious situation that the theoretical branch (grammar theory), which is obviously in need of an experimental companion (in parallel to other, more mature branches of science, as for instance theoretical and experimental biology/chemistry/physics), does without psycholinguistics. In the present day situation, a theoretical linguists is not obliged to put to test a novel claim in an experiment that produces clear-cut behavioural data of a representative group of test subjects. The scientific community of the grammar theory camp seems to be content with example sentences and complex arguments that are meant to show that properties of these example sentences follow from a set of highly intricate assumptions.[15]

Why should this be so? One reason Bornkessel-Schlesewsky and Schlesewsky (2007: 320) formulate as follows:

> "experimental data may be superior to intuitions in terms of their reliability, but they still *require interpretation*. They allow just as much misinterpretation as intuitions."

Just like native speaker judgements, the reactions of the test subject to the stimuli

> "reflect the *endpoint* of an interaction between a variety of linguistic and extralinguistic factors, thus rendering *direct* conclusions from grammatical theory just as useful or just as problematic as those drawn from careful intuitive judgements" (Bornkessel-Schlesewsky and Schlesewsky 2007: 321).

A spontaneous but inappropriate reaction could be this: if the data produced by psycholinguistic experiments are just as indirect as native speaker judgements, we can just as well stick to the latter and forget about the former. This reaction overlooks the essential point, however. Psycholinguistic data are not superior because of their guaranteed success or their higher significance; they are superior because of their experimentally controlled acquisition on the one hand, and the (not yet fulfilled) opportunity of getting closer to the immediate mental source of the grammatical properties of the data, on the other hand.

Computer-based techniques of investigating the brain activities in language processing have become standard tools in the past two decades for psycho- and neurolinguistic research. These methods[16] provide insights into the temporal dynamics (ERP) of processing activities and the coarse localisation of foci of task-related activities in the brain. The ERP method concentrates on signatures (changes in the electric potential measured on the scalp, in terms of charge polarity, latency and power change) in the signal and their correlation with types of linguistic processing activities (see Friederici 2002 for an overview).

Dogil et al. (2002) present results of, and a general methodological background for, an fMRI approach to language processing. In particular, the aim of the series of experiments presented in the paper was to locally differentiate the processing sites for phonological, syntactic and semantic operations. In sum, the results confirmed for the intact brain what has been surmised already on the basis of the results from patholinguistic research on brain lesions.

The ERP method, from the beginning, concentrated on the difference between the brain's reactions on deviant versus well-formed stimuli and the correlates thereof in the recorded signals. So, this comes close to what we are looking for, namely an indicator of ungrammaticality that is tightly associated with the relevant brain activities. Roehm and Haider (in press) tried to focus their investigation on this issue, with the following design.

The crucial question was this: can we find a reliable correlate in the EEG activities for the difference between a potentially resolvable conflict in contrast with a grammatically fatal conflict. The area of grammar we used for the stimulus selection is the interaction between the V2 property of a German finite clause and the distribution of verbal particles. In a declarative clause, a single categorically arbitrary clause-initial phrase is followed by the finite verb. If the verb is a verb with a 'separable' particle, the particle is stranded in the clause final base position of the verb (20b):

(20) a. *Hier beginnt ein Satz mit einem Adverbial*
here starts a sentence with an adverbial

b. *Hier fängt ein Satz mit einem Adverbial an*
here catches a sentence with an adverbial on ('on catch' = begin)

c. *[Mit einem Adverbial anfangen] kann man einen Satz ja immer*
[with an adverbial oncatch] can a sentence PRT always

In German, the infinitival form and the finite form of the verb in present tense 2nd and 3rd person plural is identical. So, a sentence like (21a) is temporarily ambiguous between a continuation as in (21b) or in (21c):

(21) a. *Den Satz beginnen ...*
the sentence begin

b. *Den Satz beginnen*$_{3rd.P.pl.}$ *sie diesmal am Besten mit einem Adverbial*
the sentence begin you this-time at best with an adverbial

c. *[Den Satz beginnen*$_{Inf.}$*]*$_{VP}$ *könnten sie diesmal mit einem Adverbial*
the sentence begin could you this-time with an adverbial

d. *Den Satz anfangen könnten sie auch mit einem Adverbial*
the sentence on-catch could you also with an adverbial

If, however, the verb is accompanied by a particle (21d), the presence of a particle is an unambiguous signal that the verb cannot be finite, since the finite verb would strand the particle (20b). A fronted particle verb must be (part) of a fronted phrase (20c). So, the experiment contrasted the following four pattern types.

(22)	a.	*Die Mauern entfeuchten*$_{present}$ ... the walls dehumidify	morphologically ambiguous complex verb
	b.	*Die Mauern entfeuchteten*$_{pret.}$ ... the walls dehumidify	morphologically unambiguous complex verb
	c.	*Die Farbe anfeuchten*$_{present}$ ... the paint on-moisten	morphologically ambiguous particle verb
	d.	**Die Farbe anfeuchteten*$_{pret.}$ the paint on-moisted	morphologically unambiguous particle verb

According to an 'early commitment' model of parsing, the human parser will identify the potentially finite verb in (22a), as the actual finite verb and will have to revise the assumption if (22a) develops into a pattern like (21c). If, as in (22c), the verb is accompanied by its particle, it is clear that it cannot be finite verb since in this case the particle would have to be stranded. The finiteness assumption can be revised, however, since there is a possible grammatical continuation. On the other hand, a verb with an unambiguously finite form, as the preterite (22d), plus the particle is irreparably flawed. Unlike (22a), there is no continuation that could save this sentence.

(22a) becomes a case of a temporary but resolvable conflict if the first verb is parsed as the finite verb and it turns out that this decision must be revised. (22d), on the other hand, is a case of an irresolvable conflict. Morphology tells that the verb is finite, but there is no structure that accepts a fronted finite verb accompanied by its particle. Figure 3 presents the plots of the ERP responses to the four types of stimuli.

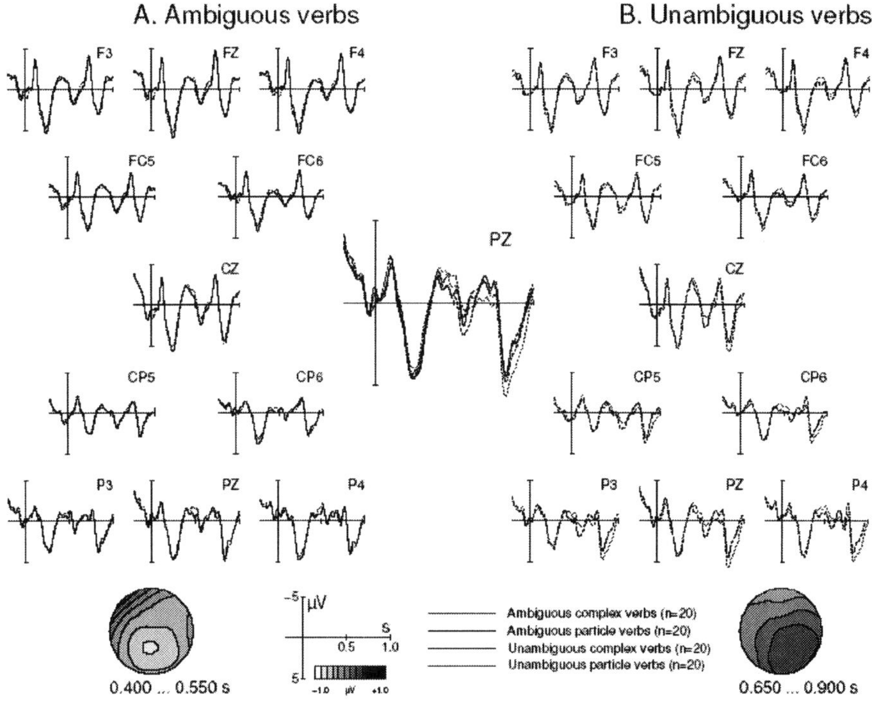

Figure 3.

The ERP-plots show a bi-phasic change in the measured potential. The irresolvable conflict triggered by the pattern (22d) correlates with a left anterior negativisation followed by a positivisation. For the pattern with the first verb as part of a fronted VP, an increased negativity is characteristic for (22c) and also for (22a), namely in those cases in which a following finite auxiliary makes it clear to the parser that the supposedly finite verb is a non-finite one in the given sentence.

The data demonstrate that explicit morphosyntactic indicators (finiteness and particle separability) are immediately taken into account by the parser insofar as they provide information that is *incompatible* with the parser's predictions. When an input string is ambiguous or underspecified, the parser proceeds according to its minimality preferences.[17] Thus, from the perspective of the parser, potential ambiguities are ignored as long as they do not have to be resolved in order to backtrack from a parse that leads into a conflict.

The resolvable conflict (type 21c) produces only an anterior negativity. The same ERP response is produced by the type (21d). Only the irresolvable conflict of the type (22d) triggers the biphasic pattern.[18] The late positivity is a reflex of the parser's failure to repair the conflict. Is this the objective behavioral correlate of the theoretician's asterisk assigned to an allegedly ungrammatical sentence? Unfortunately things are not that simple.

No ERP signature of linguistic processing activities (e.g. P600, N400, or LAN) is a signature of ungrammaticality and nothing but ungrammaticality. Each of these signatures are attested with grammatical sentences as well. N400, for instance, has been found with a scrambled order in comparison with an unscrambled one (Frisch and Schlesewsky 2001, Kutas and Federmeier 2000). P600 has been attested for sentences with a topicalized object in comparison with the variant with a topicalized subject (Frisch et al. 2002). As for LAN, Ueno and Kluender (2003) report this signature for scrambling, measured at the site of the gap, in comparison with unscrambled order.

It is not a single special signature of the EEG activities that could be interpreted as the red traffic light in processing that correlates with the impression of ungrammaticality. The signatures of ungrammaticality come in various patterns of brain reactions. It is the task of the researcher to prove that the signatures indeed are what he claims them to be in each case.

4. Conclusion

The self-understanding of linguists as members of the scientific community of the cognitive sciences sharply contrasts with the established working traditions. If linguistics is to be grounded as a branch of science, grammar theory will have to give up its 'splendid isolation' with respect to the experimental camp. The theoreticians must acknowledge that the practice that proved successful in the pioneering phase of the past decades, namely introspection and eclectic feed-back from informants, has reached its limits.

If they do not actively seek the cooperation with experimental research, it is at least their responsibility to clearly point out what are empirically testable implications of their model. It is not enough to present novel and bold hypotheses and embed them into a set of assumptions that is complex enough to make an experimenting linguist immediately resign.

In the neighboring disciplines of linguistics, standards for empirical research have been established. Since Wundt's days, psychology, but not linguistics, has successfully set up generally accepted standards of data assessment in cognitive science. In linguistics, this task could be postponed for a long time, but it surely cannot be postponed forever.

Notes

1. „Es ist ganz in die Hand der Psychologen gegeben, dafür zu sorgen, dass diese Fehler mehr und mehr ganz verschwinden. Es ist dazu nur das eine nötig, daß sie [...] sich der experimentellen Methode [...] bemächtigen."
2. „Die eine Eigenschaft ist der Hochmuth. Es gibt ja immer noch einige Leute, die das Experimentieren für eine banausische Kunst halten, mit der man sich nicht befassen dürfe, wenn man nicht des Privilegiums, im Aether des reinen Gedanken zu hausens, verlustig gehen wolle."
3. „Die andere Eigenschaft ist die falsche Bescheidenheit. Jede Kunst scheint in der Regel dem, der sie nicht versteht, viel schwerer als sie wirklich ist."
4. „Es ist aber in der experimentellen Psychologie nicht anders, als in anderen Wissenschaften auch. Die Antworten, die man erhält, sind nicht bloß von den Hülfsmitteln, über die man verfügt, sondern auch von den Fragen abhängig, die man stellt. Wer keine oder nur verkehrte Fragen zu stellen weiß, der darf sich nicht wundern, wenn er nichtssagende oder unbrauchbare Antworten erhält."
5. In both readings of this ambiguous term.
6. Featherston (2007: 410) points out that in principle, the choice of the method does not influence the results. The data from informant intuitions (judgements) and from other experimental methods converge.
7. This test, of course, cannot be limited to the contrasts in (2a–c). It has to consider strongly distinct wh-phrases as in i) as well as embedded wh-clauses in constrast with direct questions.
   (i) *As for your students, which books did you request whom to read and summarize?*
   (ii) *As for your students, it is unclear to them which books you requested whom to read and summarize.*

8. For example: English has V2 declaratives, but only under exceptional circumstances (with fronted negated quantified objects). It has finite verbs that *move* to higher functional head positions, but the majority of verbs do not. For the verbs that do not move, an *expletive auxiliary* is used instead ('do-support'). It has subject expletives but their distribution is so much restricted that an intransitive passive is unavailable in English.
9. A corollary of Murphy's law: for every complex problem, there is a simple, easy to understand, wrong solution: 'all languages have the same basic clause structure' that is modulated by syntactic processes (see Kayne 1994).
10. For more details see Featherston (2005) and my comment (Haider in press) and Featherston's reply in the same volume.
11. Chomsky (1981: 236) notes that a wh-subject is illformed in situ, independent of superiority considerations since in the following example sentences, superiority is not involved.
    (i.) **It is unclear* <u>*who*</u> *thinks (that)* ***who*** *saw us*
    (ii.) *I don't know* <u>*who*</u> *would be happy if he/****who*** *won the prize*

12. V-cluster nominalization must be distinguished from VP-nominalization. The latter is possible in English, too, of course. Thanks to Sam Featherston for providing example iii).
    (i.) das Verstreichenlassenmüssen der/von deadlines (=12d) VC nominalization
    (ii.) dein [die Deadlines verstreichen lassen müssen] $_{VP/NP}$ VC nominalization
    your [the deadlines$_{ACC}$ expire let must]
    iii) This [letting deadlines expire]$_{VP/NP}$ gives the department a bad name.

13. The relative clause obviously is opaque for principle C. So c-command is irrelevant here, since binding does not apply. In fact, adverbial clauses show the same property:
    (i.) *Ich werde ihn^i, wenn ich Max^i treffe, damit konfrontieren*
    I shall him if I meet Max with-it confront ('I shall confront him with it, if I meet Max')
    (ii.) *Ich habe ihr^i, als ich Maria^i traf, gratuliert*
    I have her when I Mary met congratulated (‚I have congratulated her when I met Mary')

14. This is the author's translation of the published version: „Die Schwierigkeit der Methode des schwarzen Kastens besteht darin, dass man – sofern das Innere des Kastens nicht sehr einfach strukturiert ist – sehr bald ein Stadium erreicht, in dem unterschiedliche Theorien alle beobachtbaren Resultate gleich gut zu erklären vermögen. Versuche, zwischen den Theorien zu entscheiden, schlagen fehl, weil neue Experimente nur neue Komplexitäten zutage fördern. Man hat dann keine andere Wahl, als sich in den Kasten hineinzutasten."
15. Not every observer formulates his discontent as squarely as Liebermann (2007: 435): "In short [...] the linguistic enterprise, like the Ptolemaic astronomical theory, will in time be regarded as fruitless an exercise in logic and disjoint from reality."

16. There are mainly two kind of methods: i) EEG measurement of event related potentials (ERP) that provide characteristic signatures in terms of latency, polarity and amplitude of the signal, and ii), imaging methods like functional magnetic resonance imaging (fMRI), which records the supposedly task-triggered differences in the regional cerebral bloodflow.
17. Assign the input to the minimally convergent structure. For the verb this means that if the first verb is potentially finite, it is assigned to the position of the finite verb in the declarative clause structure. At this point, the parser does not consider the potential alternative of a complex fronted VP.
18. Frisch and Schlesewsky (2001) found the same biphasic response with ungrammatical sentences that contained two nominatives instead of a nominative and an accusative.

References

Bornkessel-Schlesewsky, Ina and Mathias Schlesewsky
2007 The wolf in sheep's clothing: against a new judgement-driven imperialism. *Theoretical Linguistics* 33: 319–333.

Brody, Michael
2004 "Roll-up" structures and morphological words. In: Katalin É. Kiss and Henk van Riemsdijk (eds.), *Verb clusters: a study of Hungarian, German and Dutch*, 147–171. Amsterdam: Benjamins.

Crick, Francis H.C.
1979 Gedanken über das Gehirn. *Spektrum der Wissenschaft* 11: 147–150.

Culicover, Peter W. and Michael S. Rochemont
1990 Extraposition and the Complement Principle. *Linguistic Inquiry* 21: 23–47.

Chomsky, Noam
1977 On Wh-movement. In: Peter W.Culicover, Thomas Wasow and Adrian Akmajian (eds.), *Formal syntax*, 71–132. New York: Academic Press.
1981 *Lectures on Government and Binding*. Dordrecht: Foris.

Dogil Grzegorz, Ackermann Hermann, Grodd Wolfgang, Haider Hubert, Kamp Hans, Mayer Jörg, Riecker Axel, and Wildgruber Dirk
2002 The Speaking Brain: a Tutorial Introduction to fMRI Experiments in the Production of Speech, Prosody and Syntax. *Journal of Neurolinguistics* 15: 1–90.

Fanselow, Gisbert
1991 Minimale Syntax. Habilitationsschrift, Universität Passau. [Published as: *Groninger Arbeiten zur Germanistischen Linguistik* 32, Rijksuniversiteit Groningen].

Featherston, Sam
2001 *Empty categories in sentence processing*. Amsterdam: Benjamins.

2005 Universals and grammaticality: wh-constraints in German and English. *Linguistics* 43: 667–711.

2007 Reply. *Theoretical Linguistics* 33: 401–413.

Friederici, Angela D.

2002 Towards a neural basis of auditory sentence processing. *Trends in Cognitive Sciences* 6(2): 78–84.

Frisch Stefan and Matthias Schlesewsky

2001 The N400 reflects problems of thematic hierarchizing. *Neuroreport* 12(15): 3391–3394.

Frisch, Stefan, Matthias Schlesewsky, Douglas Saddy and Annegret Alpermann

2002 The P600 as an indicator of syntactic ambiguity. *Cognition* 85: B83–B92.

Gleitman, Lila R. and Henry Gleitman

1970. *Phrase and paraphrase: some innovative uses of language*. New York: W. Norton & Company.

Haider, Hubert

1986 Affect alpha. *Linguistic Inquiry* 17: 113–126.

1997 Extraposition. In: Dorothee Beerman, David LeBlanc and Henk van Riemsdijk (eds.), *Rightward movement*, 115–151. Amsterdam: Benjamins.

2000 Adverb Placement – convergence of structure and licensing. *Theoretical Linguistics* 26: 95–134.

2003 V-Clustering and Clause Union – Causes and Effects. In: Pieter Seuren and Gerard Kempen (eds.), *Verb Constructions in German Dutch*, 91–126. Amsterdam: Benjamins.

2004 The superiority conspiracy. In: Arthur Stepanov, G. Fanselow and R. Vogel (eds.), *The Minimal Link Condition*, 167–175. Berlin: Mouton de Gruyter.

2005 How to turn German into Icelandic – and derive the VO-OV contrasts. *The Journal of Comparative Germanic Linguistics* 8: 1–53.

in press Exceptions and Anomalies. In: Wiese Heike and Horst Simon (eds.), *Expecting the unexpected – Exceptions in Grammar*. Berlin: de Gruyter.

Koopman, Hilda and Szabolcsi, Anna

2001 *Verbal Complexes*. Cambridge, Mass.: MIT Press.

Kayne, Richard

1994 *The antisymmetry of syntax*. Cambridge, Mass.: MIT Press.

Kutas, Marta and Kara D. Federmeier

2000 Electrophysiology reveals semantic memory use in language comprehension. *Trends in Cognitive Sciences* 12: 463–470.

Labov, William

1978 Sociolinguistics. In: William Orr Dingwall (ed.), *A survey of linguistic science*, 339–372. Stanford, Connecticut: Greylock.

Levelt, Willem J. M., J. A. V. M. van Gent, A. F. J. Haans and A. J. A. Meijers
1977 Grammaticality, paraphrase, and imagery. In: Greenbaum, Sidney (ed.), *Acceptability in language*, 87–101. The Hague: Mouton.

Liebermann, Philip
2007 The hermetic nature of linguistic research. *The Linguistic Review* 24: 431–435.

Müller, Gereon
1995 *A-bar syntax. A study in movement types*. Berlin: Mouton de Gruyter.

Müller, Gereon and Wolfgang Sternefeld
1993 Improper movement and unambiguous binding. *Linguistic Inquiry* 24: 461–507.

Newmeyer, Frederic
1983 *Grammatical Theory*. Chicago: University of Chicago Press.

Pesetsky,David
1987 Wh-in-situ: Movement and Unselective Binding. In: E. Reuland and A. ter Meulen (eds.), *The Representation of (In)definiteness*, 98–129. Cambridge, Mass.: MIT Press.

Poeppel, David and David Embick
2005 Defining the relation between linguistics and neuroscience. In: Ann Cutler (ed.), *Twenty-first century psycholinguistics: four cornerstones*, 103–120. Hillsdale, New Jersey: Erlbaum.

Roehm, Dietmar and Hubert Haider
in press Small is beautiful: the processing of the left periphery in German. (to appear in *Lingua*).

Reinhart, Tanya
1983 *Anaphora and Semantic Interpretation*. London: Croom Helm.

Richards, Norvin
1997 What moves where when in which language. Ph.D. Dissertation, MIT.

Riemsdijk, Henk van and Edwin Williams
1981 NP Structure. *The Linguistic Review* 1: 171–217

Ueno, Mieko and Robert Kluender
2003 Event-related brain indices of Japanese scrambling. *Brain and Language* 86: 243–271.

Wasow, Thomas and Arnold, Jennifer
2005 Intuitions in linguistic argumentation. *Lingua* 115: 1481–1496.

Wiltschko, Martina
1997 Scrambling, D-linking and Superiority in German. In: W. Abraham (ed.), *Groninger Arbeiten zur Germanistischen Linguistik (GAGL)* 41: 107–162.

Wundt, Wilhelm
1888 *Selbstbeobachtung und innere Wahrnehmung*. Philosophische Studien, Bd. IV, 292–309.

Wurmbrand, Susi
2001 *Infinitives – Restructuring and Clause Structure*. Berlin: Mouton de Gruyter.

Annotating genericity: How do humans decide? (A case study in ontology extraction)

Aurelie Herbelot and Ann Copestake

1. Introduction

In computational linguistics, the task of ontology extraction deals with acquiring factual statements from natural language text. Those statements are traditionally added to knowledge bases (so-called 'ontologies') in the form of relationships linking one or several concepts together. The relations can either take the form of general statements such as 'whale – is a – mammal' or of more anecdotal information such as 'whale – escape from – zoo'.

The research presented here is part of a project aimed at the construction of a tool able to summarise – or rather sketch – the general ideas of a domain using such an ontological representation. The final software is expected to:

- transform a domain-specific corpus into a light ontology consisting of generic triples of the type 'A does B' (by 'generic', we mean that we are not interested in anecdotal or exemplary information, but in general statements about the world – the 'beliefs' of the domain).
- conflate related triples into topical clusters, to give the main 'themes' of the discourse
- find evidence for or against individual statements using the web and return them as basic 'critiques' of the ontology
- allow the user to query the ontology in their own words (a query on 'houses' should also return statements on 'homes'.)

This paper deals with the first point, the extraction of generic statements from corpora. There is no proposal in the current ontological research for distinguishing generic from specific statements at extraction stage. If this does not generally affect systems dealing with strictly-defined relations (like those acquiring chemical reactions, Nobel Prize winners or company president successions), it does have an impact on the performance of systems extracting more general relations (like taxonomy or meronymy) and those attempting to give some ontological representation of a given text.

Table 1 a list of relationships that might be extracted from the following paragraph (taken from the Wikipedia article on grey whales):

Table 1. Relationships extracted from a Wikipedia article

	Relationship	Incorrect?
1	Grey whale – feed on – benthic crustaceans	
2	Grey whale – eat – benthic crustaceans	
3	Grey whale – turn on – grey whale's side	×
4	Grey whale – scoop up – sediments from the sea floor	
5	Grey whale – classified as – baleen whale	
6	Grey whale – has – baleen	
7	Grey whale – has – whalebone	
8	whalebone – act like – sieve	
9	baleen – capture – amphipods	
10	animal – feed in – northern waters	×
11	animal – live off – extensive fat reserves	×
12	ARG1 – capture – Gray Whale	×
13	ARG1 – release – Gray Whale	×

> The grey whale feeds mainly on benthic crustaceans which it eats by turning on its side (usually the right) and scooping up the sediments (usually on the right) from the sea floor. It is classified as a baleen whale and has a baleen, or whalebone, which acts like a sieve to capture amphipods taken in along with sand, water and other material. Mostly, the animal feeds in the northern waters during the summer; and opportunistically feeds during its migration trip, and mainly lives off its extensive fat reserves. [...] In 1972, a 3-month-old Gray Whale named Gigi was captured for brief study, and then released near San Diego.

Relationship 3) cannot be considered a general fact and sounds odd in isolation – using Carlson's (1977) terminology, the relationship refers to a stage of the whale and not to the individual. Relations 10) and 11) are incorrect as one would infer from them that they are applicable to all animals. Relations 12) and 13) are not incorrect as such but, considering that all the other relationships are about the kind 'Grey Whale', it would be tempting to believe that those similarly apply to the species – leading to false statements. We will not be discussing the problem of 3) in this work – and won't attempt to classify predicates. However, the 'genericity value' of the noun phrase is important to us: we want to know, for instance, when the information is about the kind 'grey whale' – as opposed to one particular whale – and to resolve referents as in the animal/whale example (referent resolution, as we will see later, is not limited to anaphora.) What we ideally want is a tool to annotate each noun phrase with its 'genericity value'.

In the next section, we will first give an overview of the issues linked to the automatic annotation of genericity, and show that the first step towards our end goal is to devise an appropriate, manual annotation scheme. The subsequent sections cover our attempts at designing such a scheme. We start by motivating our choice of labels for the annotation and go on to present our initial scheme, mostly based on few, intuitive questions. The issues encountered in using this scheme lead us to propose another, more complex scheme, which gives us better interannotator agreement. We finish with a short discussion of how our annotations correspond to particular ontological representations.

2. The automatic annotation of genericity: issues

A typical way to perform automatic linguistic annotations in computer science is machine learning. A program is given a corpus manually annotated by human experts and attempts to learn statistically significant rules which will then be tested on a separate corpus.

It is necessary to have a sufficiently large corpus, with a wide variety of examples, to perform such training. In the case of genericity, there is no corpus that we know of which would give us the required data. The ACE corpus (2005) is possibly an exception, but it only makes a distinction between generic and non-generic entities, which, as we will see later, is too vague for our purposes. The GNOME corpus (Poesio, 2000) is another example but it is limited in genres (the annotation guidelines are also specific to those genres) and again, it only has two genericity-related labels. It is therefore necessary to construct a separate training corpus for ontology extraction. Furthermore, manual annotation allows us to investigate distinctions that can be made on linguistic grounds and motivate them by individual examples, empirically grounded by exhaustive annotation of corpus data. The use of multiple annotators leads to increased clarity and precision in such distinctions.

Annotating genericity, as we found out in our own initial attempts, is no trivial task. There are clear instances of non-generic entities such as proper nouns or narrative objects and clear instances as well of generic ones such as Latin species names, but when one starts considering every noun phrase in a corpus, things are far less obvious. Consider the following two sentences, taken again from a Wikipedia article:

(1) *Later still, Hebrew scholars made use of simple monoalphabetic substitution ciphers.*

(2) *Cryptography has a long tradition in religious writing.*

In the first sentence, it is not clear whether the article speaks of some Hebrew scholars or Hebrew scholars in general. Only detailed world knowledge of the topic would help us resolve this. In the second sentence, it may seem quite clear that the text talks about cryptography in general and it is probably difficult to imagine instances of the concept cryptography but there is only one entity in the world called cryptography and if one thinks of the difference between generics and non-generics as a matter of quantification, there is nothing that distinguishes the concept 'cryptography' from the Eiffel Tower. We would however want to argue that cryptography here is generic in the way that the sentence 'cryptographic messages have a long tradition in religious writing' refers to cryptographic messages in general. We found many other difficult examples in the course of the project.

Because it is difficult to rely on human intuition for this kind of annotation, we came to the decision that a precise scheme was needed, which would allow us to track the decision process made by humans when considering genericity, and which would eventually give us a quantifiable idea of how much agreement can be reached between two annotators.

3. Choosing labels

The first decision that we had to make was the choice of labels for the annotation. Krifka et al (1995) identify differences between genericity and non-genericity as well as between specificity and nonspecificity. Both object and kind-level entities can have a specificity value:

(3) *A lion (as in 'A lion has a bushy tail')* is non-specific and non-kind-referring.[1]

(4) *Simba/a lion, namely Simba*, is specific and non-kind-referring.

(5) *A cat* (in the taxonomic reading, as in 'a cat shows mutations when domesticated') is kind-referring but non-specific.

(6) *The lion/a cat, namely the lion* (taxonomic reading) is kind-referring and specific.

(Examples taken from Krifka et al, in Carlson and Pelletier, 1995).

As far as ontology creation is concerned, the difference between specific and non-specific readings for generic entities is not relevant. Theoretically, the information in (5) will be attached to the class 'cat1', that is, the node in the ontology which is parent to the nodes 'tiger', 'lion' and 'cat2', and whatever predicate comes after (6) will be linked to the class 'lion' in exactly the same way:

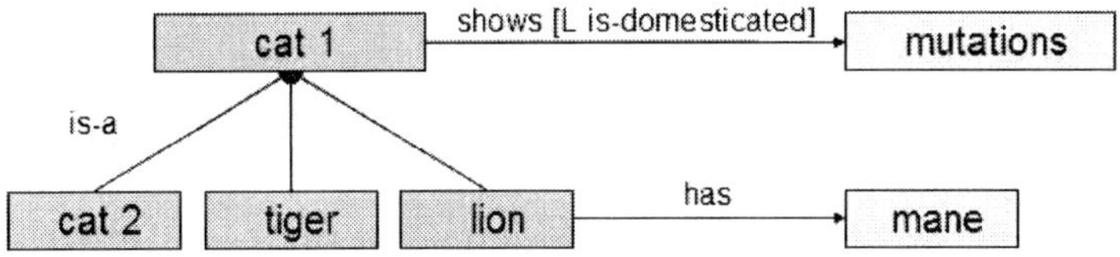

Figure 1. A cat ontology

The notion of specificity is more interesting for object-level items, however, because if we attempt to merge nodes which refer to the same entity, only those nodes which are specific should be allowed to merge. See for instance the following three sentences (let's assume from the same text) and attached diagram:

(7) *Flipper whistles on national TV.*

(8) *This dolphin has made a career!*

(9) *Mrs Smith has found a dolphin in her bath tub.*

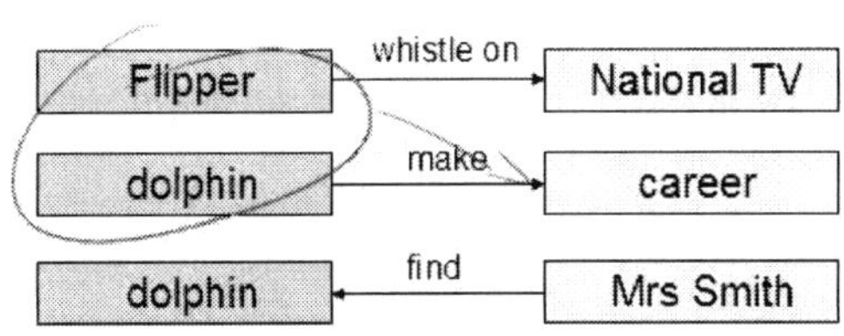

Figure 2. A dolphin ontology

Here, only two out of three nodes should be allowed to merge, as the third dolphin is not specified and cannot be assumed to correspond to Flipper. From these initial distinctions, we get three possible labels:

- GEN: generic entities
- SPEC: non-generic, specific entities
- NON-SPEC: non-generic, non-specific entities.

We have mentioned in the course of the previous sections that some entities could be ambiguous between generic and non-generic (see the Hebrew scholars example) and that the referent of the noun phrase under consideration could be more specific than the lexical realisation appears to be (see the grey whale/animal example). We therefore introduced two further labels to deal with those cases:

- AMB: ambiguous between generic and non-generic
- GROUP: the text is referring generically to a subgroup of the noun phrase. So for instance, in the example of Section 1, the noun phrase 'the animal' refers to 'all of some' animals, namely all grey whales.

Finally, we also experimented with the idea that some concepts were not 'well established': the notion of a well-established concept comes from some work on definite singulars. Krifka et al (1995) show, for instance, that a definite singular can be used generically on a well-established kind only:

(10) *The Coke bottle has a narrow neck.*

(11) **The green bottle has a narrow neck.*

(Examples attributed to Barbara Partee.)

We found the notion of well-established entity attractive from the point of view of ontology extraction, as we would like to be able to avoid the creation of dubious classes (for instance, we found in our training corpus the NP 'gimcrack affair', which in our view did not make for a stable concept with clear hyponyms).

It seems worth mentioning that when we are attributing a particular label to a noun phrase, we are only saying that the label applies to that noun phrase in context, i.e. to an instance of a grammatical construct such as bare plural or indefinite singular. In this respect, we are not making assumptions about the general features of any construct: in particular, when we are saying that a noun phrase is ambiguous between an existential and a generic reading, we do not mean to make a claim about whether bare plurals as a linguistic construct can be regarded as ambiguous or not. Similarly, if asked to annotate the noun phrase 'a lion' in 'a lion has a bushy tail', we would annotate it as a generic entity, even though Krifka et al (1995) argue that this is a non-kind-referring entity on the basis that the sentence is characterising and that the genericity does not occur at the level of the noun phrase. As far as this scheme is concerned, the lion in that sentence does not (necessarily) refer to a particular lion but rather to all lions, and we would therefore annotate it as generic.

4. Initial scheme

4.1. Instructions

Our initial scheme dealt with the distinction between generics and non-generics only, ignoring the problem of specificity. It used the four labels SPEC, GROUP, GEN and NON-WE. We give the complete scheme in Appendix 1 and comment next on the main points.

The non-generics were identified using a test of distinguishability: if an item X in the text can be distinguished from other Xs, then the noun phrase is probably at object-level (Step 1). The idea requires that unique individuals be dealt with separately in Step 2 (the Eiffel Tower cannot be distinguished from other Eiffel Towers, but it is nevertheless non-generic). We defined a unique object as a concept that doesn't have either children classes or instances. Well-established entities (Step 3) were identified with respect to their potential for being topics of information (could the noun phrase in the text be the headline of an encyclopaedia article?) Finally, groups were separated from real generics by considering the referent of the noun phrase (Step 4).

4.2. Results

The scheme was evaluated by presenting six annotators with four sections of the Wikipedia article 'The History of Cryptography', totalling 100 noun phrases, the boundaries of which were marked by one of the authors prior to annotation (this includes embedded NPs). The annotators were all students, with no formal knowledge of linguistics and with no previous experience of annotating genericity. Agreement was calculated for each pair of annotators according to the Kappa measure (Cohen, 1960):

$$\kappa = \frac{\mathrm{Pr(a)} - \mathrm{Pr(e)}}{1 - \mathrm{Pr(e)}}$$

where Pr(a) is the actual, observed agreement and Pr(e) is the expected figure if annotators were acting independently and any agreement was due to chance. (There are different versions of Kappa depending on how multiple annotators are treated and how the probabilities of classes are calculated to establish P(e): here we use the simple unweighted Kappa, Cohen 1960.) In practice, this means calculating the 'chance' confusion matrix from the annotation confusion matrix for a pair of annotators and then computing:

$$\kappa = \frac{\textit{Actual-Expected}}{\textit{TotalAnnotations-Expected}}$$

where *Actual* is the number of times that the two annotators agreed, *Expected* is the number of times that they would have agreed by chance, and *TotalAnnotations* is the total number of annotations performed. Note that taking chance into account means that there is no straight correspondence between plain percentages of agreement (*Actual/TotalAnnotations*) and Kappa values. Landis and Koch (1977) provide an interpretation of Kappa which is commonly used and that we summarise in Table 2.

Table 2. An interpretation of the values of Kappa

Kappa	Interpretation
< 0	No agreement
0 - 0.2	Very low agreement
0.21 – 0.4	Low agreement
0.41 – 0.6	Moderate Agreement
0.61 – 0.8	Full Agreement
0.8 – 1.0	Perfect Agreement

The evaluation gave us 15 Kappa figures ranging from 0.31 to 0.62, with percentage agreement ranging from 56% to 78%. Full results are available in Table 3. The figures in the top right-hand side triangle are the Kappas while the figures in the bottom left-hand side triangle are the plain percentages of agreement.

Table 3. Interannotater agreement, first scheme

	1	**2**	**3**	**4**	**5**	**6**
1		.62	.40	.37	.51	.52
2	78		.39	.36	.48	.38
3	61	62		.31	.36	.45
4	60	61	56		.48	.43
5	68	67	57	65		.43
6	65	56	62	60	58	

4.3. Discussion

We carried out an analysis of the areas of stronger disagreement by picking out all NPs without majority. That is, we selected all phrases for which fewer than four of the six annotators agreed on a label. We then attempted to understand the reason for each annotation and derived a rough map of issues.

We found that for 72 phrases out of 100, at least four annotators were in agreement. The remaining 28 phrases formed the core of our analysis. The following conclusions could be derived:

- A portion of the disagreements could have been covered by an 'ambiguity' label. In those cases, there is a genuine ambiguity between specificity and genericity, which is not resolved in the text. For instance, in the sentence *'Later still, Hebrew scholars made use of simple mono-alphabetic substitution ciphers'*, it is not clear whether all Hebrew scholars or some specific people are involved.
- Our simple definition of genericity in Step 4 ('all or any' of the instances of the concept expressed by the lexical item) produces confusions between GROUP and GEN labels. In the sentence *'The Greeks of classical times are said to have known of ciphers'*, 'ciphers' was labelled by some annotators as GROUP, presumably because the Greeks would not have known of all ciphers in existence.
- The semantic interpretation of the copula differs depending on the annotator. Some assume that the second argument of the copula has automatically the same scope as the first argument, while others prefer to see it as a class (and therefore a generic entity). An example of such disagreement occurs for the NP 'examples of cryptography' in the sentence *'Herodotus tells us of secret messages [...] these are not proper examples of cryptography.'* Out of the two annotators who marked 'secret messages' as specific, one marked the last NP as generic, the other as specific.
- In some cases, the disagreement is simply due to slight differences in the resolution of the referent in context, as in *'Gilbert Vernam proposed a teletype cipher in which a previously-prepared key [...] is combined character by character with the plaintext message.'* When annotating the NP 'the plaintext message', opinions differed between SPEC and GEN labels (with an odd GROUP), presumably because of interpreting the sentence as either an exemplary, specific event or as generic instructions.

The last point deserves some elaboration. It is interesting to note that all the issues above relate, in one way or another, to the resolution of the referent in context. Either the annotators do not realise the ambiguity of the noun phrase, or they disagree on the resolution. This accounts for the confusions between group and generic labels: in the previous example, *'The Greeks of classical times are said to have known of ciphers'*, some people resolved 'ciphers' to 'all ciphers at all times' while others interpreted it as 'ciphers in ancient Greece'. The issue relating to the copula can be similarly interpreted, where the second argument is seen as referring to the first one in one case, or to a class of objects in the other case. In order to track this problem, we attempted in further schemes to give rules on how the referent should be resolved and asked the annotators to provide a written record of each noun phrase's referent. The issue is further discussed in Section 5.

Finally, we found that the notion of 'well-established' entity was particularly difficult to explain and to exemplify in a structured scheme – it proved to be the source of many preliminary queries from our annotators. Note that there are also now arguments against the idea of well-established kinds on the grounds that sentences starting with a definite article such as the following are possible (Hofmeister, 2003):

(12) *The newly-hatched fly is a lazy insect.*

(13) *The well-crafted bottle has a narrow neck.*

Considering the mediocre results given by this label, and the lack of strong basis for its linguistic motivation, we abandoned it in subsequent experiments.

5. A revised scheme

5.1. Instructions

We found that our Wikipedia article, although giving us a fair proportion of both specific and generic instances, was lacking many types of expression that we had noted elsewhere in text. We suspected that this was due to the set encyclopedic style of Wikipedia and turned to a different corpus. The new scheme was developed using material which would give us better examples of the range of expressions found in general text: we produced a development corpus by selecting 10 paragraphs out of 10 different genres in the British National Corpus and marking 50 noun phrases for their variety of expressions. This corpus is available at http://www.cl.cam.ac.uk/~ah433.

Having gone through several development iterations, our scheme now contains 14 steps and caters for specific cases such as existentials, proper nouns and copula constructions. We give the full scheme in Appendix 2 and discuss here the main points.

– We have now a step dedicated to referent resolution (Step 4). The annotator is required to perform not only simple anaphora resolution but also spatial and temporal resolution in context. Pronouns, and in particular possessive pronouns, must refer to an entity in the text.

- Unique entities are dealt with in two steps (7 and 8), one to assert the uniqueness of the noun phrase and the other to filter through class names which could be interpreted as unique objects: our initial experiments, for instance, showed that the concept of 'cryptography' had been marked as specific by some annotators because 'there are not several cryptographies' (see Section 3).
- A label for non-specifics has also been added (Step 12): our initial definition of generics as 'any' or 'all' of a class instances created problems when annotating sentences such as 'I want a new bike', where 'bike' is 'any bike' but certainly not a generic entity. We now require that entities that refer to a particular object be classified as either specific (identifiable) or non-specific (non-identifiable). We explain this distinction further at the end of the section.
- The differentiation between groups and generics is now made simple by comparing the textual entity P with its referent resolution P2: when P = P2, we have a generic entity, otherwise a group (Step 14).
- Finally, there is an explicit ambiguity label which can be applied to bare plurals (Step 15). Non-specific entities in bare plurals must be reconsidered and the annotator is asked whether there is a reading of the sentence where the entity might refer to a class of objects.

Some comments must be made about the tests for specificity and non-specificity. As argued by Jorgensen (2000), specificity is not a well-defined concept. The idea behind the notion is that specific entities are identifiable while non-specific ones are not. Jorgensen, however, quotes Krifka et al (1995) to show that there is no good consensus on what the definition actually is:

> The actual specific/non-specific distinction (if there is just one such distinction) is extremely difficult to elucidate in its details. It is for this reason that we wish to remain on a pretheoretic level. Even so, we had better point out that we take, e.g., a lion in 'A lion must be standing in the bush over there' to be specific rather than nonspecific, even if there is no particular lion that the speaker believes to be in the bush.

Jorgensen himself proposes a definition centred on the speaker: what he calls J-specificity separates the cases where the speaker has the means to identify the referent and/or believes it to be unique from cases where neither necessarily apply. The latter cases are non-specific. We adopted that approach and chose to have a test for specificity after the test for distinguishability: if an entity can be distinguished from other similar entities (ie, if it is unique in Jorgensen's sense) and if it is identifiable, then it is specific; if the entity can be distinguished from other similar entities but is not identifiable, then it is non-specific.

5.2. Results

The test corpus comes from the BNC, like the development corpus (see Section 5.1). Our software randomly selects 10 different genres in the BNC, randomly extracts one paragraph for each genre, produces a syntactic parse of each sentence using the RASP software (Briscoe and Carroll, 2000) and identifies full NPs in the output. At this stage, it is necessary to manually weed incorrect NPs due to parsing errors. In our first trial, we found that out of 552 noun phrases, 131 were incorrect, yielding an accuracy of 76%. We also decided that when two NPs were co-ordinated, they should be considered in isolation.

In order to measure Kappa on the new scheme, we extracted the first 48 noun phrases out of the 421 left after parsing and manual correction, and presented them to two annotators. We obtained a Kappa of 0.744, corresponding to an agreement of 83%. The confusion matrix for this annotation is shown in Table 4.

Table 4. Confusion matrix for final annotation

	SPEC	**NON-SPEC**	**GEN**	**GROUP**	**AMB**
SPEC	25	0	0	0	0
NON-SPEC	0	6	0	2	0
GEN	0	0	3	1	1
GROUP	0	2	2	6	0
AMB	0	0	0	0	0

5.3. Discussion

Most of the disagreements left at this stage relate to the resolution of the referent. See for instance the sentence:

(14) *Under the agreement, enhancements to the libraries will be developed to address such areas as performance, ease-of-use, internationalisation and support for multi-threading.*

One annotator resolved ‘enhancements to the libraries’ as ‘enhancements to the Tools.h++ libraries[2] ‘while the other resolved it to ‘enhancements that will be developed under the agreement’, producing a NON-SPEC annotation in the first case and a GROUP annotation in the second case. We found that disagreements were often due to differences in world knowledge, simple omissions, and interpretation of the semantics of certain verbs. For instance, in a sentence of the type ‘X consists of Y’, some people tend to resolve Y as being ‘the Y in X’ while others will resolve it as just Y. This corresponds roughly to the two paraphrases 'X consists of a certain amount of Y' and 'X is made out of the general material called Y'.

We expect reference resolution to be one of the major problems in the design of a program for the annotation of genericity, as automatic reference resolution beyond anaphora is currently limited (see Vieira and Poesio, 2000 for a description of the difficult problem of processing bridging descriptions). We argue, however, that considering the referent is absolutely necessary to provide accuracy to the results. As a short investigation of how the referent affects the annotation, we decided to perform an experiment where the same 48 noun phrases would be annotated, first with and then without the reference resolution step. The results showed major differences: the group labels, which we would have ideally liked to see transferred to generic labels, were transferred to specifics and non-specifics. Out of 48 noun phrases, it was judged that the annotation for 15 of them was incorrect beyond argument when ignoring the reference resolution step.

6. Interpreting genericity

We have so far related the phenomenon of genericity to a basic ontological structure, with classes and instances. For instance, a generic will refer to a concept, or class, which can have instances. An entity marked as specific will be taken as being an instance of a class in the ontology. Some specifics will even be marked as unique instances of that concept: for example, there is only one instance of the concept 'Great Wall of China'. Non-specifics will also refer to instances, but those will be random instances of a concept rather than identifiable ones. In the end, the various annotations can be paraphrased as follows:

- X is specific: X is an instance of a concept (or unique instance of that concept, depending on the path followed for the annotation)
- X is non-specific: X is a random instance of a concept
- X is generic: X is a class
- X is a group: X refers to some instances of a class which themselves form a subclass.

The problem that has not yet been explored in this work is that of providing a particular interpretation of genericity such as, for instance, quantification, rules or induction (see Cohen, 2002). The reason that such interpretations cannot be directly linked to the notions of quantification or inference that they appeal to is that generic statements differ in the extent to which they apply to individuals in a class. See for instance:

(15) *Turtles are reptiles.* (All turtles are reptiles.)

(16) *Turtles lay eggs.* (Female turtles lay eggs.)

(17) *Turtles live over 100 years.* (Some turtles, in rare cases, live over 100 years.)

It is clear that examples (16) and (17) cannot be treated as involving universal quantification over individual turtles. However this is a highly complex issue with no clear solution which we will not discuss further here.

7. Conclusion

This paper has presented a scheme for the manual annotation of genericity, with the ultimate aim of using human annotations to train an automatic classifier. Our current scheme produces reasonable interannotator agreement with a Kappa of 0.74. We noted that the resolution of the noun phrase's referent has much to do with the way it is annotated by humans and we predict that this might be the main bottleneck in automating the annotation. Finally, we showed how the annotations could relate to the concept nodes of an ontology and remarked that the notion of generic class would have to be further formalised to take into account all possible interpretations of genericity. We leave this problem as further work, together with the construction of a machine learner able to automatically reproduce human annotations.

Appendix 1

The annotation scheme is designed as a list of 4 steps, to be taken in turn. Annotators should start at Step 1 and follow instructions in each subsequent step. When one of the four labels SPEC, GEN, GROUP or NON-WE appears, the noun phrase should be marked appropriately and the annotator should stop.

Step 1. Can the entity be singled out from similar entities in the real world? If yes, annotate as SPEC.
Examples:
[The development of cryptography] has been paralleled by the development of cryptanalysis: 'the development of cryptography' cannot be separated from

other potential 'developments of cryptography' in this context, so go to next step without annotation.
[Many scholars] believe it's a concealed reference to the Roman Empire: those 'many scholars' can probably be distinguished from other scholars, so annotate as SPEC.
[The Chinese] invented the firework: There is only one Chinese people and it doesn't make sense to talk about another entity called 'the Chinese', so go to next step without annotation.

Step 2. Is it possible to imagine instantiations or specialisations of the expression (is the expression a class)? Try to instantiate the phrase P with 'this P' (or 'these' if plural), or 'this form of P', which produces another referent. If the instantiation does not make sense, annotate as SPEC.
Examples:
Until the 1970s, [secure cryptography] was largely the preserve of governments: 'this form of secure cryptography' is acceptable, so go to next step without annotation.
The breaking of [codes] and ciphers: 'this code' is acceptable, so go to next step without annotation.
Allied reading of Nazi Germany's ciphers shortened [World War II]: 'this World War II' or 'this form of World War II' is nonsensical, so annotate as SPEC.

Step 3. Is the expression a 'well-established entity'? I.e. can you define the entity in a way that most people would agree with, or could you imagine an encyclopaedia article about it – or at least a webpage on the topic? If not, annotate as NON-WE
Examples:
The subsequent introduction of electronics and computing has allowed [elaborate schemes of still greater complexity]: it is difficult to imagine what an article about 'elaborate schemes of still greater complexity' would look like, so annotate as NON-WE.
[Methods of encryption that use pen and paper]: although very constrained, this is a definable topic, so go to next step without annotation.
Methods of encryption that use [pen] and paper: 'pen' is a concept that would have a definition in a dictionary, so go to next step without annotation.

Step 4. Can the information contained in the text apply to the entity in general (that is, to all or any of its instances), or is it only relevant to a subgroup? If yes, annotate as GEN, otherwise, annotate as GROUP.

Examples:
It's a concealed reference to the Roman Empire (and so to [Roman persecution policies]): this is a reference to all Roman persecution policies, therefore annotate as GEN.
[The key] in every such system had to be exchanged between the communicating parties: this is not applicable to all keys, or any key, but to certain keys in certain systems, therefore annotate as GROUP.
The destination of the whales is California where they breed and [the young] are born: this is not applicable to all young but only to all whale youngs, therefore annotate as GROUP.

Appendix 2

The annotation scheme is designed as a list of 14 steps. Each step corresponds to a test, the answer to which decides of the next step to take. Annotators should start at Step 1 and follow instructions in each subsequent step. When one of the five labels SPEC, NON-SPEC, GEN, GROUP or AMB appears, the noun phrase should be marked appropriately and the annotator should stop unless a further step is specified.

In what follows, the letter P refers to the noun phrase being annotated.

1. Does P appear in an existential construct of the type 'there [be] (a) P(s)' where the existential describes a particular situation in space and time? The copula 'be' can appear conjugated in any tense and there may be other phrases separating it from its logical subject and object. Yes → SPEC No → 2.
Examples: *There are daffodils in the garden. There is a car parked across the road.*

2. Is P a proper noun? Yes → SPEC No → 3.
Examples: *John Smith, War and Peace, Easter Island, World War II ...*

3. Does P start with an indefinite quantifier other than 'all' or 'a'? This includes some, a few, few, many, most, one of, a couple of, etc. Yes → NON-SPEC No, quantifier is 'all' → read 4 and jump to 13 No → 4.

4. It will often be the case that P refers to something more specific than it seems. We will call that more specific reading P2. Consider the following cases:
Make sure you have a hammer at hand. The tool will be needed in step 4. The tool = the hammer.
The cathedral is magnificent. The stained-glass windows date from the 13th century. The stained-glass windows = the stained-glass windows of the cathedral X.

(In a book about 19th century Europe) *Women could not vote.* Women = women in 19th century Europe.

It helps to ask whether the entity could be 'any P in existence'. If not, there is probably a more specific reading involved (P2). Sometimes, it is difficult to answer the question (for instance if the entity is not a familiar concept). In this case, try to specify as much as possible using explicit location/time details from the context. If the word is an anaphoric reference to a previous word, let P2 be the previous word. If the identity of P can be specified, through context or general knowledge, record the specified entity in P2. Possessives should also be resolved:

his car = Paul's car.

If P cannot be precised further, then P2 = P. Go to step 5.

5. Does P appear in a construct of the type 'A [be] P(s)'? The copula be can appear conjugated in any tense and there may be other phrases separating it from its logical subject and object. Implicit copulas also call for an affirmative answer: for instance, 'X classified as Y' or 'X named Y' will, in certain cases, mean 'X is a Y.' Yes → 6 No → 7.

6. In the identified construct, 'A [be] P (s)', are A and P two names for the same thing? Consider for example: Elizabeth II is the Queen of England or The Morning Star is the Evening Star. Yes → 7 No → 13.

7. Does the lexical realisation of P2 refer to an entity which is unique in the world? (Plurals are necessarily non-unique.)Yes → 8 No → 9. (If unsure, go to 9.)

The Daily Mail was looking for a new chief editor. Paul went for the job. There are not several jobs of chief editor for the Daily Mail, so this is unique.

The lion bit my toe. There is more than one lion in the world, possibly even more than one lion who bit my toe, so this is not unique.

8. Is P2 a common noun that could have taxonomical children? (When considering complex entities, e.g. 'X of Y', the taxonomical child must belong to the head of the phrase – X in the example.)Yes → 13 No → SPEC.

Psychology: yes, because experimental psychology and behavioural psychology are forms of psychology.

Mozart's death: no, nothing is a form of Mozart's death.

9. Does P have a determiner? Yes → 10 No → 11.

10. Does P2 refer to a particular object, or group of objects, in the world? Ie, out of all possible P2s, is the text only talking about one/some of them? (The determiner is sometimes a very good clue.) Yes → 12 No → 13.

Can you see the lion? (Assuming P2=the lion at London zoo.) Particular object = the lion being pointed at, as opposed to all possible lions at London zoo.
The lion is a mammal. Non-particular = this is talking about lions in general.

11. Is there a reading of the sentence where the P2(s) in the text can be distinguished from other P2s (or group of P2s)? Ie, out of all possible P2s, is the text only talking about some of them? Yes → 12 No → 13. (See examples in step 10.)

12. Is/Are the P2(s) in the text identifiable or is the text talking about, potentially, any of them? Identifiable → SPEC Not identifiable and last step = 10 → NON-SPEC Not identifiable and last step = 11 → NON-SPEC + 14.
Mary has a new bike. Identifiable = one bike, Mary's bike.
I would like a new bike. Not identifiable = one bike, but any will do.

13. Is P2 = P? Yes → GEN No → GROUP.

14. Is there a reading of the sentence where P2 means 'all' P2(s)? Yes → AMB No → STOP.

Notes

1. Although we follow the Krifka et al general classification, we do not agree with the classification of this particular example. See our comments later in this section.
2. For non-computer scientists: the Tools.h++ library is a piece of software designed for programmers who write in the C++ language, mentioned in the text prior to sentence (14).

References

ACE (Automatic Content Extraction)
2005 English Annotation Guidelines for Entities, Version 5.6.1 2005.05.23.

Briscoe, Ted, Carroll, John and Watson, Rebecca
2006 The Second Release of the RASP System. In: *Proceedings of the COLING/ACL 2006 Interactive Presentation Sessions*, Sydney, Australia, 2006.

Carlson, Greg
1977 A Unified Analysis of the Bare English Plural. *Linguistics and Philosophy* 1: 413–457.

Carlson, Greg and Pelletier, Francis.
1995 *The Generic Book.* University of Chicago Press.

Cohen, Axel
2002 Genericity. *Linguistische Berichte*, 10.

Cohen, Jacob
1960 A coefficient of agreement for nominal scales. *Educational and Psychological Measurement* 20: 37–46.

Hofmeister, Philip
2003 Generic Singular Definites. Available at http://www.stanford.edu/~philiph/skeleton.pdf. Last accessed on 24 April 2008.

Jorgensen, Stig
2000 Computational Reference. Ph.D Dissertation, Copenhagen Business School.

Krifka, Manfred et al.
1995 *Genericity: An Introduction.* In: G. Carlson and F. Pelletier, eds., *The Generic Book.* Chicago: University of Chicago Press.

Landis, J. R. and Koch, G. G.
1977 The measurement of observer agreement for categorical data. *Biometrics* 33: 159–174.

Poesio, Massimo
2000 Annotating a corpus to develop and evaluate discourse entity realization algorithms: issues and preliminary results. In: *Proceedings of the Third Conference on Language Resources and Engineering*, Athens.

Vieira, Renata and Poesio, Massimo
2000 Corpus-based development and evaluation of a system for processing definite descriptions. In: *Proceedings of the 18th COLING*, Saarbruecken, Germany.

Canonicity in argument realization and verb semantic deficits in Alzheimer's disease*

Christina Manouilidou and Roberto G. de Almeida

1. Introduction

In this paper we argue that argument realization requires different types of information and that the mapping from meaning-to-form may be disrupted when knowledge necessary for its fulfillment breaks down as a result of brain damage. More specifically, we discuss the performance of a population suffering from a semantic deficit (i.e. Alzheimer's patients), in a sentence completion task with predicates that involve non-canonical argument realization.

The study of thematic (or semantic) roles is one of the most challenging topics in linguistic investigations, bringing together lexical, syntactic and semantic issues. Thematic roles label the ways in which entities are involved in, or related to, predicates. Their main function is to mediate between syntax and semantics, and to guide the mapping of semantic representations to syntactic structures. In other words, thematic roles are in part responsible for transferring meaning to the level of form. However, despite the general agreement on their crucial role in the syntax-semantics mapping, the way this mapping is achieved varies according to different approaches. Part of the problem lies in the fact that there is no general consensus as to how many, and what kind of, thematic roles exist. The majority of researchers working on thematic roles use labels such as *Agent*, *Theme*, *Patient*, *Goal*, *Instrument*, *Source*, *Location*, *Benefactive*, and *Experiencer*. Theories that make use of thematic roles target the interpretation of any noun phrase (NP) in a sentence, according to its syntactic position (*thematic hierarchy,* e.g. Fillmore, 1968; Grimshaw, 1990; Jackendoff, 1990), its general semantic content (*proto-roles,* e.g. Dowty, 1991), and its properties of animacy and definiteness (*animacy hierarchy,* e.g. Croft, 2003)[1]. These approaches are not mutually exclusive but often overlap.

In this paper we explore the effects of "canonicity" in argument realization, as stemming from the requirements of hierarchical relations (i.e. *thematic* and *animacy* hierarchies as well as proto-roles) in syntax-semantics mapping by examining how patients with Alzheimer's disease (AD) interpret sentences. We discuss experimental evidence (mostly from Manouilidou, de Almeida, Schwartz, and Nair, 2009) from patients' performance with verbs whose argument realization follows canonical thematic hierarchy compared to their performance with verbs whose argument realization deviates from canonical hierarchy (*psych* verbs; e.g. *fear*, *frighten*). The study we discuss provides evidence for the role of canonicity in sentence processing and stresses the difficulties associated with structures deviating from canonical argument realization for brain-damaged populations, such as AD patients.

The paper is organized as follows: In section 2, we provide an overview of the role of various hierarchies in canonical argument realization. In section 3, we briefly describe the linguistic structures we investigated (i.e. psychological verbs and passive voice) and we show that they demonstrate non-canonical argument realization. Our experimental evidence from patients with AD is described in section 4. Finally, in section 5, we discuss our findings with respect to canonical argument realization and the semantic deficits of AD patients; we suggest that AD patients are sensitive to deviations from canonicity not only in terms of thematic hierarchy but also in terms of the [+/– agentive] verb feature.

2. Linguistic canonicity in argument realization

In this section, we describe some crucial issues on the principles that guide argument realization. We focus on the hierarchical relations of canonical argument realization based on the prerequisites of thematic and animacy hierarchies as well as proto-roles.

2.1. Thematic hierarchy

Proponents of the role of *thematic hierarchy* in argument realization claim that meaning-to-form mapping is based on hierarchical relations between thematic roles. Thematic hierarchy is the most widely used method to explain the mapping between an ordered list of semantic roles and an ordered list of grammatical relations, thus allowing for a particular argument of a verb to be referred to in terms of its function (e.g. subject or object), instead of in terms of its semantic role (e.g. *Agent* or *Patient*) (Levin and Rappaport Hovav, 2005: 155). For instance, Fillmore (1968) suggests that in a verb predicated of an *Agent*, an *Instrument* and a *Theme* argument, the preferred choice of subject is *Agent* > *Instrument* > *Theme/Patient*, meaning that whenever there is an *Agent* in the sentence, it occupies the subject position (e.g. *The boy opened the door*), and, in the absence of an *Agent*, it is the *Instrument* that occupies the subject position (e.g. *The key opened the door*); otherwise the subject is the *Theme* or *Patient* (e.g. *The door opened*).

Table 1. Sample thematic hierarchies.

Study	Thematic hierarchy*
Fillmore (1968)	*Ag > Ins > Th*
Jackendoff (1972)	*Ag > G/S/L > Th*
Givón (1984)	*Ag > Ben > Pat > L > Ins*
Belletti and Rizzi (1988)	*Ag > Exp >Th*
Baker (1989)	*Ag > Ins > Th/Pat > G/L*
Grimshaw (1990)	*Ag > Exp > G/S/L > Th*
Van Valin (1990)	*Ag > Eff > Exp > L > Th > Pat*
Jackendoff (1990)	*Act > Pat/Ben > Th > G/S/L*

* *Ag (Agent), Exp (Experiencer), Ins (Instrument), Pat (Patient) G (Goal), S (Source) L (Location), Ben (Benefactor), Th (Theme), Eff (Effector).*

For Levin and Rappaport-Hovav (2005), thematic hierarchies emerge as the result of embedding relations among arguments in an event structure. These relations are always respected in argument realizations. Thus, it appears that more embedded arguments usually receive less prominent syntactic realizations. More recently, other thematic roles, such as *Goal, Source*, and *Location*, have been taken into consideration, resulting in multiple ways of forming thematic hierarchies (e.g. Baker, 1989, 1997; Givón, 1984; Grimshaw, 1990; Jackendoff, 1972, 1990; Van Valin, 1990; see Table 1 for a sample of thematic hierarchies). Although there is considerable variability in the ranking of various thematic roles, the only point of agreement found among them is the fact that whenever there is an *Agent*, it occupies the subject position. This observation leads us to the notion of *canonicity in argument realization* and deviations thereof.

In a *canonical* thematic hierarchy, then, the *Agent* thematic role occupies the most prominent position in the sentence. In the absence of an *Agent*, *atypical* argument realization emerges. Deviations from canonical argument realization can be observed at two levels: when the default *Agent* argument is missing such as in (1) and when there is a *mismatch* between the thematic hierarchy requirements and the actual argument realization, such as in (2). Thus, we will be using the term "non-canonical" to refer generally to two distinct levels of deviations from thematic hierarchy, calling the former case *atypical* argument realization, and the latter *non-canonical* argument realization proper.

(1)	The key opened	the door	
	⟨*Ins*⟩	⟨*Th*⟩	*atypical* argument realization
(2)	The door opened with	the key	
	⟨*Th*⟩	⟨*Ins*⟩	*non-canonical* argument realization

Although thematic hierarchies may provide an appealing way to describe various linguistic phenomena and regularities across languages, it seems to be impossible to formulate a thematic hierarchy which will capture all generalizations involving the realization of arguments in terms of their semantic roles. For instance, in a sentence such as (3), it is not clear whether *Agent* or *Instrument* should be assigned to the first NP. In order for the proper role to be assigned, one would need to know the actual nature of the event – e.g. whether the victim was dead or alive, whether or not an agent used the victim's hands as instrument, etc.

(3) The victim's hand opened the door

In addition, it is not clear which semantic and perhaps "world-knowledge" factors should enter into the determination of the proper characterization of thematic roles. It seems clear that, beyond the syntactic information about the number and the grammatical class of the arguments, more semantic information will be recruited for the realization of each argument. Thus, specific semantic properties of the arguments such as *sentience* and *causal order* also appear to become relevant. The crucial role of these properties in argument realization is assumed by proponents of animacy hierarchy and thematic proto-roles, which are discussed next.

2.2. Animacy Hierarchy

Hierarchical relations between arguments also appear to be regulated by animacy constraints. A hierarchy of animacy has been proposed by various authors to account for different grammatical phenomena. For instance, Morolong and Hyman (1977) use such a hierarchy to determine the object status of arguments, and Silverstein (1976) uses it in a typology of split ergativity systems. The exact characterization of the hierarchy varies from author to author. Animacy hierarchy involves several distinct but related grammatical dimensions, such as *person hierarchy*, in which first and second person outrank third person, *NP-type hierarchy*, in which pronouns outrank common nouns, and finally what Croft (2003: 130) calls the *animacy hierarchy proper*. In this last type of hierarchy, for SVO languages such as English, humans outrank nonhuman animates, which in turn outrank inanimates. Animacy hierarchy is not an ordering of discrete categories, but rather a more or less continuous category ranging from "most animate" to "least animate". In most languages, the animacy of NPs is closely related to particular thematic roles normally assigned by particular verbs. For instance, the thematic properties of the verb *to eat* dictate that it must assign the role of

Agent to an animate NP, while the role of *Theme* would more likely be assigned to an inanimate NP. The role of animacy has been observed both in language acquisition (e.g. Diessel, 2007; Ozeki and Shirai, 2007) as well as in language processing of adults (e.g. Kuperberg et al., 2007; Lamers, 2007) suggesting that animacy constraints on verbs' arguments are computed online and can affect verb processing. Thus, we should consider any structure consisting of an inanimate noun in the subject position and an animate noun in the object position, such as in (4), as deviation from the animacy hierarchy.

(4) The question amazed the journalist

Closely related to animacy hierarchy is Dowty's (1991) proposal about proto-roles, which is outlined below.

2.3. Proto-roles

Proponents of the importance of proto-roles in argument realization assume the existence of only two generalized thematic roles, labeled *macroroles* (Foley and Van Valin, 1984) or proto-roles (Dowty, 1991) – one for the *Agent* and one for the *Patient* (proto-*Agent* and proto-*Patient*). According to this view, thematic roles are not discrete categories, but rather are "cluster concepts" (Dowty, 1991: 571) drawing from a pool of basic semantic properties such as *sentience*, *volition*, and *movement*. No single thematic role necessarily has all of these properties, and some have more than others. Using a series of diagnostics, Dowty has suggested that each of these properties (or "entailments"), listed in Table 2, can be isolated from the others, and so should be treated as distinct. When the predicate of an active sentence takes two arguments, the one with more proto-*Agent* properties appears as the subject, even if both arguments could make good *Agents*. When

Table 2. Proto-*Agent* and proto-*Patient* properties from Dowty (1991)

Proto-Agent properties	**Proto-Patient properties**
Volitional involvement in the event or state	Undergoes change of state
Sentience (and/or perception)	Incremental theme
Causing an event or change of state in another participant	Causally affected by another participant
Movement (relative to another participant)	Stationary relative to movement of another participant
Exists independently of the event named by the verb	Does not exist independently of the event, or at all

a predicate takes three arguments, the non-subject argument with the fewest proto-*Patient* properties appears as the oblique or prepositional object, while the one with the most proto-*Agent* properties appears (as usual) as the subject.

Dowty's proto-roles proposal has several appealing qualities; most important among them is a decrease in the number of thematic roles. Arguments identified as true *Agents* have all or most of the Proto-*Agent* properties and few or none of the proto-*Patient* properties; other thematic roles have few Proto-*Agent* properties, or mixed proto-*Agent* and proto-*Patient* attributes. For example, the only Proto-agent property of a subject *Experiencer* verb, such as in *John admires the statue,* is sentience. Another attractive quality of the proto-roles proposal is that it captures all event properties that are of particular interest to humans in order to interpret the specific event. For instance, when confronted with an event, we tend to care a great deal about the volition of the participants in that event; about who caused what to happen; about participants' perception of, and attitude towards, an event; about whether an event was completed; and about what changes, if any, took place as the result of an event. Thus, canonicity in terms of proto-roles would be defined in a manner similar to canonicity in terms of animacy hierarchy, with the argument carrying more proto-*Agent* properties figuring in the subject position and the argument carrying more proto-*Patient* properties occupying the object position.

There are, however, some potential problems with this theory. One concerns the *ontology* of the features that give rise to the proto-roles. Dowty treats these properties or features as "entailments" of the predicates, i.e., he treats them as the types of information that predicates entail about the nature of their constituent arguments. To put it simply, a predicate such as *kick* would select for an agent role which entails some of the properties listed in the first column of Table 2; for instance, it would entail *volition* and *causation* of the agent. It is not clear how these entailments work in the representation of the predicates – i.e., whether or not they are represented as part of the concept that a particular verb labels – nor is it clear what is the function of these entailments in the representation of the sentence formed by a particular predicate.[2] Another potential problem for understanding the nature of proto-roles is their function in language use, that is, what role they play in interpreting a sentence during linguistic perception. We defer some of these issues for later discussion in light of the data on AD patients' sentence processing.

Thus far, we outlined three basic principles for guiding the form-to-meaning mapping. These approaches suggest that there is a variety of factors that affect argument realization. A central question is how these different types of information come together to form a representation of meaning as we process language and what happens when some of the knowledge that is required for argument realization breaks down as a result of brain damage. Some of these questions are addressed below, when we discuss a study on the performance of AD patients on linguistic structures that deviate from canonical argument realization. Since ADs are supposed to have difficulties with semantic – but not syntactic – aspects of language processing, we investigated how their alleged deficit interacts with the processing of non-canonical sentences. We compared sentences with *psych* verbs to sentences with agentive verbs, in both active and passive voice. More specifically, we used non-reversible sentences where the *Experiencer* is always an animate entity and the *Theme/Causer* an inanimate one, such as *the statue fascinated the public / the public admired the statue.* We now turn to a discussion on the nature of argument realization in *psych* verbs and in passive structures, which constitute the main type of materials employed in our study with AD patients.

3. Non-canonical linguistic structures

3.1. Psych Verbs

Psychological predicates have constituted one of the most fertile testing grounds for understanding the nature of the mapping between argument structure and thematic roles. According to Belletti and Rizzi (1988), *psych* verbs are divided in three distinct categories:

a.	Class I:	Nominative experiencer, accusative theme. *John loves Mary.*
b.	Class II:	Nominative theme, accusative experiencer. *The show amused Bill.*
c.	Class III:	Nominative theme, dative experiencer. *The idea appealed to Julie.*

In formulations of the hierarchies that include an *Experiencer* (e.g. Belletti and Rizzi, 1988; Grimshaw, 1990; Van Valin, 1990), this role is ranked higher than the *Theme.* Hence, subject-*Experiencer* verbs, as in (5a), demonstrate *atypical* argument realization – with *Experiencer* rather than *Agent* assigned to the first NP –, whereas object-*Experiencer* verbs, as in (5b), demonstrate non-canonical argument realization, in the sense that there is a mismatch between thematic hierarchy and argument realization (i.e., *Theme* appearing before *Experiencer*). Thus, it appears that the two types of psych verbs described above provide us with two distinct cases of thematic hierarchy violations.[3]

(5) a. John loves Mary
 b. The show amused Bill

Most interestingly, one can find minimal pairs of *psych* verbs sharing similar semantic content but differing in the way their thematic roles are realized, such as the *fear-frighten* pair. Both *fear* and *frighten* refer to a "fright" situation seen from two different perspectives: from the perspective of the person who is in this mental state (the *Experiencer* in examples 6–9a), and from the perspective of the causer of the mental state (the *Theme* in examples 6–9b). Hereafter, we will be referring to subject-*Experiencer* verbs as "*fear*-type verbs" and to object-*Experiencer* verbs as "*frighten*-type verbs".

(6) a. Jane *fears* the thunder.
 b. The thunder *frightens* Jane.

(7) a. The public *admires* the statue.
 b. The statue *fascinates* the public.

(8) a. The children *enjoy* the music.
 b. The music *amuses* the children.

(9) a. The class *ponders* the equation.
 b. The equation *perplexes* the class.[4]

Although the classification of psych verbs proposed by Belletti and Rizzi (1988) has been widely adopted in the literature (e.g. Pesetsky, 1995; Baker, 1997; Landau, 2002; 2005), this has not been done without essential modifications. Belletti and Rizzi call the thematic roles involved in psychological predicates *Experiencer* and *Theme.* However, Pesetsky (1995) suggests that the subject argument of the object-*Experiencer* class bears the role *Causer*[5]. For the same class of psych verbs, Landau (2005: 5) also claims that they are transitive, projecting a little *v* and an external argument, a *Causer*[6]. The analysis treating the subject *frighten* as *Causer* has been widely adopted and it is now considered as standard. Thus, following this analysis, pairs like *fear* and *frighten* do not differ only in the way their arguments are realized, but they essentially bear different kinds of arguments. This has further implications regarding their predictions with respect to thematic and animacy hierarchy violations.[7]

That is, while Belletti and Rizzi's (1988) model suggests that object-*Experiencer* verbs produce a mismatch between the requirements of thematic hierarchy and their argument realization (with the *Theme* preceding the *Experiencer* argument), the analyses of Pesetsky (1995) and Landau (2005) do not allow us to make the same statement. In contrast, it appears that there is no violation, since the *Causer* argument, being closer to an *Agent* proto-role, precedes the *Experiencer.* This approach thus claims that psych verbs do not really violate the thematic hierarchy; they just demonstrate atypical argument realization (no *Agent*) in the subject-*Experiencer* constructions.

When it comes to psych verbs, Dowty (1991: 579–80) points out that pairs such as *fear-frighten* represent arbitrariness in argument realization. Both *fear* and *frighten* have equal Proto-*Agent* entailments: the sentience of the *Experiencer* and the causation of *Theme/Stimulus*. Thus, the two arguments are not distinguished by other entailments, and, therefore, it is not clear which one will occupy the subject and which one will occupy the object positions. Either realization at the subject position does not violate any Proto-*Agent* principle. However, *fear* and *frighten* have different entailments when it comes to the Proto-*Patient* role. These entailments are related to the eventive reading of object-*Experiencer* verbs extensively observed in the literature. The eventive reading of this verb class is associated with a change of state on the part of *Experiencer,* which is a Proto-*Patient* property. Thus, although the two arguments are equal in terms of proto-*Agent* properties, it is their difference in the Proto-*Patient* properties that determines their realization. Therefore, in Dowty's terms, causation outranks sentience in determining canonical argument realization.

In terms of animacy hierarchy, while the subject of *fear*-type verbs is most of the time an animate *Experiencer,* the subject of a *frighten*-type verb could be either animate (*John frightened Mary*) or inanimate (*the thunder frightened Mary*). Thus, the only case we may consider as a deviation from canonical animacy hierarchy is related to *frighten*-type verbs when an *inanimate* NP occupies the subject position and an *animate* NP occupies the object position, such as in the sentence *the thunder frightened the children*.

3.2. Passives

In an investigation of non-canonical argument realization, passive voice cannot be left aside. The process of passivization, as described below, results in the externalization of internal argument, which is usually a *Theme*, and the suppression of the original external, usually *Agent,* argument. The sentences in (10) and (11) describe the same basic event with the same semantic participants:

(10) Philip bit the dog

(11) The dog was bitt**en** (by Philip)

Sentences in (10) and (11) describe a biting event. The *biter* (*Agent*) is *Philip* and the *bitee* (*Theme*) is *the dog.* At least on the surface, then, these two sentences seem to involve the same thematic information. However, on closer examination, one would notice that in (11) the *Agent* is represented by an optional prepositional phrase headed by the preposition *by*. This turns the *Agent* from an argument into an adjunct and as such it is not included in the basic thematic grid of the verb and it is therefore not subject to the theta criterion (Chomsky, 1981). It thus seems that the sentences in (10) and (11) have different thematic properties. The active sentence in (10) has an *Agent* and a *Theme*, while the passive sentence in (11) lacks the *Agent* argument in its thematic grid. This theory of the passive does not however claim that the *Agent* argument is totally deleted. It is instead supposed to be absorbed or suppressed by the passive morpheme *-en*. This morphological operation thus triggers the surfacing of the *Theme* in the subject position in order to satisfy the EPP (external projection principle).

In the case of *psych* verbs, the issue of their passivization has generated much controversy in the literature and it is beyond the scope of this chapter to discuss the details of this controversy. We adopt Landau's (2002, 2005) proposal that it is *eventiveness* and not *agentivity* that is a determining factor in the passivization of *psych* verbs (2005: 49). In *psych* passives, the suppressed argument is the *Experiencer/Theme* (as in *The statue was admired/The sculptor was threatened).* Thus, the fact the *psych* verbs passivize cannot be taken as evidence for them being agentive.

Defining canonicity is a fairly straightforward task for agentive structures, for all approaches discussed above share the same assumption as to what constitutes a canonical argument realization. Passives of agentive verbs result in non-canonical argument realization, with the *Theme* figuring in the subject position and the *Agent* being suppressed and represented by an adjunct *by*-phrase. It is more difficult to determine canonicity with passives of *psych* verbs. Passives of *fear*-type verbs bear the *Theme* argument at the subject position, thus resulting in a non-canonical argument realization. Passives of *frighten* verbs normally externalize the *Experiencer* argument and canonicity depends on whether the second argument is a *Causer* or a *Theme*. In the former case, non-canonical argument realization emerges, while in the latter case, there is no deviation. Table 3 summarizes the structures that result in non-canonical argument realization.

4. Non-canonicity in brain damaged populations

The role of canonicity in terms of thematic hierarchy as a determining factor for sentence comprehension in patients with Broca's aphasia was addressed by Piñango (e.g. Piñango, 2006). The main language symptom of Broca's aphasia is impaired sentence production and comprehension when it comes to the

Table 3. Non-canonicity in *psych* verbs and in passives

Sentence Type	Example	Belletti and Rizzi (1988) Thematic Hierarchy	Pesetsky (1995) Thematic Hierarchy	Dowty (1991) Proto-Roles	Croft (2003) Animacy Hierarchy
Fear-active	The children feared the thunder	+ <Exp, Th>	– <Exp, Caus>	– <Exp, Caus>	+ <An, In>
Fear-passive	The thunder was feared by the children	– <Th, Exp>	+ <Caus, Exp>	+ <Caus, Exp>	– <In, An>
Frighten-active	The thunder frightened the children	– <Th, Exp>	+ <Caus, Exp>	+ <Caus, Exp>	– <In, An>
Frighten-passive	The children were frightened by the thunder	+ <Exp, Th>	– <Exp, Caus>	– <Exp, Caus>	+ <An, In>
Agent-active	The gang stole the car	+ <Ag, Th>	+ <Ag, Th>	+ <Ag, Th>	+ <An, In>
Agent-passive	The car was stolen by the gang	– <Th, Ag>	– <Th, Ag>	– <Th, Ag>	– <In, An >

+ = *canonical argument realization*
– = *non-canonical argument realization*

interpretation of complex syntactic structures. For instance, agrammatic aphasics have been found to have difficulties both with *psych* verbs (e.g. Piñango, 1999, 2000) and passives (e.g. Grodzinsky, 1995; but see Berndt, Mitchum, and Haendiges, 1996). More specifically, agrammatics have problems with *frighten*-type verbs (12), and also with passives of agentive (13) and *fear*-type verbs (14).

(12) The noise frightened Mary.

(13) Mary was pushed by John.

(14) Mary is admired by John.

Piñango (2006), adopting Belletti and Rizzi's (1988) analysis of object-*Experiencer* verbs, postulates that agrammatic patients experience difficulties with passives and *psych* verbs due to these structures' deviations from canonical argument realization. Piñango suggests that these specific constructions violate the principle of linking between semantic representation and syntactic structure (along the lines of Levin and Rappaport Hovav, 2005). The basic principle is that prominent structural positions are occupied by elements which are also prominent in other dimensions, such as semantic role and animacy, leaving the less prominent items for the non-subject position. That is why *Agent* and *Experiencer* arguments precede *Patients/Themes* and *Recipients*.[8] Thus, when syntactic representation violates the canonical order of arguments, agrammatic aphasics perform poorly. However, Piñango's reasoning holds only within Belletti and Rizzi's analysis of *psych* verbs, which treats the non-*Experiencer* argument as *Theme,* and does not explain the pattern of results when this argument is treated as *Causer.*

We examined effects of canonicity in argument realization in terms of both thematic and animacy hierarchy by looking at the performance of AD patients, a brain-damaged population that is supposed to have retained their syntactic abilities, but generally, to have lost their semantic skills (Manouilidou et al., 2009). This combination of preserved syntax and impaired semantics allowed us to examine a different aspect of argument realization and thematic-role mapping, one that mostly relies on semantic resources. A general description of how AD affects linguistic and cognitive abilities of patients is provided in the following section.

4.1. Clinical and linguistic description of patients with AD

Alzheimer's disease (AD) is a progressive neurodegenerative condition characterized by neuropathological changes in the cortex and marked neuronal loss. The observation of excessive quantities of neurofibrillary tangles and senile plaques, formed by increased tau phosphorylation, is sufficient for a diagnosis of AD. Furthermore, hippocampal atrophy, often detected before dementia onset by MRI studies (Fox, Warrington, Stevens, and Rossor, 1996; Visser et al., 1999), is believed to result to clinically identifiable dementia (Fox et al., 1996). Individuals with AD also manifest alterations in various cognitive domains. Deficits are seen in episodic memory (Chen et al., 2001), executive function (Chen et al., 2001), perceptual speed (Fox, Warrington, Seiffer, Agnew, and Rossor, 1998), visuospatial skill (Chen et al., 2001) and attention (Levinoff, Saumier, and Chertkow, 2005; Perry and Hodges, 2000; Pignatti et al., 2005).

AD patients often manifest deficits in language processing very early in the disease course. Deficits are seen in verbal fluency (for a review, see Henry, Crawford, and Phillips, 2004), naming (Laiacona, Barbarotto, and Capitani, 1998), particularly of biological items (Zannino et al., 2006) semantic knowledge (Mauri, Daum, Sartori, Riesch, and Birbaumer, 1994; Garrard, Patterson, Watson, and Hodges,1998), and discourse-level processing (for a review, see Caramelli, Mansur and Nitrini, 1998). Syntactic and phonological abilities, on the other hand, are relatively preserved (Bayles, 1982; Schwartz, Marin and Saffran, 1979 etc.).

Taking into account the claim that AD patients have preserved syntactic but impaired semantic abilities, we studied their performance in a sentence completion task involving *psych* verbs. Based on data from this study, we will discuss the evidence for these hierarchies in language processing by brain damaged populations and argue for their psychological reality.

4.2. The Experimental Data

In a recent study investigating the verb deficit in AD, Manouilidou et al. (2009) tested the performance of 10 AD patients in a sentence completion task by using two types of *psych* verbs, in active and passive voices. Our strategy was to test AD patients' ability to assign thematic roles to the various NPs associated with verbs in different thematic-grid configurations. Based on the fundamental role that hierarchical relations appear to play in the mapping between semantic participants and syntactic structures, we predicted that patients would have difficulty with predicates that require non-canonical argument realization, given the pervasive semantic deficits in AD. The focus of our investigation was patients' performance in sentences that required subject-*Experiencer* (*fear*) verbs, which call for *atypical* argument realization (no *Agent*), and object-*Experiencer* (*frighten*) psych verbs which entail *non-canonical* argument realization (mismatch between the thematic hierarchy and the actual realization of the arguments, with *Theme* preceding *Experiencer*).

In this study we presented participants with sentences with the verb missing marked by a blank line (e.g. *The boy____the thunder*). They had to choose the correct verb from a list of four verbs, which included the two main alternatives (e.g. *fear* and *frighten*), one syntactically anomalous (e.g. *sleep*) and one semantically unrelated (e.g. *cook*). In total, patients were required to complete 72 active and passive written sentences (see Appendix). All verbs used in the study were controlled for frequency (Kucera and Francis 1982). Materials were divided into 6 conditions, with 12 sentences in each of them: (1) subject-*Experiencer* verbs (e.g. *fear*); (2) the reverse equivalent of subject-*Experiencer* verbs, i.e. object-*Experiencer* verbs (e.g. *frighten*); (3) and (4) were the passive equivalent of (1) and (2), respectively (e.g. *was feared* and *was frightened*); (5) subject-agent verbs (e.g. *kick*); (6) the passive equivalent subject-*Agent* verbs (e.g. *was kicked*). Patient performance was compared to that of 11 healthy controls, matched for age, education, and demographics, and to that of 49 young controls.

We scored correct verb selection and analyzed the data taking into account participants and materials (sentence types) as random variables. Our analyses first contrasted the performance of the three groups (AD patients, matched elderly controls, and young controls). The analyses of the three groups revealed significant differences between them. The young controls, however, performed at ceiling, so all our other contrasts were made taking into account only the performance of the other two groups. For these analyses we focused on two main variables, the predicate type (distinguished by subject thematic role) (*Agent*, *Experiencer* subject, and *Experiencer* object) and voice (active and passive).

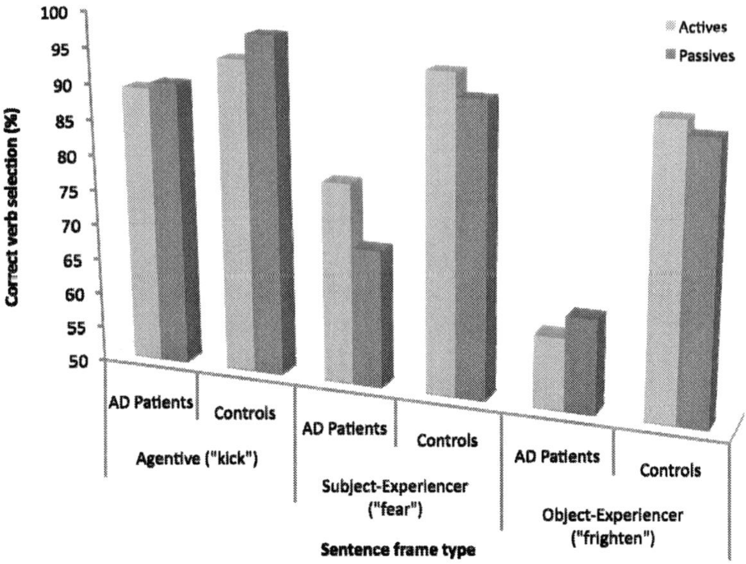

Figure 1. Correct verb selection by Alzheimer's patients and age-matched controls

There were no significant differences between AD patients and controls in the performance of agentive sentences. The differences between the two groups were in the performance of sentences with *psych* verbs. We plotted the performance of the two groups across all conditions in Figure 1.

As can be seen, AD patients committed many more errors than their controls in both *psych* verb sentence types in both active and passive constructions. More importantly, in the analysis of the AD patient data there was a main effect of subject thematic role, which was independent of voice, suggesting that the effects are due to thematic role, not syntactic frame. Taking into account only the AD patient data, we also found a significant effect of subject thematic role. Given that patients performance in sentences with *Agent* roles was not significantly different from that of their controls, we analyzed only the two *psych*-verb frames. Here too we found a significant difference – with more errors in the object-*Experiencer* (*frighten*) frame than in the subject-*Experiencer* (*fear*) frame.

The differences observed in the subject-*Experiencer* and object-*Experiencer* constructions – together with the lack thereof in the case of agentive frames – highlight the difficulty AD patients have with the non-canonical argument realization projected by *psych* verbs. In order to better understand the nature of the difficulty AD patients have with these verbs, we looked at the errors they

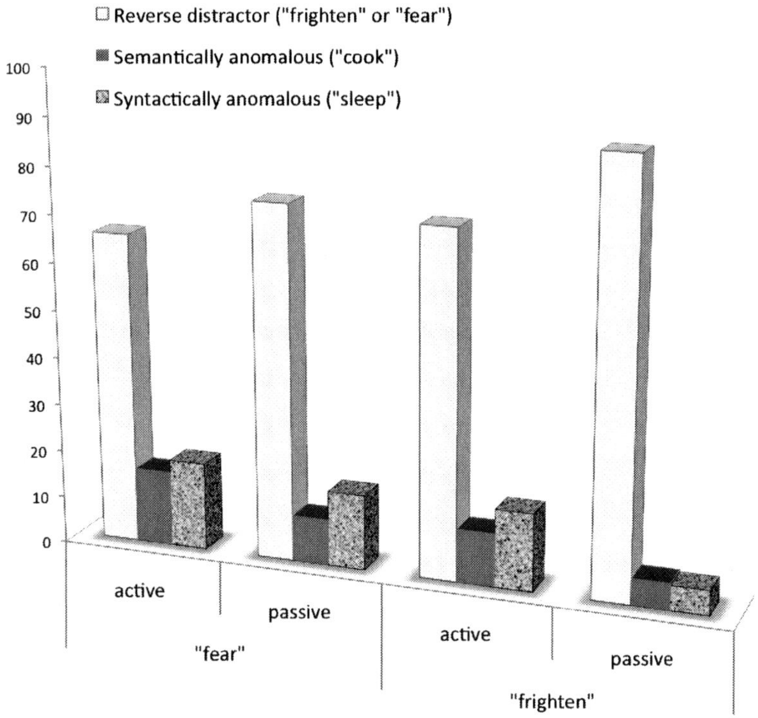

Figure 2. Distribution of errors (%) committed by AD patients when selecting a verb for a sentence frame (e.g. percentage of times in which the reverse distractor *frighten* was chosen in place of the correct *fear* in active and passive frames).

committed when choosing a verb for each frame. The distribution of these errors is shown in Figure 2.

When AD patients opted for an incorrect *psych* verb, they most often selected the verb with the reverse thematic roles (e.g. when the target verb was *fear*, they often chose *frighten*). They very rarely selected the unrelated distractors in both active and passive voice sentences. We suggest that AD patients had no difficulty determining the semantic content of the verbs, for they clearly made their selection between the two competing verbs. The pattern of data supports the view that their deficit is in the assignment of verb thematic roles.

5. Argument Realization and Canonicity

The primary goal of the present study is to discuss different views on argument realization in light of the performance of brain-damaged populations supposedly suffering from a semantic deficit, such as AD patients. Patients' performance was examined with verbs whose argument realization deviate from canonical (*Agent* first) structure, such as psychological predicates. We started off by briefly presenting three main views on argument realization (thematic hierarchy, animacy hierarchy and proto-roles), and outlined their assumptions of canonicity in hierarchical relations between arguments. In order to shed light on the potential role of hierarchical relations in sentence representation, in the present section we discuss the results of our empirical study from the perspective of the theories that have been put forth to account for argument realization.

As we have seen, the results of Manouilidou et al. (2009) show that patients have difficulties with non-canonical structures, as evidenced by the errors they made when they had to complete a sentence with a *psych* verb of either subject-*Experiencer* or object-*Experiencer* type. In contrast, their performance was similar to that of healthy controls when confronted with agentive verb sentences, either in active or in passive voice. A closer look at the pattern of results – which are summarized in Table 4 – allows us to observe that the findings do not entirely support any of the hierarchical theories of argument realization discussed. Instead, it seems that both thematic hierarchy and animacy hierarchy should be considered in a complementary way in order to account for the results.

Table 4. AD patient performance against the predictions of different thematic/animacy hierarchies

Sentence Type	AD Performance Compared to controls	Belletti and Rizzi (1988) Thematic Hierarchy	Pesetsky (1995) Thematic Hierarchy	Dowty (1991) Proto-Roles	Croft (2003) Animacy Hierarchy
Fear- active	*Impaired*	+ <Exp, Th>	✔ – <Exp, Caus>	✔ – <Exp, Caus>	+ <An, In>
Fear- passive	*Impaired*	✔ – <Th, Exp>	+ <Caus, Exp>	+ <Caus, Exp>	✔ – <In, An>
Frighten- active	*Impaired**	✔ – <Th, Exp>	+ <Caus, Exp>	+ <Caus, Exp>	✔ – <In, An>
Frighten- passive	*Impaired*	+ <Exp, Th>	✔ – <Exp, Caus>	✔ – <Exp, Caus>	+ <An, In>
Agent- active	*Normal*	✔ + <Ag, Th>	✔ + <Ag, Th>	✔ + <Ag, Th>	✔ + <An, In>
Agent- passive	*Normal*	– <Th, Ag>	– <Th, Ag>	– <Th, Ag>	– <In, An >

\+ = *canonical argument realization (predicted to be sparred in AD)*
– = *non-canonical argument realization (predicted to be impaired in AD)*
✔ = *predictions supported by the results*
* = *performance also worse than* fear-*active constructions*

Moreover, the results point to the importance of the *Agent* argument, albeit not necessarily at the subject position, emphasizing the complexity of sentence interpretation for AD patients in terms of factors that come into play.

More specifically, thematic hierarchy, under Belletti and Rizzi (1988)'s analysis fails to account for participants' impaired performance in *fear*-actives, *frighten*-passives, and agentive passives. The same holds for animacy hierarchy. However, Pesetsky (1995)'s thematic hierarchy and the theory of proto-roles correctly predict patients' performance in the above structures, but fail to account for their performance in *frighten*-active and *fear*-passive sentences. Finally, none of the proposals for argument realization accounts for patients' ceiling performance with agentive passives. Thus, we cannot maintain that non-canonicity, as strictly defined by hierarchical relations, affects patient performance to a decisive degree. In contrast, AD patients are sensitive to deviations from canonicity in argument realization, when canonicity is not defined in terms of thematic hierarchy but mostly in terms of *agentivity*. The pattern of results seems to suggest that there is a dissociation between [+agentive] verbs (relatively preserved) and [–agentive] verbs (significantly more impaired). This pattern was consistent for both active and passive voice constructions.

In relation to the lack of voice effect, we should emphasize patients' performance on passives. Patients performed normally completing semantically non-reversible passives with agentive verbs, while their performance with non-reversible *psych* passives was impaired. This result casts doubt on the hypothesis of impaired mapping procedures and difficulties in assigning verb arguments in non-canonical sentences. Note that non-reversible passives typically involve animate and inanimate entities whose role in the sentence is easily predictable. For instance, in the sentence *The public was fascinated by the statue* there is only one way to interpret the thematic role of the NPs. However, AD patients were clearly impaired when confronted with these types of *psych* sentences. In contrast, when confronted with non-reversible agentive passives, e.g. *The car was stolen by the gang* there was no confusion as to the selection of the correct verb based on the position of the NPs in the sentence. Even though this sentence is non-canonical in terms of thematic hierarchy, animacy hierarchy and proto-roles, AD patients had no difficulty selecting the correct verb. It seems that the AD patients could use the syntactic cues – e.g. the *by* phrase – to determine the correct position of the *Agent*.[9] Thus, regardless of how non-canonical – in terms of hierarchical relations – the output is, because the verb calls for an agentive interpretation, AD patients show no difficulty understanding that the *Agent* position in the sentence is after the verb, in the *by*-phrase. The normal performance of AD patients on this type of sentences is perfectly in line with their spared abilities on [+agentive] verbs and [+agentive] sentences. One could argue, then, that the difference in the type of thematic roles [+agentive] and [–agentive] verbs can take is responsible for AD patients' pattern of performance. Thus, AD patients' performance would be impaired only when the subject of the verb maps onto a thematic role different from that of *Agent*.

Another way of accounting for the pattern of performance of the Manouilidou et al. (2009) study is that AD patients suffer from a category-specific semantic deficit related to *psych* verbs. Their spared abilities would be sufficient to allow access to the meaning of agentive verbs and of all verbs used as distractors. However, the subjects' performance fails when confronted with a *psych* verb. According to this account, AD patients would perform worse on *psych* verbs simply because they have a selective impairment in this verb category. In fact, naming of subject-*Experiencer* perception verbs (*smell, listen*) was found to be impaired in another group of AD patients (de Almeida, Mobayyen, Kehayia, and Schwartz, 2009). These patients performed better at naming events using lexical causatives and motion verbs. Perception verbs also lack the *Agent* argument. Thus, impaired naming on perception verbs also supports our claim about impaired [–agentive] verbs. If this is the case, then it strongly suggests that a range of factors may affect AD patients' performance in the sentence completion task, and one of them is the presence or absence of the *Agent* argument in the sentence. Hence, it seems that AD patients suffer from a semantic deficit restricted to [–agentive] verbs and [–agentive] sentences. This deficit occurs in the context of spared abilities in active and passive agentive sentences. We cannot at this point determine if the AD patients' deficit involves thematic roles that are different from that of *Agent* or if it simply involves the [–agentive] verb feature per se. If they have a deficit with thematic roles that are not *Agent*, patients should have difficulty with thematic roles assigned to the object of agentive sentences.[10] The pattern of results of our study, however, does not support this hypothesis. Thus, a [–agentive] verb feature deficit seems to be the best way to account for our data.[11]

Most interestingly, the above finding does not cancel out any possible effects of hierarchical relations in argument realization and sentence interpretation by AD patients. Before concluding on the defining role of *agentivity* in guiding AD patients' sentence interpretation, we should account for the difference between *fear* and *frighten* active sentences. Patients performed better on *fear*-actives than on *frighten*-actives. This finding suggests a sensitivity of AD patients to argument realization that deviates from animacy hierarchy and from canonical thematic hierarchy for subject-*Experiencer* verbs, following Belletti and Rizzi's analysis. That is, because *frighten* actives have an argument realization with a *Theme* figuring before *Experiencer*, these verbs present greater difficulty than *fear* verbs, which have an atypical but still canonical argument realization. While agentivity appears to be a defining factor in leading AD patients' performance, canonicity stemming from thematic hierarchy also appears to play a role. Thus, sentence interpretation by AD patients appears to be subject to multiple constraints, with first among them the presence of an *Agent* followed by the presence of an animate entity in the subject position. Evidently, these constraints are subject to different degrees of violability, which could be described in a, practically, optimality theory way, as applied in syntax by Aissen (2003).

This finding allows us to argue for the existence of thematic hierarchy as a linguistic entity that guides argument realization and to address certain issues pertaining to the nature of thematic roles. The role of hierarchical relations in argument realization has been put into question by various researchers (e.g. McCarthy, 2002; Newmeyer, 2002) mostly because of a lack of agreement regarding its formulation and also because of an inability to be proven as "innate and functionally motivated" (Newmeyer, 2002: 60). The results of the study we discuss cannot argue for the innateness of hierarchical structures, but they do argue for the functional motivation of these hierarchies. Sensitivity to their violations by brain-damaged populations provides support for the psychological reality of such structures. The mapping from meaning to form is not random, but it complies with hierarchical regularities related to semantic properties of each argument. This observation together with the selective impairment of AD patients in [–agentive verbs] gives further support to the existence of thematic roles as entities that are not merely labels (Rappaport and Levin, 1988) for lists of arguments of a predicate, but also crucially assist in the mapping of form to meaning. While we can argue for the existence of thematic hierarchy based on this specific study, we cannot argue that argument realization can be fully accounted for in a theory that relies on proto-roles (Dowty, 1991). In the proto-roles approach, *causation* outranks *sentience,* while we have shown evidence for the opposite realization.

In conclusion, we have shown that deficits arising from neurologically impaired individuals provide us with the opportunity of observing how a particular domain of knowledge can be selectively affected. Although the performance of AD patients cannot be taken as the only – nor necessarily the best – evidence for the nature of thematic hierarchy and argument realization, it does provide us with a window into how these patients unravel the phrase structure rules of their native language and sheds light on the nature of the mapping between arguments and their thematic roles. We have evidence that AD patients are sensitive to deviations from canonicity in linguistic structures. This canonicity is mostly defined in terms of *agentivity* with the role of thematic hierarchy still being significant. It is the presence of the *Agent* argument that leads comprehension. When there is no *Agent*, then thematic hierarchy seems to guide sentence comprehension.

Thus, it appears that the semantic properties of a verb's arguments cannot exhaustively account for argument realization. In contrast, mapping from form to meaning requires different types of information, which may be disrupted when some of the knowledge that is required for argument realization breaks down as a result of brain damage.

Appendix

This appendix contains sample materials used in the experiment by Manouilidou et al. (2009)

Sentence frames were presented for verb selection, and participants had to choose the correct alternative among four verbs presented in random order. The verb options for each sentence below are the following: the first verb represents the correct answer, the second is the main distractor, the third is the semantically inappropriate distractor and the forth is the syntactically inappropriate distractor. Passive versions employed the same verb materials as in the active sentences but with passive frames presented to participants (e.g., The statue was *admired/fascinated/rode/slept* by the public).

fear active

1) The public *admired/fascinated/rode/slept* the statue.
2) The children *feared/frightened/melted/bloomed* the thunder.
3) The scientist *liked/pleased/froze/smiled* the fossil.
4) The minister *pitied/saddened/saved/screamed* the poverty.
5) The spectators *enjoyed/amused/licked/lived* the performance.
6) The class *pondered/perplexed/cooked/coughed* the equation.
7) The students *dreaded/intimidated/brushed/whispered* the exam.
8) The actress *envied/tempted/poured/chatted* the singer's voice.
9) The elderly *hated/bothered/danced/agreed* the hospitals.
10) The author *resented/disappointed/sipped/frowned* the editor's remarks.
11) The community *tolerated/disturbed/murdered/existed* the differences.
12) The listeners *detested/disgusted/hit/stood* the commentator's opinion.

frighten active

1) The exam *intimidated/dreaded/brushed/whispered* the students.
2) The singer's voice *tempted/envied/ poured/chatted* the actress.
3) The hospitals *bothered/hated/danced/agreed* the elderly
4) The editor's remarks *disappointed/resented/sipped/frowned* the author
5) The differences *disturbed/tolerated/murdered/existed* the community.

6) The commentator's opinion *disgusted/detested/hit/stood* the listeners.
7) The statue *fascinated/admired/rode/slept* the public
8) The thunder *frightened/feared/melted/bloomed* the children.
9) The fossil *pleased/liked/froze/smiled* the scientist.
10) The poverty *saddened/pitied/shaved/screamed* the minister
11) The performance *amused/enjoyed/licked/lived* the spectators.
12) The equation *perplexed/pondered/cooked/coughed* the class.

agent active

1) The teacher *accompanied/arrived/grew/yawned* the students.
2) The gardener *cultivated/sprouted/decided/babbled* the carrots.
3) The company *fired/resigned/concurred/drifted* many employees.
4) The hostess *illuminated/glittered/divorced/gossiped* the room.
5) The hunter *killed/died/descented/sneezed* the deer.
6) The lifeguard *saved/survived/expressed/snored* the swimmer.
7) The king *expelled/departed/moaned/wrinkled* the poets.
8) The policeman *chased/fled/kissed/spoke* the criminal.
9) The thief *stole/vanished/helped/stuttered* the painting.
10) The cleaner *pushed/fell/mopped/barked* the bucket.
11) The mom *tickled/giggled/cured/revolved* the kid.
12) The movie *bored/yawned/carved/nodded* the audience.

Notes

* We are grateful to George Schwartz and N.P.V. Nair, from the Douglas Hospital, in Montreal, for facilitating our access to Alzheimer's patients, and to Levi Riven for assistance during the preparation of this chapter. We would also like to thank Sam Featherston, Paul Hirschbhüler and Marie Labelle for detailed comments. Financial support for research reported here was provided by grants from the Social Sciences and Humanities Research Council of Canada.

1. Hierarchical relations are especially important for SVO languages which do not allow free word order, such as English, the language under investigation in the present paper. While the mapping from meaning to form for other languages is marked by inflectional morphology, in English it depends heavily on the position of the NP in the sentence.
2. Dowty assumes that these roles are compiled as "prototypes", much like the prototype theory in psychology (e.g. Rosch and Mervin, 1975). However, Dowty's use of the term "prototype" is slightly different. The term "proto-roles" refers to higher-order generalizations about lexical meanings without suggesting that individual lexical meanings themselves are prototypes (Dowty, 1991: 577).

3. We will use the term "violation" to refer to both cases of deviation although we do not consider an atypical argument realization a violation, but a deviation from the most typical case of argument realization.
4. We are not claiming that the verbs constituting these minimal pairs are synonymous with reversed thematic roles. It is beyond the scope of the present paper to determine the content properties of these verbs or to account for the notion of content similarity between the members of the pairs. The strategy used in our study was to employ verb pairs that allow for the reverse thematic roles while keeping the nature of the state predicated by the verbs as close as possible.
5. Pesetsky (1995: 55) also renames the object argument with the subject-*Experiencer* class either as *Target of Emotion* or *Subject Matter*. This difference is not relevant for the purposes of our study and we will not further elaborate on it.
6. Notice that the majority of object-*Experiencer* verbs are ambiguous between stative and eventive readings. However, there are some verbs that are unambiguously stative, such as *interest* and *concern*. Following Landau (2002) we assume that only these verbs lack a "causer" argument in their thematic grid.
7. It should be noted that this analysis also runs into problems if *Causer* is somewhat taken as part of the semantic representation of the object-*Experience* sentence. Fodor (1970) has long observed that constructions such as (ia) and (ib) are not synonymous, for their distributional properties are not the same. Compare (ii) and (iii).

   (i) a. The article angered Bill
   b. The article caused Bill to become angry
   (ii) a. The article angered Bill and it surprised me that it did so
   b. The article caused Bill to become angry and it surprised me that it did so
   (iii) a. *The article angered Bill and it surprised me that he did so
   b. The article caused Bill to become angry and it surprised me that he did so

8. This applies to all languages in which subject precedes object (such as SVO).
9. The preposition *by* is lexically ambiguous, introducing a NP that can be assigned the thematic role of an *Agent* or *Location* among others (*found by the river*). However, discourse expectation, verb bias, and mostly a frequency bias from the preposition itself favor the role of *Agent*. A bias for interpreting the *by* argument as an *Agent* is also found in on-line experiments of sentence processing by using eye-tracking (Tanenhaus, Spivey-Knowlton, and Hanna, 2000) indicating that a *by* phrase following a passive verb provides overwhelming support for the agentive interpretation. In the same study, Tanenhaus et al. (2000) found effects of individual verb biases. Agent-biasing verbs strengthened the preference for an agent completion in all conditions.
10. Even though we only have two arguments, we are still in position to judge whether incorrect responses stem from the subject thematic role and not from the object thematic role, simply because a difficulty with the object thematic role would equally affect agentive and non-agentive sentences.
11. Deficits affecting only [–agentive] verbs were found with aphasic patients as well (Finocchiaro, 2002).

References

Aissen, J.
2003 Differential object marking: iconicity vs economy. *Natural Language and Linguistic Theory*, 21: 435–483.

Baker, M.
1989 Object Sharing and Projection in Serial Verb Construction, *Linguistic Inquiry*, 20: 513–553.
1997 Thematic roles and syntactic structure. In: Liliane Haegeman (ed.), *Elements of Grammar: Handbook of Generative Syntax*, pp. 73–137, Dordrecht: Kluwer.

Bayles, K.
1982 Language function in senile dementia. *Brain and Language*, 16: 265–280.

Belletti, A. and Rizzi, L.
1988 Psych-Verbs and Theta-Theory. *Natural Language and Linguistic Theory* 6: 291–352.

Berndt, R. S., Mitchum, C. C., and Haendiges, A. N.
1996 Comprehension of reversible sentences in "agrammatism": A meta-analysis. *Cognition* 58: 289–308.

Caramelli, P., Mansur, L. L., and Nitrini, R.
1998 Language and communication disorders in dementia of the Alzheimer type. In: B. Stemmer and H. A. Whitaker (eds.), *Handbook of Neurolinguistics*, pp. 463–473. San Diego, CA: Academic Press.

Chen, P., Ratcliff, R., Belle, S.H., Cauley, J.A., DeKosky, S.T., and Ganguli, M.
2001 Patterns of cognitive decline in presymptomatic Alzheimer's disease: a prospective community study. *Archives of General Psychiatry* 58: 853–8.

Chomsky, N.
1981 *Lectures in government and binding.* Dordrecht: Foris.

Croft, W.
2003 *Typology and universals, second edition.* (Cambridge Textbooks in Linguistics.) Cambridge: Cambridge University Press.

de Almeida, R. G., Mobayyen, F., Kehayia, E., and Schwartz, G.
2009 *Category-specific verb semantic deficit: Evidence from a dynamic action naming task.* Manuscript in preparation.

Diessel, H.
2007 Frequency effects in language acquisition, language use, and diachronic change. *New Ideas in Psychology* 25: 108–127.

Dowty, D.
1991 Thematic Proto-Roles and Argument Selection. *Language* 67: 547–619.

Finocchiaro, C.
2002 Sensitivity of [–/+agentive] feature: the case of an aphasic subject. *Journal of Neurolinguistics* 15: 433–446.

Fillmore, C. J.
1968 *Lexical entries for verbs*. Dordrecht, Holland: D. Reidel.

Finocchiaro, C.
2002 Sensitivity to the verb [+/–agentive] feature: the case of an aphasic subject. *Journal of Neurolinguistics* 15: 433–446.

Fodor, J.
1970 'Three Reasons for Not Deriving 'Kill' from 'Cause to Die', *Linguistic Inquiry* 1: 429–438.

Foley, W. A. and Van Valin, R., Jr.
1984 *Functional syntax and universal grammar*. Cambridge: Cambridge University Press.

Fox, N.C., Warrington, E.K., Stevens, J.M., and Rossor, M.N.
1996 Atrophy of the hippocampal formation in early familial Alzheimer's disease. A longitudinal MRI study of at-risk members of a family with an amyloid precursor protein 717 ValGly mutation. *Annals of the N Y Academy of Science* 777: 226–32.

Fox, N.C., Warrington, E.K., Seiffer, A.L., Agnew, S.K., and Rossor, M.N.
1998 Presymptomatic cognitive deficits in individuals at risk of familial Alzheimer's disease. A longitudinal prospective study. *Brain* 121: 1631–9.

Garrard, P., Patterson, K., Watson, P., and Hodges, J. R.
1998 Category-specific semantic loss in dementia of Alzheimer'stype. Functional-anatomical correlations from cross-sectional analyses. *Brain* 121: 633–646.

Givón, T.
1984 *Syntax: A Functional-typological Introduction*, vol. 1. Amsterdam: John Benjamins.

Grimshaw, J.
1990 *Argument Structure*. Cambridge, MA: MIT Press.

Grodzinsky, Y.
1995 Trace deletion, theta roles, and cognitive strategies. *Brain and language* 51: 469–497.

Henry, J.D., Crawford, J.R., and Phillips, L.H.
2004 Verbal fluency performance in dementia of the Alzheimer's type: A meta-analysis. *Neuropsychologia* 42: 1212–1222.

Jackendoff, R.
1972 *Semantic Interpretation in Generative Grammar*. Cambridge, MA: MIT Press.
1990 *Semantic Structures*. Cambridge, MA: MIT Press.

Kucera, H. and Francis, W. N.
1982 *Computational Analysis of Present-Day American English.* Providence, RI: Brown University Press.

Kuperberg, G., Sitnikova, T., and Lakshmanan, B.
2007 Semantic violations of action and morphosyntactic agreement violations recruit an overlapping neural network: Evidence from functional magnetic resonance imaging. *submitted.*

Laiacona, M., Barbarotto, R., and Capitani, E.
1998 Semantic category dissociation in naming: Is there a Gender effect in Alzheimer disease? *Neuropsychologia* 36: 407–419.

Lamers, M.
2007 Verb type, animacy and definiteness in grammatical function disambiguation. *Linguistics in the Netherlands*, 125–137.

Landau, I.
2002 A typology of psych passives. In: Hirotani, M. (Ed.), *Proceedings of the 32nd Conference of the North Eastern Linguistic Society*, 271–286, GLSA, UMASS, Amherst.
2005 *The locative syntax of Experiencers.* Ms. Available at http://www.bgu.ac.il/~idanl/

Levin, B. and Rappaport Hovav, M.
2005 *Argument Realization.* Cambridge: Cambridge University Press.

Levinoff, E.J., Saumier , D., and Chertkow, H.
2005 Focused attention deficits in patients with Alzheimer's disease and mild cognitive impairment. *Brain and Cognition* 57: 127–130.

Manouilidou, C., de Almeida, R. G., Schwartz, G., and Nair, N. P. V.
2009 Thematic hierarchy violations in Alzheimer's disease: The case of psychological predicates. *Journal of Neurolinguistics* 22: 167–186.

Mauri, A., Daum, I., Sartori, G., Riesch, G., and Birbaumer, N.
1994 Category-specific semantic impairment in Alzheimer's disease and temporal lobe dysfunction: A comparative study. *Journal of Clinical and Experimental Neuropsychology* 16: 689–701.

McCarthy, J.
2002 *A thematic guide to optimality theory.* Cambridge: Cambridge University Press.

Morolong, M. and Hyman, L.
1977 Animacy, objects and clitics in Sesotho. *Studies in African Linguistics* 8: 199–218.

Newmeyer, F.
2002 Optimality and Functionality: A critique of functionally-based optimality-theoretic syntax. *Natural Language and Linguistic Theory* 20: 43–80.

Ozeki, H. and Shirai, Y.
2007 Does the Noun Phrase Accessibility Hierarchy predict the difficulty order in the acquisition of Japanese relative clauses? *Studies in Second Language Acquisition* 29: 169–196.

Perry, R. J. and Hodges, J. R.
2000 Differentiating frontal and temporal variant frontotemporal dementia from Alzheimer's disease. *Neurology* 54: 2277–2284.

Pesetsky, D.
1995 *Zero Syntax*. MIT Press.

Pignatti R., Rabuffetti M., Imbornone E., Mantovani F., Alberoni M., Farina E. et al.
2005 Specific impairments of selective attention in mild Alzheimer's disease. *Journal of Clinical Experiemental Neuropsycholy* 27: 436–48.

Piñango, M.
1999 Syntactic displacement in Broca's aphasia comprehension. In: R. Bastiaanse and Y. Grodzinsky (eds.), *Grammatical disorders in aphasia: A neurolinguistic perspective*. London: Whurr.
2000 Canonicity in Broca's sentence Comprehension: The Case of Psychological Verbs. In: Y. Grodzinsky, L. Shapiro, and D. Swinney (eds.) *Language and the Brain: Representation & Processing*. New York: Academic Press.
2006 Thematic roles as event structure relations. In: I. Bornkessel, M. Schlesewsky, and A. Friederici (eds.), *Semantic Role Universals and Argument Linking: Theoretical, Typological, and Psycholinguistic Perspectives*. Berlin: Mouton.

Rappaport, M. and Levin, B.
1988 What to do with theta-roles. In: W. Wilkins (ed.), *Syntax and Semantics 21: Thematic Relations*, 7–36. Academic Press, New York, NY.

Rosch, E., and Mervin, C.
1975 Family resemblances: Studies in the internal structure categories. *Cognitive Psychology* 8: 382–439.

Schwartz, M. F., Marin, O. M., and Saffran, E.
1979 Dissociations of language deficits in Dementia. A case study. *Brain and Language* 7: 277–306.

Silverstein, M.
1976 Hierarchy of features and ergativity. In: R. M. W. Dixon (ed.), *Grammatical categories in Australian Languages*, 112–171, New Jersey.

Tanenhaus, M. K., Spivey-Knowlton, M. J., and Hanna, J. E.
2000 Modeling thematic and discourse context effects on syntactic ambiguity resolution within a multiple constraints framework: Implications for the architecture of the language processing system. In: M. Pickering, C. Clifton and M. Crocker (eds.), *Architecture and mechanisms of the language processing system*, Cambridge: Cambridge University Press.

Van Valin, R. D. Jr.
1990 Semantic Parameters of Split Intransitivity, *Language* 66: 221–260.
Visser, P. J., Sheltens, P., Verhey, F. R. J., Schmand, B., Launer, L. J., Jolles, J., and Jonker, C.
1999 Medial temporal lobe atrophy and memory dysfunction as predictors for dementia in subjects with mild cognitive impairment. *Journal of Neurology* 246: 477–485.
Zannino, G.-Z., Perri, R., Pasqualetti, P., Carlesimo, G., and Caltagirone, C.
2006 (Category-specific) semantic deficit in Alzheimer's patients: The role of semantic distance. *Neuropsychologia* 44: 52–61.

Automated collection and analysis of phonological data

James Myers

1. Introduction

The past decade has seen renewed interest in the empirical basis of theoretical syntax, sparked in part by the publication of Schütze (1996) and Cowart (1997). However, a similar empirical revolution began in phonology about a decade earlier, with the publication of Ohala and Jaeger (1986) and Kingston and Beckman (1990). Today a significant proportion of the theoretical phonology papers published in the major linguistics journals employ experimental methods (e.g. S. Myers and Hansen 2007), quantitative corpus analysis (e.g. Uffmann 2006), or both (e.g. Zuraw 2007).

This dramatic change in the course of the phonological mainstream raises the key question of how the new phonological methods relate to the old traditional ones. Whatever the answer may be, it is not being made clearly to many phonology students, who in introductory classes continue to practice testing hypotheses against small data sets from dictionaries, and yet when they begin to read the contemporary literature they are confronted with the very different empirical vocabulary of psycholinguistic experiments, electronic corpora, and quantitative analysis.

Fortunately for those living through this age of methodological transition, differences between the old and new ways are more a matter of degree than of kind. In particular, native speaker intuitions of acceptability represent experimentally elicited psycholinguistic data (as noted even in the otherwise highly critical review of Labov 1975), and the analyses of small data sets in phonology represent a form of corpus analysis (albeit using dictionaries compiled from speech rather than samples of this speech itself). Moreover, the arguments that phonologists make on the basis of such data are implicitly quantitative, as when rarity is used to identify exceptionality.

Clearly, however, the quantitative arguments used in the new methods are of a much higher degree of sophistication than the informal rules of thumb that have traditionally been used. It is precisely here where many theoretical linguists and their students face their greatest stumbling blocks in adapting to the new methodological world. Linguists are generally the sort of people who love words, not numbers, and it is my impression that those few who love both are naive to think that the rest will follow their lead by example alone, without bridges clearly linking the old and new worlds.

In this chapter I describe one way in which such bridges might be built. On the theoretical side, the key is to recognize that traditional phonologists are already doing quantitative corpus analyses and psycholinguistic experiments, even though they don't think of them in these terms. On the practical side, the key is automation: phonologists would benefit from special-purpose software that allows them to maintain many of their familiar habits, while, mostly hidden from view, powerful algorithms put their theoretical hypotheses through rigorous quantitative tests.

While the ideal versions of such software still lie a bit in the future, working prototypes already exist: MiniCorp (Myers 2008b) for the analysis of phonological corpora, and MiniJudge (Myers 2007a) for the design and analysis of linguistic judgment experiments. Both tools are free and open-source; currently the most frequently updated versions are written in JavaScript running in the user's Web browser, and have been tested most extensively in Firefox for Windows. The statistics are handled by R, the free, open-source statistics package (R Development Core Team 2008) that is fast becoming the de facto standard in quantitative linguistics (Baayen 2008, Johnson 2008). MiniCorp and MiniJudge may be found at http://www.ccunix.ccu.edu.tw/~lngproc/MiniGram.htm.

I start the discussion in section 2 with a brief overview of traditional methods in phonology, and why they remain worthy of respect. Section 3 then describes the principles behind MiniCorp, the corpus analysis tool, and section 4 does the same for MiniJudge, the judgment experiment tool. These tools are then demonstrated in section 5 in a study of Mandarin phonotactics. Section 6 concludes and points towards the future.

2. Traditional phonological methods

The most common method in phonology has traditionally been the study of dictionaries (discussed in 2.1), though phonologists have sometimes also made use of acceptability judgments (2.2). In this section I show why phonologists have tended to prefer the former, and how both methods, even in their traditional forms, are akin to the more sophisticated techniques becoming more common in the phonological literature.

2.1. Corpus analysis

Despite early generative arguments that certain aspects of phonological competence can only be discovered via acceptability judgments, such as the preference of English speakers for the unattested *blick* over the equally unattested *bnick* (Chomsky and Halle 1965), phonologists have generally remained unaffected by the revolution in data sources sparked by Chomsky (1957). Even Chomsky and Halle (1968) rely heavily on dictionary data (specifically, Kenyon and Knott 1944). As I show in this section, however, the traditional favoring of pre-existing samples (i.e. corpora) in phonology turns out to be surprisingly well justified.

Dictionary data have often been criticized by methodological reformers, because systematicity in a lexicon does not suffice to show that the patterns are part of synchronic phonological competence; they could instead be relics of sound change operating without the help of grammatical competence (Ohala 1986, Blevins 2004). This alternative view has recently been challenged by experiments using nonlexical items (e.g. Zuraw 2007, Moreton 2008), but it is less well recognized that the relevance of corpus data to competence theories can actually be defended on the basis of corpus data alone. For example, Kiparsky (2006) argued that sound change unguided by universal grammatical principles predicts lexical patterns that are apparently unattested (contra Blevins 2006). More generally, ascribing synchrony to diachrony undermines diachronic reasoning itself, since many reconstructions depend on assumptions about what makes a plausible synchronic grammar.

Another important reason for phonologists to focus on corpus data is that language learners do so as well. Understanding language acquisition, often cited as a central goal of linguistic theory (Chomsky 1965), means finding the one "true" corpus analysis used by actual children. This insight has recently fueled research on phonological acquisition models (e.g. Tesar and Smolensky 1998, Boersma and Hayes, 2001, Hayes and Wilson 2008), which take phonological corpora as input.

Finally, the traditional study of dictionaries is also worthy of respect because it relies on the same sort of quantitative logic used in computational corpus linguistics. In particular, phonologists often test claims using corpus type frequencies and probability theory, even though they rarely recognize that this is what they are doing. Thus a generalization with few or no exceptions is acknowledged to be more convincing than one with many. Likewise, what the traditional notion of the systematic gap represents is a type frequency much lower (perhaps zero) than expected by chance, given the combinatorial possibilities of the phonological units in the language. For example, *bnick* represents a systematic gap in English because the free combination of /b/ and /n/ (the null hypothesis) predicts many more /bn/ words than are actually found (zero). Phonologists intuitively understand that just as a grammatical claim can be supported by a robust generalization, the absence of evidence can be interpreted as evidence of absence if one has a model of chance probability.

2.2. Native speaker judgments

Phonologists also occasionally use native speaker judgments. Experimental data, including elicited judgments, have many familiar advantages over corpus data, in addition to those noted above: They make it much easier to test synchronic productivity (e.g. Frisch and Zawaydeh 2001) and phrasal phonology (e.g. Keller and Alexopoulou 2001), and new experiments can be devised whenever new questions arise (Ohala 1986). Here I address a less often discussed advantage of collecting phonological judgments in particular, as well as some important limitations.

The view of linguistic theory as the search for the child's preferred corpus analysis algorithm, alluded to in the previous section, predicts two types of mismatches between corpus patterns and judgments. On the one hand, speakers may be able to distinguish between forms that are equally unattested in the corpus, which is what the *blick* vs. *bnick* contrast is intended to show. This type of mismatch is related to the argument from the poverty of the stimulus (Chomsky 1980), and in this guise it has recently received renewed attention in the experimental phonology literature (e.g. Zuraw 2007). On the other hand, speakers may also ignore information in the input if their grammar learning algorithm is not designed to pick up on it. A version of this is seen in the child language literature, where children may reject negative evidence even when it is explicitly offered (e.g. Morgan, Bonamo, and Travis 1995). The result for the adult are judgment patterns that neglect certain statistically robust corpus patterns.

Although such theoretically important mismatches can only be detected with the help of judgments, they depend just as much on corpus data. Moreover, if we seriously view a mature grammar as the result of the single "true" corpus-analysis algorithm, the baseline condition in a judgment experiment should not be chance alone, but rather the predictions made by alternative corpus-analysis algorithms. This is why formal phonological judgment experiments typically control for phonotactic probability, relating to the probability of the internal components of target items relative to real words, and neighborhood density, relating to the overall similarity of target items to real words (e.g. Frisch and Zawaydeh 2001). Though both are known to affect phonological processing (e.g. Vitevitch and Luce 1999), they are assumed to reflect extra-grammatical factors. Thus the interpretation of a phonological judgment experiment typically depends on a corpus analysis quantifying these potential confounds.

The importance of corpus analysis to phonology means that the design of judgment experiments poses greater challenges to the phonologist than to the syntactician. As shown later in this chapter, the vagaries of actual lexicons and the rigidity of phonotactic constraints typically make it difficult to follow strict factorial designs when creating wordlike materials for a judgment experiment. Despite the many benefits of experimentation for testing phonological hypotheses, then, it is entirely understandable that phonologists continue to focus less on judgment data than syntacticians.

3. Automating phonological corpus analysis

The main purpose of the MiniCorp software tool is to extend and automate the quantitative logic underlying the traditional analysis of dictionary data (for related discussion, see Myers 2007b, 2008a, 2008b). The "mini" in the name indicates that it is designed for limited analyses of small corpora. In particular, MiniCorp tests whether a hypothesized phonological grammar is statistically supported by patterns in an electronic dictionary.

MiniCorp is not an automated grammar learner. Rather than exploring the corpus for patterns, it starts with a user-entered grammar and computes the probability that observed differences in the sizes of corpus categories (i.e. type frequencies), as defined by the proposed grammar, could have arisen by chance. To constrain the space of possible grammars, MiniCorp (at least in its current version) adopts the theoretical framework of Optimality Theory (OT; Prince and Smolensky 2004). As explained in section 3.1, not only is OT the contemporary lingua franca of theoretical phonology, but it has mathematical properties that make it convenient for statistical hypothesis testing; the relevant statistical techniques are explained in 3.2. MiniCorp also uses a standard search algorithm to annotate corpus items for analysis, as explained in 3.3. Finally, as discussed in 3.4, MiniCorp calculates certain (presumably extra-grammatical) lexical statistics so that they can be factored out in judgment experiments.

3.1. Modeling grammar

Despite lingering challenges (opacity being the most notorious), OT has proven itself a highly productive and flexible tool for describing patterns in dictionary data and beyond. Moreover, it has two very convenient mathematical properties: OT constraints describe surface forms (though ironically, this is why OT has trouble with opacity), and they are ranked so that lower-ranked constraints only have a say if higher-ranked constraints are noncommittal. These properties link OT to the older connectionist-inspired theory of Harmonic Grammar (HG; Legendre, Sorace, and Smolensky 2006), and have led to recent advances in OT acquisition modeling (Hayes and Wilson 2008, Coetzee and Pater 2008). They also allow MiniCorp to test the statistical significance of grammatical hypotheses.

OT constraint ranking is a special case of the constraint weighting of HG, where the overall evaluation score for a candidate output form is given by summing the products of each weight with the severity of its violation; the higher this score, the worse the candidate, with the lowest-scoring (most "harmonic") candidate chosen as final output. For example, the grammar in the first row in the tableau in (1a), with the constraints Cons_1, Cons_2, Cons_3 and weights w_1, w_2, w_3, will choose Out_1 as output. This is because (1a) is equivalent to the equations in (1b).

(1) a.

	Cons_1 $w_1 = 3$	Cons_2 $w_2 = 1$	Cons_3 $w_2 = 1$
Out_1		*	*
Out_2	*		

b. $\text{Evaluation}(\text{Out}_i) = \Sigma w_j \times \text{Violation}(\text{Out}_i, \text{Cons}_j)$, i.e.:
$\text{Evaluation}(\text{Out}_1) = (3)(0) + (1)(1) + (1)(1) = 2$
(more harmonic than)
$\text{Evaluation}(\text{Out}_2) = (3)(1) + (1)(0) + (1)(0) = 3$

Note that the winning candidate in (1a) would also win in an OT grammar where $\text{Cons}_1 \gg \{\text{Cons}_2, \text{Cons}_3\}$. This follows from the fact that $w_1 > w_2 + w_3$, so the two lower-ranked constraints cannot override the higher-ranked one (Prince 2007). A different choice of constraint weights may not have this property, so OT is a special case of HG.

Automated HG learners set the constraint weights by exposure to a corpus (Hayes and Wilson 2008, Coetzee and Pater 2008). Although MiniCorp is not a grammar learner, it also sets weights on the basis of corpus data, but here the weights are taken as measures of a pre-given grammar's statistical reliability rather than as components of the grammar itself. That is, the constraint weights set by MiniCorp reflect the type frequencies associated with the generalizations, exceptions, systematic gaps, and accidental gaps predicted by the user-defined grammar. Only if a weight is sufficiently different from zero is the associated constraint considered to be statistically reliable, and only if the weight of one constraint is significantly higher than that of another is a hypothesized constraint ranking considered to be supported by the data.

MiniCorp thus provides a quantitative formalization of core aspects of traditional phonological methodology, expressed in terms of the currently most familiar phonological framework. As explained in the next section, setting and evaluating constraint weights consistent with this logic can be accomplished using well-established statistical methods.

3.2. Loglinear modeling

Type frequencies are discrete, countable values, and thus represent categorical data; such data are often handled statistically with loglinear modeling (Agresti 2002). Loglinear modeling is a generalization of linear regression, so called because it attempts to relate the independent (predictor) and dependent (predicted) variables in terms of a straight line. Regression can be applied to categorical data with the proper transformation of the dependent variable and the proper random distribution. Loglinear models use the logarithmic transformation, and when the dependent variable represents type frequencies, the appropriate distribution is the Poisson distribution, which unlike the normal distribution is discrete and tends to be positively skewed (because counts cannot go below zero).

The relevance here of these well-established techniques is that the right side of a (log)linear regression equation is highly reminiscent of the right side of the HG equations in (1b). Namely, they contain the sum of the products of regression coefficients (here, constraint weights) and independent variables (here, constraint violations). The weights are set so that the right side of the equation fits the observed (transformed) type frequencies as closely as possible, and the contribution of each constraint is evaluated in the context of all of the others.

Loglinear modeling (though not Poisson regression) is also used to set constraint weights in the HG learner proposed by Hayes and Wilson (2008), but since the goal of MiniCorp is hypothesis testing rather than grammar learning, there are two important differences. First, as with regression models generally, Poisson regression allows MiniCorp to test the statistical significance of each constraint (relevant to hypothesis testing but not necessarily to learning). Second, Poisson regression also makes it possible to test the statistical significance of a proposed OT constraint ranking (irrelevant to HG and thus to HG-based learners).

MiniCorp tests a ranking hypothesis by comparing a regression equation in which the constraints are free to take any weight, as in (2a), with an equation in which the weights must be identical, as in (2b) (the notation Y $\sim$ X means "Y varies as a function of X"). Only if the model in (2a) does a significantly better job at fitting the data (as evaluated by a likelihood ratio test, another standard statistical technique) can we reject the null hypothesis that $w_1 = w_2$ and conclude that the constraints may indeed be ranked. (A bit of algebra shows that (2a) is the same as (2b) with the addition of a term, the significance of which is what the likelihood ratio test is actually testing, and with further algebra we can generalize the logic to grammars with multiple and multiply violated constraints; see Myers 2008a.)

(2) a. Counts $\sim w_1\text{CONS}_1 + w_2\text{CONS}_2$

b. Counts $\sim w_1\text{CONS}_1 + w_2\text{CONS}_2,\ w_1 = w_2$

In its current version, MiniCorp (like MiniJudge, described below) runs the analyses in R, the free statistical programming language (R Development Core Team 2008).

3.3. Corpus annotation

As in most corpus analyses, the analyses performed by MiniCorp depend on annotations marking linguistically relevant abstract features, in this case, annotations indicating which OT constraints are violated by which lexical items. Corpus annotation can be the most labor-intensive aspect of corpus preparation, but fortunately mathematical properties again make it possible for MiniCorp to automate the task through a well-established algorithm.

It is an empirical fact about human language that phonological patterns can be described with regular expressions (Bird and Ellison 1994). Regular expressions also happen to be commonly used for pattern matching in text searches. Regular expression notation includes symbols representing wildcards (which match to any string), repetition, disjunction, the start and end of strings, and so on. Since violations of OT structure constraints represent classes of substrings, Karttunen (1998) noted that they can also be encoded as regular expressions.

MiniCorp exploits these observations in a tool (using the regular expression engine built into JavaScript) that automatically searches for, and then annotates, corpus items for OT constraint violations. This method works best for output structure constraints. It cannot reliably annotate faithfulness constraints, which reflect relationships with representations not available in the corpus itself, and its success depends partially on manual annotations like syllable boundaries (relevant to constraints like ONSET and NOCODA). Nevertheless, as will be demonstrated in 5.2, the regular expression tool does greatly simplify the annotation of constraint violations.

3.4. Quantifying lexical confounds

Though the central purpose of MiniCorp is to test a pre-specified grammar, it also helps compute extra-grammatical lexical statistics to be factored out in phonological judgment experiments. Here I discuss only one of these lexical statistics, neighborhood density.

The reason for focusing on this particular variable is to limit the risk of throwing out the baby with the bathwater. Just because certain patterns can be detected in a corpus by a presumably extra-grammatical algorithm does not mean that they are not also detected by the child's grammar-learning algorithm. Factoring out an extra-grammatical lexical variable that mimics the results of grammar-learning too closely may cause us to miss genuine evidence for grammar in judgments.

With neighborhood density the risk of this happening is low, since this lexical statistic seems to reflect exemplar-driven analogy, not grammar. First, neighborhood density evaluates forms holistically; phonotactic probability, by contrast, is similar to OT constraints in analyzing forms into substrings. Second, psycholinguistic experimentation suggests that neighborhood density only affects phonological processing after the lexicon has been contacted, whereas phonotactic probability plays a prelexical role (Vitevitch and Luce 1999), and thus is, like grammar, partially independent of the lexicon. Finally, there has recently been some interest in incorporating probabilistic phonotactics inside grammar itself (e.g. Coetzee and Pater 2008).

The current version of MiniCorp applies the simplest possible definition of neighborhood density, namely the number of lexical items differing from a target item by deletion, insertion, or replacement of one phonological unit (Luce 1986). This definition is not only simple, but it is akin to the MAX, DEP, and IDENT correspondence constraints familiar to OT phonologists.

4. Automating phonological judgment experiments

As with MiniCorp, the purpose of MiniJudge is to build on traditional linguistic methodology, in this case the collection of native speaker judgments of acceptability (Myers 2007a). Its scope is also minimalist, helping the linguist to design, run, and statistically analyze experiments with relatively few speakers judging relatively few items on a binary good/bad scale. The tool was originally developed for syntax, where judgments have historically played a more important role, but in this section I highlight the special characteristics of MiniJudge when used for phonological judgments, in terms of material design (4.1) and the collection and statistical analysis of data (4.2).

4.1. Material design

MiniJudge guides the researcher to choose the experimental factors and materials instantiating them, and includes tools to deal with the special challenges posed by phonological judgment experiments.

Because grammatical hypotheses often involve the relationship between two elements, the typical MiniJudge experiment involves two factors, each representing one of the elements; the theoretical hypothesis then relates to the interaction between them. For example, an experiment on the constraint against **bnick* in English could involve two factors, one representing onset /b/ (in contrast to /s/, say) and the other onset /n/ (in contrast to /l/, say). The hypothesized constraint would predict lower acceptability for /bn/ relative to /sn/, /bl/, /sl/; the results could not then be explained away as constraints against /b/ and/or /n/ themselves.

Theoretical linguists are already familiar with the basic logic of factorial experimental design, as instantiated by the minimal pairs and minimal sets of examples cited in research papers. Starting a MiniJudge experiment thus involves entering such a basic set of matched materials. To help generate the additional sets needed for generalizability, MiniJudge detects the structural contrasts implicit in the initial material set, so that the user only has to enter in new matching components rather than create new sets from scratch (risking typos).

For example, the factors in a **bnick* experiment, schematized in (3a), could be instantiated with the material set in (3b), where the items are identical except for the properties defined by the factors. The repeated elements are those listed in (3c), each of which can be replaced by a functionally equivalent element as in (3d) (assuming that **bnick* is a special case of *[–cont][+nas]). By substituting these new elements for the old ones, MiniJudge derives the new set in (3e).

(3)	a	[+b+n]	[+b–n]	[–b+n]	[–b–n]	
	b.	bnick	blick	snick	slick	
	c.	b	s	n	l	ick
	d.	k	s	m	l	oss
	e.	kmoss	smoss	kloss	sloss	

It should be obvious from this example that the design of wordlike materials for judgment experiments face serious challenges (such problems do not arise for syntax or phrasal phonology). First, there is nothing to prevent an item generated by the above algorithm from being an actual word (e.g. *slick*). Testing phonological judgments on real words is notoriously problematic because real words have many memorized properties that are difficult to control for, including lexical frequency and semantics (Bailey and Hahn 2001). If real words and nonwords are mixed together, lexical status becomes a confounding factor as well (though perhaps it may be explicitly recognized and factored out, as in Myers and Tsay 2005).

A related challenge, ironically, is phonotactics itself, which makes it difficult to avoid real words and maintain the experimental design at the same time. For example, if *bnick* and *blick* are included in a two-factor design, we really have no choice but to make the other two items *snick* and *slick*, despite the fact that both are real words. This is because the only consonant that appears before a nasal in English is /s/, and the only sonorant available as a control (to be minimally different from the nasal), and which appears after /s/ as required by the factorial design, is /l/ (aside from non-nativized borrowings like *Sri Lanka*).

MiniJudge's sister program MiniCorp provides some assistance with such challenges, since as a collateral benefit of calculating the neighborhood density for each experimental item, it also detects whether this item is listed in the lexicon. The researcher is then alerted to any sets containing real words (including less familiar ones like *snick*), and may choose to replace them or counterbalance the distribution of real words across sets to minimize confounding with the experimental factors.

Neighborhood density itself is easier to deal with. After computing the values with MiniCorp, the MiniJudge user may choose either to match materials on this lexical statistic, or to keep the original materials and allow MiniJudge to factor out neighborhood density as a covariate in the statistics (as explained in 4.3).

4.2. Data collection and analysis

After MiniJudge has helped to create a judgment experiment, it then helps to run and analyze it. Here I briefly review these steps, highlighting the special characteristics of phonological judgment experiments where relevant.

MiniJudge generates surveys presenting items in different random orders for each experimental participant to reduce the confounds of fatigue, practice, and cross-item priming. While this is standard psycholinguistic practice, the current version of MiniJudge has three built-in limitations that are somewhat nonstandard. First, experiments can have at most two factors, and factors must be binary. Secondly, there is currently no option for filler items or counterbalanced lists, methods recommended in the experimental syntax literature to prevent participants from detecting, and perhaps responding atypically to, the patterns of theoretical interest (e.g. Cowart 1997). Finally, judgments must be made on a binary good/bad scale, rather than on the ordinal or continuous-valued scales often advocated in the experimental syntax literature (though see Weskott and Fanselow 2009 for arguments that a binary scale can suffice).

All three limitations exist solely to keep MiniJudge experiments as simple as possible, both conceptually and practically, for both the experimenter and the participants. In particular, just as the algorithm for generating materials described in 4.1 allows users to start with the sort of minimal set already familiar from traditional linguistic practice, the choice of a binary judgment scale is intended to link MiniJudge with the most commonly used acceptability diacritics in the linguistics literature (* vs. blank). Future versions of MiniJudge will convert these limits into mere defaults, while providing more flexible options for the more experienced experimenter.

MiniJudge surveys themselves can currently be distributed on paper or by email, as long as participants understand that they must judge items in the order in which they are presented. While these modes are presumably sufficient for collecting syntactic judgments from literate participants, it is reasonable to wonder whether phonological judgments would be better elicited using auditory stimuli (or video, in the case of sign languages). Implementing this suggestion would merely require a bit more software; the deeper question is how to interpret modality effects if any are found. Bailey and Hahn (2001) found very little effect of modality (auditory vs. written) in English nonword judgments, whereas Myers and Tsay (2005) found a stronger modality effect in judgments on Mandarin syllables (auditory vs. written in a quasi-phonemic orthography, described below). Auditory stimuli presumably engage the phonological processor more directly than written stimuli, but written stimuli have the advantage of eliminating acoustic ambiguity, and they perhaps also encourage judgments to be made at a more abstract, amodal level, rather than solely at a perceptual level.

After the raw results have been collected, MiniJudge reformats them so that they can be analyzed using mixed-effects logistic regression, another member of the loglinear family (Agresti 2002, Baayen 2008). This is a generalization of logistic regression, the statistical technique at the core of the sociolinguistic software tool VARBRUL (Mendoza-Denton, Hay, and Jannedy 2003), but as a mixed-effects model it takes random variation across participants (and items) into account along with the fixed experimental factors. It therefore permits by-participants and by-items analyses to be run simultaneously, and because these random variables are included inside the model, their contributions can be tested by likelihood ratio tests. Thus it may sometimes happen that item sets don't differ much in their effect on judgments, and a by-participants analysis is sufficient. Mixed-effects models have the further advantage over separate by-participants and by-items analyses in that they are more sensitive in small experiments, since statistical reliability depends on the total number of observations, which is the product of the numbers of participants and items.

As a species of regression, mixed-effects logistic regression also permits non-categorical independent variables. By default MiniJudge includes the order of item presentation as a covariate, to help reduce the influence of shifting judgment scales over the course of the experiment, and interactions between presentation order and the experimental factors can be analyzed as well, if desired (see Myers 2007a,c for why this may be useful).

Phonologists are also given the option to factor out lexical covariates, in particular neighborhood density. A hypothesized constraint that continues to have a significant effect on judgments even when neighborhood density is factored out is more likely to represent an actual grammatical component, rather than merely the effects of exemplar-driven analogy.

5. A demonstration

Now that the philosophical underpinnings and technical details of MiniCorp and MiniJudge have been clarified, we can turn to an application with real data, involving a phonotactic pattern in Mandarin. The decision to look at phonotactics is dictated solely by the choice of language; Mandarin has relatively few alternations or prosodic phenomena (Duanmu 2007). MiniCorp and MiniJudge are not limited to examining phonotactics, however; any hypothesis that can be expressed in a standard OT grammar can be studied with MiniCorp, and any hypothesis predicting judgment contrasts can be studied with MiniJudge.

After proposing an OT analysis of the phonotactic pattern in Mandarin (5.1), I then describe how it was tested in a MiniCorp analysis (5.2) and in a MiniJudge experiment (5.3).

5.1. A pattern in Mandarin phonotactics

Mandarin syllable structure may be schematized as in (4), where C represents a consonant, V a vowel, and X either; the only obligatory element is a nuclear vowel.

(4) (C)(V)V(X)

Virtually all Mandarin morphemes are monosyllabic, so phonotactic patterns are syllable-internal. The most relevant to the one tested here are the following. As in many languages, vowels outside the sonority peak must be high, namely /i/ (front unrounded), /u/ (back rounded), or /y/ (front rounded); two high vowels cannot be adjacent in a syllable. In diphthongs and triphthongs, the nuclear vowel must be low (/a/) or mid, in the latter case agreeing in rounding and backness with the following vowel. The vowel /y/ can appear prevocalically, but not postvocalically. Thus the only two possible syllable-final diphthongs are /ou/ and /ei/.

With these exceptionless patterns as background, the phonotactic pattern tested here concerns the combinations of high vowels permitted in triphthongs. The pattern is illustrated in Table 1 (superscripts indicate the conventional numbering for the four lexical tones: 1 = high level, 2 = rising, 3 = low dipping, 4 = falling). The cells marked * represent unattested triphthongs. The pattern here is also seen with consonant-initial syllables.

Table 1. Cooccurrence restrictions on Mandarin triphthongs

		First vowel		
		i	u	y
Last vowel	i	*iei (some speakers)	uei^4 'for'	*yei
		*iai (some speakers)	uai^4 'outside'	*yai
	u	iou^4 'again'	*uou	*you
		iau^4 'want'	*uau	*yau

The generalization is clear: triphthongs cannot start and end with vowels identical in backness or rounding (Duanmu 2007). However, some speakers have an apparent exception in the morpheme for 'cliff', pronouncing it /iai^2/. There are three further low-frequency exceptions cited in Mandarin dictionaries, all homophonous with this one. Other speakers pronounce the morpheme for 'cliff' as /ia^2/, consistent with the generalization.

This generalization is an instantiation of the Obligatory Contour Principle (OCP; S. Myers 1997). Within the OT framework, the fact that the OCP can be violated for some Mandarin speakers implies a grammar in which it is blocked by a higher-ranked faithfulness constraint. This blocking constraint must be indexed to apply only in an arbitrary lexical class (see Pater forthcoming for analyses like this). Thus we end up with an OT grammar with the structure in (5) (the faithfulness constraint is kept vague since theory-internal details are not relevant).

(5) $\text{F}{\scriptstyle\text{AITH}}_{\text{Exceptions}} \gg \text{OCP}$

While this grammar is trivially simple, and the arguments for it familiar and rather banal, it raises two sets of difficult methodological questions. The first concerns the reliability of the grammar in (5) as a description of the Mandarin lexicon, the very data source that suggested it in the first place. Doesn't the mere existence of lexical exceptions cast doubt on the OCP being a genuine component of Mandarin grammar? Yet at the same time, aren't the number of exceptions too few (a mere four morphemes) to provide convincing evidence for an exception-specific $\text{F}{\scriptstyle\text{AITH}}_{\text{Ex}}$ constraint? Finally, even if both constraints prove to give statistically reliable descriptions of the Mandarin lexicon, is their claimed ranking supported as well? After all, the very fact that the OCP is rarely violated implies that it provides better coverage of the data than the hypothesized exception constraint. Can this state of affairs truly be handled by ranking the latter over the former?

The second set of questions concerns the synchronic relevance of the grammar. Even if one or both of the constraints accurately describes the Mandarin lexicon, are they still reflected in contemporary native speaker judgments? If so, does the evidence for grammar in judgments remain even if analogy, as measured by neighborhood density, is taken into account? Finally, if the corpus and judgments prove to differ in what they say about the hypothesized grammar, how should this mismatch be interpreted?

5.2. A MiniCorp analysis

The MiniCorp analysis began by entering a list of 13,607 Mandarin monosyllabic morphemes (Tsai 2000), transcribed using IPA for the segments and using the conventional single-digit notation for the four tones.

The next step was to annotate the corpus in terms of constraint violations. Given the grammar proposed in (5), there should be no violations of the undominated constraint $\text{F}{\scriptstyle\text{AITH}}_{\text{Ex}}$. The OCP should be violated by any morpheme both ending and beginning in /i/ or /u/ (/y/ can be ignored, since it cannot appear in triphthongs at all). Violations can thus be found with help of the regular expression in (6), where "." is the wildcard symbol (here representing the nucleus mid or low vowel) and "|" represents disjunction.

(6) (i.i)|(u.u)

This regular expression adds a violation mark to four items, namely the morpheme for 'cliff' and its homophones. The researcher can sort the corpus items according to violations to make sure that the annotations are correct; changes can be made by toggling violations on and off in the interface shown in Figure 1 (currently, this interface assumes that each form violates a constraint at most once, an obvious limitation to be fixed in the next version).

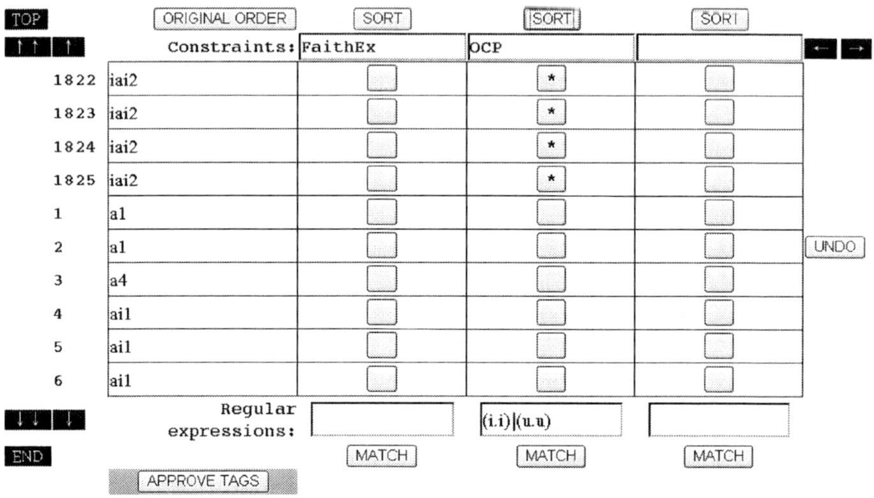

Figure 1. MiniCorp interface for annotating lexical items for constraint violations

After the annotated corpus has been saved, MiniCorp generates an R script to classify lexical items by all possible combinations of constraint violations and count the associated type frequencies. The result here is shown in Table 2, where 1 in the constraint columns indicates violation and 0 indicates non-violation. Since loglinear models like Poisson regression cannot provide reliable coefficients if there are perfect correlations (Agresti 2002), the script converts all zero counts

Table 2. Adjusted type frequencies associated with constraint violations

Counts	Faith_{Ex}	OCP
13603	0	0
4	0	1
1	1	0
1	1	1

into one, as in the last two cells of the counts column (this weakens the statistical power only slightly).

The R script then analyzes the frequency table using Poisson regression, as explained earlier in section 3.2, and outputs the results summary shown in (7); a more detailed statistical report is saved in an offline file. Ranking is tested in terms of the position of each constraint relative to all constraints hypothesized to be ranked lower. Thus for the grammar proposed in (5), we only need to test the ranking of FAITH$_{\text{Ex}}$ (relative to the OCP).

(7) a. Constraint test:

Constraints	Weights	p	
FaithEx	–8.8252	0	*
OCP	–7.9087	0	*

(* significant constraint)

b. Ranking test:

Constraints	p
FaithEx	0.2491

(No significant rankings)

The results in (7a) show that both constraints provide significantly reliable descriptions of the data (*p* values below .05), even the FAITH$_{\text{Ex}}$ constraint, which is only relevant in four morphemes. The weights for both constraints are negative, indicating that, as desired, they are obeyed more often than violated (that is, counts are lower when the independent variable is coded as 1 rather than 0).

Note also that the magnitude of the FAITH$_{\text{Ex}}$ constraint is slightly larger than that of the OCP, consistent with the ranking hypothesis. Unfortunately, as shown in (7b), this difference in constraint magnitude is not great enough to be significantly different by the likelihood ratio test. Thus we are not justified in positing the ranking in (5).

Without this ranking, however, the FAITH$_{\text{Ex}}$ hypothesis itself loses support, since the only reason this constraint was posited in the first place was to block the OCP in an arbitrary lexical class. The failure here does not mean that the concept of exception-specific faithfulness constraints is inherently flawed, though. Simulated data varying lexicon size and number of exceptions shows that a mere seven exceptions can suffice to provide statistically significant evidence (with the usual $p < .05$ criterion) for the undominated ranking of an exception-specific constraint.

5.3. A MiniJudge experiment

Despite problems with other aspects of the proposed OT grammar, the MiniCorp analysis showed that the OCP is a statistically reliable pattern in the Mandarin lexicon. To determine whether it remains active synchronically, native speaker acceptability judgments were collected and analyzed using MiniJudge.

Like many grammatical generalizations, the OCP involves the relationship between two elements, here the first and last vowel in a triphthong. These can be represented by the two binary factors [±FirstU] (whether or not the first vowel is /u/ rather than /i/), and [±LastU] (likewise for the last vowel). The OCP predicts an interaction between these two factors, such that forms with same-sign factor values should be judged worse than forms with different-sign factor values. These predictions are illustrated in (8) with a set of syllables unattested in the Mandarin lexicon (transcriptions again use IPA, other than the tone marks, so /t/, like /p/ in the examples to follow, represents an unaspirated plosive).

(8)	[+FirstU, +LastU]	$tuau^2$	[unacceptable?]
	[+FirstU, –LastU]	$tuai^2$	[acceptable?]
	[–FirstU, +LastU]	$tiau^2$	[acceptable?]
	[–FirstU, –LastU]	$tiai^2$	[unacceptable?]

In order to test whether the OCP applies beyond this single quartet, three further item sets were created. However, the need to avoid lexical items while respecting other phonotactic constraints meant that the perfect matching seen in (8) was not possible for these other sets. The variant sets generated with the help of MiniJudge thus had to be adjusted manually, resulting in the material list in Table 3 ([F] and [L] stand for [FirstU] and [LastU], respectively). The nucleus varies across the items in Sets 2 and 3 in order to obey the constraint, noted earlier, that a mid vowel in a triphthong must agree in rounding and backness with the final vowel. Similarly, the onset /n/ substitutes for /p/ in the first two columns in Sets 3 and 4 because of an independent phonotactic constraint against labial-round-vowel sequences (Duanmu 2007). The variation in mid vowels is thus confounded with the [LastU] factor, while the variation in onsets is confounded with the [FirstU] factor. This situation is not ideal, but at least neither is confounded with the crucial [FirstU] × [LastU] interaction predicted by the OCP.

These sixteen items were written in *zhuyin fuhao*, the quasi-phonemic Mandarin orthography used in Taiwan (functionally much like the *Hanyu pinyin* system used across the Taiwan Strait, but written in non-Roman symbols representing onsets, rimes, and tones rather than segments). MiniJudge was then used to generate printed surveys with the items in different random orders. Twenty

Table 3. Materials in the MiniJudge experiment

Factors:	[+F+L]	[+F–L]	[–F+L]	[–F–L]
Set 1:	$tuau^2$	$tuai^2$	$tiau^2$	$tiai^2$
Set 2:	$tuou^2$	$tuei^2$	$tiou^2$	$tiei^2$
Set 3:	$nuou^2$	$nuei^2$	$piou^2$	$piei^2$
Set 4:	$nuau^2$	$nuai^2$	$piau^2$	$piai^2$

native speakers of Mandarin in Taiwan, without any linguistic training, were asked to judge each item, in order, as being "like Mandarin" (*xiang Guoyu*) or not.

After the judgments were collected, MiniJudge created a data file and wrote an R script to run mixed-effects logistic regression on it, including a likelihood ratio test to determine whether cross-item variation needed to be taken into account. This script generated the summary report in (9), along with a more detailed statistical report saved offline. Crucially, the results revealed a significant interaction between the two factors ($p < .05$). There was also a main effect of [FirstU], but there is no theoretical significance of this; it could relate somehow to the failure to match onsets in two of the four sets, though the last line of the results summary indicates that including cross-item variation in the statistical model did not affect its fit with the data.

(9) Results summary for the initial analysis, generated by MiniJudge's R script

The factor FirstU had a significant negative effect.
The interaction between FirstU and LastU had a significant negative effect.
There were no other significant effects.

The above results do not take cross-item variability into account because no confound between items and factors was detected (p > .2).

The detailed report file gives the coefficient associated with the interaction in the best-fitting model as –0.469 ($p = .001$). The negative sign is consistent with the OCP because it means that same-sign items were judged worse than different-sign items. This interaction is much easier to appreciate from the graph in Figure 2, which is also automatically generated by the R script. As predicted by the OCP, triphthongs with identical first and last vowels tended to be judged worse than triphthongs beginning and ending in different vowels.

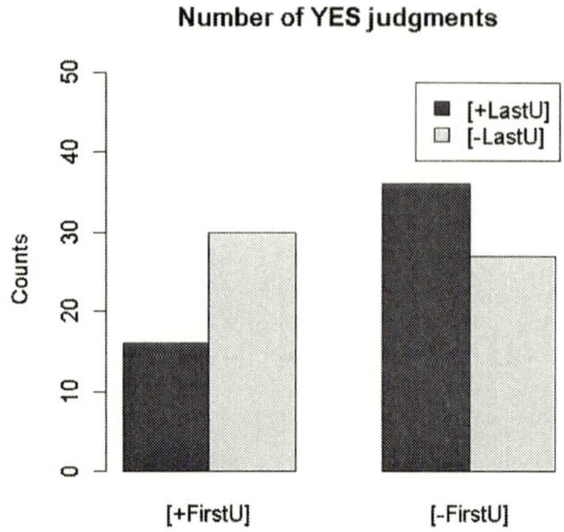

Figure 2. Graph generated by MiniJudge's R script

We have thus found evidence supporting the synchronic activity of the OCP in a very small and quick experiment, involving only twenty speakers judging sixteen items on a binary good/bad scale. However, as discussed earlier, a stricter test of claims about grammatical knowledge, as opposed to mere knowledge of superficial lexical statistics, would be to factor out analogical influences on judgments, as measured by neighborhood density. We have already seen an apparent example of the power of analogy in the Mandarin lexicon itself; recall that the exceptions to the OCP are all homophonous with each other.

MiniJudge took the neighborhood densities computed by MiniCorp for each of the sixteen experimental items, incorporated them into the data file, and generated a new R script taking them into account. The results summary was dramatically different, as seen in (10) (again the best-fitting model was by-participants only).

(10) Results summary for the analysis including neighborhood densities

Neighborhood density had a significant positive effect.There were no other significant effects.

The detailed report file shows that neighborhood density was positively correlated with the probability of acceptance (coefficient = 0.013, $p = .04$); judgments were indeed improved by analogy with real lexical items. Meanwhile, the interaction predicted by the OCP, while still negative, was no longer significant (coefficient = –0.112, $p = .62$). The disappearance of the OCP effect when neighborhood density was taken into account raises the possibility that this effect was due primarily to analogical processes, not a grammatical constraint. Of course, as a null result in a small experiment, this conclusion cannot be conclusive.

Putting the results from the MiniCorp and MiniJudge analyses together, then, it seems that although the OCP is consistent with type frequencies in the Mandarin lexicon and it correlates with native speaker judgments, these judgments may be sufficiently explained by analogy. If replicated in larger studies, the latter result may suggest that speakers do not need to actively process phonotactics in languages with syllable inventories small enough to memorize *in toto* (in contrast to languages with larger syllable inventories, where OCP-like constraints continue to affect judgments even when neighborhood density is controlled; see Frisch and Zawaydeh 2001 for Arabic, and Coetzee 2008 for English). A more extreme possibility would be that the particular variety of the OCP seen in Mandarin triphthongs represents the kind of corpus pattern that cannot be learned by the child's grammar-learning algorithm, a possibility alluded to earlier in 2.2 (in this scenario, the lexical pattern would be the result of extra-grammatical diachronic processes of the sort posited in Blevins 2004). Perhaps the most plausible possibility, however, is that Mandarin's very simple syllable structure, and consequently very small syllable inventory, means that neighborhood density is particularly tightly confounded with grammatical constraints, so factoring it out will tend to throw out evidence for genuine grammatical patterns even if they do exist. Indeed, the mean neighborhood density of the experimental items obeying the OCP (67.75) is much higher than that of the items violating it (12.25). Such observations raise the interesting methodological question of how grammatical patterns could be reliably detected in the lexical phonology of languages like Mandarin.

These conclusions, tentative though they are, are presumably of some relevance to theoretical phonology. Being based on inherently quantitative results, however, they could not have been reached without corpus analysis and formal experimentation. The contribution made by MiniCorp and MiniJudge is that they link such techniques directly with concepts and methods already familiar in theoretical phonology, including OT grammars, analogy, the analysis of dictionary data, minimally contrasting example sets, and binary acceptability judgments.

6. Conclusions and beyond

I began this chapter by asking whether the new methods currently sweeping the field of phonology are compatible with the traditional ones. I hope to have shown that they are, and that in fact the traditional methods can readily be "scaled up" to the same level of quantitative sophistication. To show how this process can be made simpler for theoretical phonologists without much quantitative experience, I described software tools designed to automate the most time-consuming and technically difficult steps, from corpus annotation to experimental material preparation to statistical analysis. The tools were then demonstrated in the testing of phonological hypotheses that could not have been tested with traditional methods alone.

The tools themselves, MiniCorp and MiniJudge, have already been used in a variety of linguistic studies, including, in the case of MiniJudge, studies on morphology and syntax (Myers 2007a,b,c, Ko 2007). However, they both continue to undergo refinement, and since both are open-source (under a GNU General Public License, permitting reuse of the code if it remains open-source), researchers impatient for upgrades are encouraged to borrow code or ideas for their own software tools.

Planned improvements include options for free corpus exploration (as in Uffmann 2006), ordinal and continuous-valued judgment scales, corpus-based testing of non-OT grammars (e.g. rule ordering tests as in Sankoff and Rousseau 1989), and tools using electronic corpora to generate matched sets of nonword items for phonological judgments. Moreover, to make the programs easier to use for inexperienced users, future versions will not require R at all, though an R interface will remain available for those wanting to extend analyses. Linguists desiring quick results would also benefit from statistical tests optimized for extremely small samples (e.g. Myers, Huang, and Tsay 2007). Finally, the interface needs to be improved; eventually MiniCorp and MiniJudge will be integrated into a single package written in Java (MiniJudge already has an alternative Java implementation).

There are many practical advantages for linking traditional methods with the quantitative techniques standard in the rest of the cognitive sciences. Linguists may find it easier to collaborate with their colleagues across disciplines, theoretical linguistics students may be less intimidated by quantitative data, and certain controversies over empirical claims may be resolved more quickly and easily. Just as important, however, is a philosophical implication: The old and new methods are truly part of a single, unified science of linguistics.

Acknowledgments. This research was supported in part by National Science Council (Taiwan) grants 94-2411-H-194-018, 95-2411-H-194-005, 96-2411-H-194-002. All versions of MiniCorp and MiniJudge are co-copyrighted by National Chung Cheng University. My thanks to Tsung-Ying Chen for helping to run the MiniJudge experiment; he and Chen-Tsung Yang also programmed the Java version of MiniJudge.

References

Agresti, Alan
2002 *Categorical Data Analysis* (2nd ed). Hoboken, NJ: Wiley-Interscience.

Baayen, R. H.
2008 *Analyzing Linguistic Data: A Practical Introduction to Statistics Using R*. Cambridge, UK: Cambridge University Press.

Bailey, Todd M. and Ulrike Hahn
2001 Determinants of wordlikeness: Phonotactics or lexical neighborhoods? *Journal of Memory and Language* 44: 569–591.

Bird, Steven and T. Mark Ellison
1994 One level phonology: Autosegmental representations and rules as finite automata. *Computational Linguistics* 20: 55–90.

Blevins, Juliette
2004 *Evolutionary Phonology: The Emergence of Sound Patterns*. Cambridge, UK: Cambridge University Press.
2006 A theoretical synopsis of Evolutionary Phonology. *Theoretical Linguistics* 32 (2): 117–166.

Boersma, Paul and Bruce Hayes
2001 Empirical tests of the Gradual Learning Algorithm. *Linguistic Inquiry* 32 (1): 45–86.

Chomsky, Noam
1957 *Syntactic Structures*. The Hague: Mouton.
1965 *Aspects of the Theory of Syntax*. Cambridge, MA: MIT Press.
1980 Rules and representations. *Behavioral and Brain Sciences* 3: 1–61.

Chomsky, Noam and Morris Halle
1965 Some controversial questions in phonological theory. *Journal of Linguistics* 1 (2): 97–138.
1968 *The Sound Pattern of English*. New York: Harper and Row.

Coetzee, Andries W.
2008 Grammaticality and ungrammaticality in phonology. *Language* 84 (2): 218–257.

Coetzee, Andries W., and Joe Pater
2008 Weighted constraints and gradient restrictions on place co-occurrence in Muna and Arabic. *Natural Language and Linguistic Theory* 26 (2): 289–337.

Cowart, Wayne
1997 *Experimental Syntax: Applying Objective Methods to Sentence Judgments*. London: Sage Publications.

Duanmu, San
2007 *The Phonology of Standard Chinese*, 2nd ed. Oxford, UK: Oxford University Press.

Frisch, Stefan A. and Bushra Adnan Zawaydeh
2001 The psychological reality of OCP-Place in Arabic. *Language* 77 (1): 91–106.
Hayes, Bruce and Colin Wilson
2008 A maximum entropy model of phonotactics and phonotactic learning. *Linguistic Inquiry* 39 (3): 379-440.
Johnson, Keith
2008 *Quantitative Methods in Linguistics*. Oxford, UK: Blackwell Publishing.
Karttunen, Lauri
1998 The proper treatment of Optimality Theory in computational phonology. *Finite-state Methods in Natural Language Processing*, pp. 1–12. Ankara.
Keller, Frank and Theodora Alexopoulou
2001 Phonology competes with syntax: Experimental evidence for the interaction of word order and accent placement in the realization of Information Structure. *Cognition* 79:301–372.
Kenyon, John Samuel and Thomas A. Knott
1944 *A Pronouncing Dictionary of American English*. Springfield, MA: Merriam.
Kingston, John and Mary E. Beckman (eds.)
1990 *Papers in Laboratory Phonology*. Cambridge, UK: Cambridge University Press.
Kiparsky, Paul
2006 Amphichronic linguistics vs. Evolutionary Phonology. *Theoretical Linguistics* 32 (2): 217–236.
Ko, Yu-Guang
2007 Grammaticality and parsibility in Mandarin syntactic judgment experiments. National Chung Cheng University MA thesis.
Labov, William
1975 Empirical foundations of linguistic theory. In: Robert Austerlitz (ed.) *The Scope of American Linguistics*, pp. 77–133. Lisse: Peter de Ridder.
Legendre, Géraldine, Antonella Sorace and Paul Smolensky
2006 The Optimality Theory – Harmonic Grammar connection. In: Paul Smolensky and Géraldine Legendre (eds.) *The Harmonic Mind: From Neural Computation to Optimality-Theoretic Grammar*, Vol. 2, 339–402. Cambridge, MA: MIT Press.
Luce, Paul A.
1986 Neighborhoods of words in the mental lexicon. Doctoral dissertation, Indiana University, Bloomington, IN.

Mendoza-Denton, Norma, Jennifer Hay, and Stefanie Jannedy
2003 Probabilistic sociolinguistics: Beyond variable rules. In: Rens Bod, Jennifer Hay, and Stefanie Jannedy (eds.) *Probabilistic Linguistics*, pp. 97–138. Cambridge, MA: MIT Press.

Moreton, Elliott
2008 Analytic bias and phonological typology. *Phonology* 25: 83–127.

Morgan, James L., Katherine M. Bonamo and Lisa L. Travis
1995 Negative evidence on negative evidence. *Developmental Psychology* 31 (2): 180–197.

Myers, James
2007a MiniJudge: Software for small-scale experimental syntax. *International Journal of Computational Linguistics and Chinese Language Processing* 12 (2): 175–194.
2007b Linking data to grammar in phonology: Two case studies. *Concentric* 33 (2): 1–22.
2007c Generative morphology as psycholinguistics. In: Gonia Jarema and Gary Libben (eds.), *The Mental Lexicon: Core Perspectives*, pp. 105–128. Amsterdam: Elsevier.
2008a Testing phonological grammars with dictionary data. National Chung Cheng University ms.
2008b Bridging the gap: MiniCorp analyses of Mandarin phonotactics. *Proceedings of the 37th Western Conference on Linguistics*, pp. 137–147. University of California, San Diego.

Myers, James, Shih-Feng Huang and Jhishen Tsay
2007 Exact conditional inference for two-way randomized Bernoulli experiments. *Journal of Statistical Software* 21, Code Snippet 1, 2007-09-02.

Myers, James and Jane Tsay
2005 The processing of phonological acceptability judgments. *Proceedings of Symposium on 90-92 NSC Projects*, pp. 26–45. Taipei, Taiwan, May.

Myers, Scott
1997 OCP effects in Optimality Theory. *Natural Language and Linguistic Theory* 15: 847–892.

Myers, Scott and Benjamin B. Hansen
2007 The origin of vowel length neutralization in final position: Evidence from Finnish speakers. *Natural Language and Linguistic Theory* 25 (1): 157–193.

Ohala, John J.
1986 Consumer's guide to evidence in phonology. *Phonology Yearbook* 3, 3–26.

Ohala, John J., and Jeri J. Jaeger (ed.)
1986 *Experimental Phonology*. Orlando, FL: Academic Press.

Pater, Joe

Forthcoming Morpheme-specific phonology: Constraint indexation and inconsistency resolution. In: Steve Parker (ed.), *Phonological Argumentation: Essays on Evidence and Motivation*. London: Equinox.

Prince, Alan

2007 Let the decimal system do it for you: A very simple utility function for OT. Rutgers University ms.

Prince, Alan and Paul Smolensky

2004 *Optimality Theory: Constraint Interaction in Generative Grammar*. Oxford, UK: Blackwell Publishing.

R Development Core Team

2008 R: A language and environment for statistical computing. R Foundation for Statistical Computing, Vienna, Austria. ISBN 3-900051-07-0, URL: http://www.R-project.org.

Sankoff, David and Pascale Rousseau

1989 Statistical evidence for rule ordering. *Language Variation and Change* 1 (1): 1–18.

Schütze, Carson T.

1996 *The Empirical Base of Linguistics: Grammaticality Judgments and Linguistic Methodology*. Chicago: University of Chicago Press.

Tesar, Bruce and Paul Smolensky

1998 The learnability of Optimality Theory. *Linguistic Inquiry* 29 (2): 229–268.

Tsai, Chih-Hao

2000 Mandarin syllable frequency counts for Chinese characters. Kaohsiung Medical University, Taiwan, ms. http://technology.chtsai.org/syllable/

Uffmann, Christian

2006 Epenthetic vowel quality in loanwords: Empirical and formal issues. *Lingua* 116: 1079–1111.

Vitevitch, Michael S. and Paul A. Luce

1999 Probabilistic phonotactics and neighborhood activation in spoken word recognition. *Journal of Memory and Language* 40: 374–408.

Weskott, Thomas and Gisbert Fanselow

2009 Scaling issues in the measurement of linguistic acceptability. In: Sam Featherston and Susanne Winkler (eds.), *The Fruits of Empirical Linguistics. Process*, pp. 229–246. Berlin: Mouton de Gruyter.

Zuraw, Kie

2007 The role of phonetic knowledge in phonological patterning: Corpus and survey evidence from Tagalog infixation. *Language* 83 (2): 277–316.

Semantic evidence and syntactic theory

Frederick J. Newmeyer

1. Introduction

This paper is concerned with the nature of the evidence relevant to the construction of a syntactic theory, where 'syntactic theory' is understood in terms of the structure-building operations of the computational system. To be specific, I argue that semantic evidence (i.e., judgments of paraphrase, ambiguity, scope, nuances of aspect and the nature of events, etc.) is, in general, inappropriate to that task.

The paper is organized as follows. Section 2 defines and motivates the concept of the 'autonomy of syntax', which has traditionally been one of the leading ideas of generative grammar. In Section 3 I note that the autonomy of syntax has generally had a methodological counterpart, namely that semantic evidence is irrelevant to the construction of syntactic theory. Section 4 documents how autonomy has come to be weakened in recent years, both substantively and methodologically, while Section 5 outlines the negative consequences of this weakening. Section 6 raises some related issues and Section 7 is a brief conclusion.

2. The autonomy of syntax

Throughout most of its history, what has distinguished generative syntax from virtually all other approaches to grammar is the hypothesis of the autonomy of syntax (AS):

(1) Autonomy of Syntax: The rules (principles, constraints, etc.) that determine the combinatorial possibilities of the formal elements of a language make no reference to constructs from meaning, discourse, or language use.

Section 2.1 provides evidence for autonomy and Section 2.2 rebuts two challenges to the concept. Section 2.3 argues that the minimalist program has not made autonomy a dead issue.

2.1. Evidence for the autonomy of syntax

What sorts of facts bear on whether syntax is autonomous? One extreme position is advocated by certain formalists, who think that all that is required is to demonstrate some mismatch between form and meaning or between form and function. But if that were sufficient, then every linguist would believe in autonomous syntax, since nobody denies that such mismatches exist. The following examples (from Hudson, et al. 1996) illustrate:

(2) a. He is likely to be late.
b. *He is probable to be late. (*likely*, but not *probable*, allows raising)

(3) a. He allowed the rope to go slack.
b. *He let the rope to go slack. (*let* does not take the infinitive marker)

(4) a. He isn't sufficiently tall.
b. *He isn't enough tall. / He isn't tall enough. (*enough* is the only degree modifier that occurs postadjectivally)

Defending the autonomy of syntax, then, clearly involves more than showing the existence of mismatches between form and meaning.

Many functionalists take the opposite extreme and believe that one can refute the autonomy of syntax simply by showing that form is in a systematic relationship with meaning and function. Consider the following quote from a leading functionalist:

> Crucial evidence for choosing a functionalist over a traditional Chomskian formalist approach [embodying the autonomy of syntax – FJN] would minimally be any language in which a rule-governed relationship exists between discourse/cognitive functions and linear order. Such languages clearly exist. (Payne 1998: 155)

But all generative theories posit a rule-governed relationship between syntactic and semantic structure. There would be no 'autonomous syntacticians' if, in order to qualify as one, one had to reject rules linking form and meaning.

In a nutshell, to motivate the autonomy of syntax, it is necessary to demonstrate the correctness of the following two hypotheses:

(5) a. There exists an extensive set of purely formal generalizations orthogonal to generalizations governing meaning or discourse.
b. These generalizations 'interlock' in a system.

In other words, a full defense of the autonomy of syntax involves not merely pointing to extensive formal generalizations, but showing that these generalizations interact in a manner graphically illustrated in (6) (where 'FG' stands for 'formal generalization'):

(6)

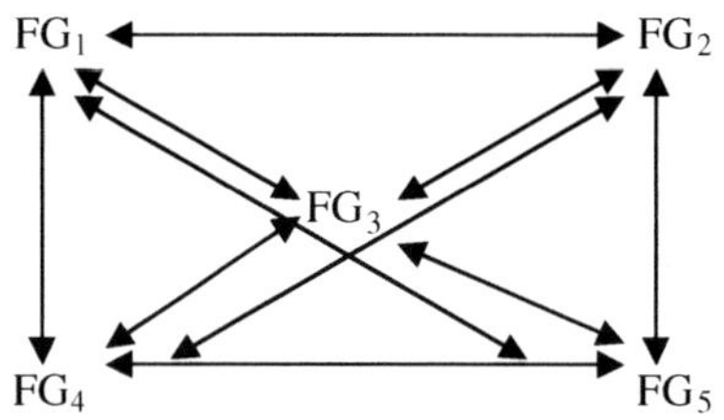

It is considerably easier, of course, to illustrate (5a) than (5b). The former is nicely illustrated by reference to structures in English with displaced *wh*-phrases, as in (7–10):

Wh-constructions in English:

Questions:

(7) Who did you see?

Relative Clauses:

(8) The woman who I saw

Free Relatives:

(9) I'll buy what(ever) you are selling.

Wh (Pseudo) Clefts:

(10) What John lost was his keys.

We have here a profound mismatch between syntactic form and the semantic and discourse properties associated with that form. In each construction type, the displaced *wh*-phrase occupies the same structural position, namely, the left margin of the phrase immediately dominating the rest of the sentence (in Principles-and-Parameters terminology, the 'Specifier of CP'):

(11)

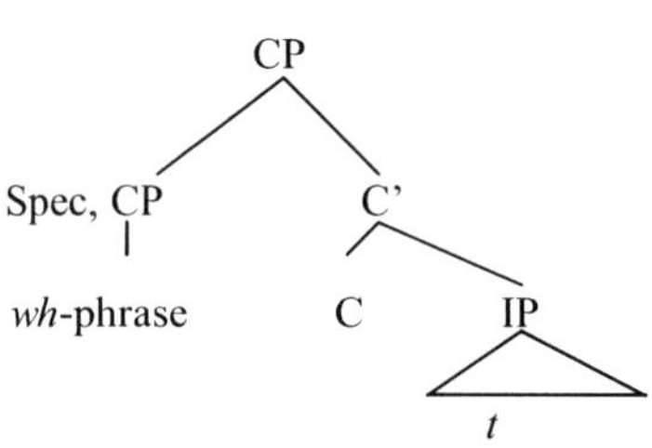

Despite their structural parallelism, the *wh*-phrases in the four constructions differ from each other in both semantic and discourse function. For example, the fronted *wh*-phrases in the different constructions play very different roles in terms of information structure. In simple *wh*-questions, the sentence-initial *wh*-phrase serves to focus the request for a piece of new information, where the entire clause is presupposed except for a single element (Givón 1990). Fronting in relative clauses, however, has nothing to do with focusing. Haiman (1985) suggests that the iconic principle that ideas that are closely connected tend to be placed together is responsible for the adjacency of the relative pronoun to the head noun. In free relatives, the fronted *wh*-phrase actually fulfills the semantic functions of the missing head noun. Semantically, the fronted *wh*-phrase in pseudo-clefts is different still. As Prince (1978) argues, the clause in which the *wh*-phrase is fronted represents information that the speaker can assume that the hearer is thinking about. But the function of the *wh*-phrase itself is not to elicit new information (as is the case with such phrases in questions), but rather to prepare the hearer for the focused (new) information in sentence-final position. In short, we have an easily characterizable structure manifesting a profound mismatch with meaning and function.

As far as their semantics is concerned, ones first thought might be that it is the (semantic) function of a fronted *wh*-phrase to set up an operator-variable configuration or to act as a scope marker. But such is true only in the least complex cases. Consider simple *wh*-questions, for example. In (12) *what* does indeed behave as a semantic operator and as a scope marker:

(12) What did Mary eat? = for what *x*, Mary ate *x*

But the full range of *wh*-constructions gives no support to the idea that the semantic role of the attracting feature *in general* is to set up operator-variable relations. So in (13), for example, with an appositive relative clause, there is no operator-variable configuration corresponding to trace and antecedent:

(13) Ralph Nader, who several million Americans voted for, lost the election.

By way of confirmation, as pointed out by Lasnik and Stowell (1991), there is no weak crossover effect with appositive relatives:

(14) a. Gerald_i, who_i his_i mother loves t_i, is a nice guy.
b. This book_i, which_i its_i author wrote t_i last week, is a hit.

Nor does the fronted *wh* element reliably act as a scope marker. Consider partial *Wh*-Movement in German and Romani (McDaniel 1989):

(15) Was_i glaubt [$_{IP}$ Hans [$_{CP}$ mit wem]$_i$ [$_{IP}$ Jakob jetzt t_i spricht]]]?
what think Hans with who Jacob now speaks
'With whom does Hans believe Jacob is now talking?'

(16) So$_i$ [[$_{IP}$ o Demìri mislinol [$_{CP}$ [kas]$_i$ [$_{IP}$ I Arìfa dikhl'a t$_i$]]
what that Demir think who the Arif saw
'Whom does Demir think Arifa saw?'

The same point can be made in cases of multiple *wh* phrases, where one is left in situ:

(17) Who remembers where we bought which book? (Baker 1970)

There are two interpretations, in neither of which the *wh*-phrase in SPEC of CP acts as a scope marker:

(18) Two interpretations of (17) (Chomsky 1973: 283):
a. For which *x, x* remembers for which *z*, for which *y*, we bought *y* at *z*
b. For which *x*, for which *y, x* remembers for which *z* we bought *y* at *z*

Indeed, Denham (2000) argues persuasively that *Wh*-Movement and scope marking are completely dissociated in UG.

Consider now evidence for (5b), namely the idea that *wh*-constructions not only have an internal formal consistency, but they behave consistently within the broader structural system of English syntax. For example, in all four construction types, the *wh*-phrase can be indefinitely far from the gap:

(19) a. Who$_i$ did you ask Mary to tell John to see ____$_i$?
b. The woman who$_i$ I asked Mary to tell John to see ____$_i$
c. I'll buy what(ever)$_i$ you ask Mary to tell John to sell ____$_i$.
d. What$_i$ John is afraid to tell Mary that he lost ____$_i$ is his keys.

And as (20) shows, each *wh*-construction is subject to principle of Subjacency, informally stated as in (21):

(20) a. *Who$_i$ did you believe the claim that John saw ____$_i$?
b. *The woman who$_i$ I believed the claim that John saw ____$_i$
c. *I'll buy what(ever)$_i$ Mary believes the claim that John is willing to sell ____$_i$.
d. *What$_i$ John believes the claim that Mary lost ____$_i$ is his keys.

(21) Subjacency

Prohibit any relationship between a displaced element and its gap if 'the wrong kind' of element intervenes between the two.

But Subjacency, as it turns out, constrains movement operations that involve no (overt) *wh*-element at all. For example, Subjacency accounts for the ungrammaticality of (22):

(22) *Mary is taller than I believe the claim that Susan is.

In other words, the formal principles fronting *wh*-phrases interlock with the formal principle of Subjacency. One might try to subvert this argument by claiming that Subjacency is a purely *functional* principle, rather than an interlocking grammatical one. In fact, there is no doubt that the ultimate roots of Subjacency are a functional response to the pressure for efficient parsing (see Berwick and Weinberg 1984, Newmeyer 1991, Kirby 1998). But over time, this parsing principle has become grammaticalized. Hence, there are any number of cases in which sentences that violate it are ungrammatical, even in the absence of parsing difficulty. Sentence (23a), a Subjacency violation, is ungrammatical, even though it is transparently easy to process. Minimally different (23b) does not violate Subjacency and is fully grammatical:

(23) a. *What did you eat beans and?
b. What did you eat beans with?

In summary, the *wh*-constructions of (7–10) are integrated into the structural system of English, of which Subjacency forms an integral part.

The autonomy of syntax is easier to motivate for highly configurational languages like English than for those like Japanese, where there are few if any structural restrictions governing the cooccurrence of two or more phrasal categories. However, even in Japanese we find important mismatches between syntactic structure and semantic structure. Consider an example involving Japanese subordination markers (Yuasa 2005; Yuasa and Francis 2003). There are essentially three classes of such markers in Japanese. The first class includes the items *kara* and *keredo*:

(24)	[Benri	da-**kara**]	kore-o	kai-masyoo
	convenient	is-because	this-Acc	buy-shall
	‘Because this is convenient, let’s buy this one’			

Syntactically the members of this class are postpositions, but semantically they are predicates. The second class includes the items *toki* and *uchi*:

(25)	[Uchi-ni	i-ru	**toki-ni**]	odenwa	kudasai
	home-at	be-Pres	time-at/when	phone	please
	‘Please call me when I am at home’				

Syntactically the members of this class are nouns, but semantically they are arguments. The third class includes the items *totan*, *toori*, *kuse*, and *ageku*:

(26)	[Uchi-o	de-ta	**totan-ni**]	ame-ga	fut-te	ki-ta
	house-Acc	left-Pst	instance-at	rain-Nom	fall-Ger	come-Past

‘It started raining right after/as soon as I left home’

Syntactically the members of this class are nouns, but semantically they are predicates. So schematically we have a situation as in (27):

(27)

	Class 1 (*kara*, *keredo*)	Class 3 (*totan*, *toori*)	Class 2 (*toki*, *uchi*)
Syntax	Postposition	Noun	
Semantics	Predicate		Argument

In other words, there is no smooth mapping between form and meaning. Syntactic notions like ‘noun’ and ‘postposition’ in Japanese need to be given a characterization independently of semantic notions like ‘predicate’ and ‘argument’. It is facts like these that argue for a level of purely formal patterning, that is, a level linking to meaning, but not subsidiary to it.

2.2. Challenges to the autonomy hypothesis

Superficially the autonomy of syntax seems to be falsified right and left. However, I would argue that most of the cases where it looks like a syntactic process is sensitive to meaning, something more subtle is going on. Consider passivization, for example. An old problem is that English measure verbs (*cost, weigh, measure,* etc.) do not passivize:

(28) a. The book cost a lot of money.
b. John weighed 180 pounds.

(29) a. *A lot of money was cost by the book.
b. *180 pounds was weighed by John.

Examples like these are at first blush a prima facie refutation of the autonomy of syntax. It looks like a syntactic process is sensitive to the meaning of the items involved. But in fact there are a number of analyses, which are most likely notational variants of each other, that attribute the deviance of (29a–b) to interface conditions, that is to conditions governing the syntax-semantics boundary, rather than to the computational system per se. In this regard, *a lot of money* in (28a) and *180 pounds* in (28b) have been analyzed as being locations (Jackendoff 1972), predicate attributes (Bresnan 1978), and quasi-arguments (Adger 1992; 1994). Principles interfacing form and meaning prevent such structures from occupying subject position if a true argument has adjunct status. There is no violation of the autonomy of syntax here.

Consider another – somewhat trickier – challenge to the autonomy of syntax. There are a number of contexts in which Subject-Aux Inversion in English is triggered. One of the most common is the presence of a negative adverbial or PP in fronted position:

(30) a. Rarely would she talk about her job.
b. *Every day of the week would she talk about her job.

(31) a. Under no circumstances would he yodel.
b. *Given any opportunity would he yodel.

Subject-Aux Inversion in negative contexts poses two potential problems for the autonomy of syntax:

(32) a. Semantic negation appears to be triggering inversion.
b. Auxiliary inversion is possible only when the nonoccurrence of the main clause event is entailed (Lakoff and Brugman 1987):
i. For no money would she sky-dive. (She wouldn't.)
ii. For no money, she would sky-dive. (She would.)

In other words, it looks as though semantic conditions need to be placed on whatever statement in the grammar is responsible for inversion. Such is not necessarily the case, however. The impossibility of (30b) and (31b) would be a problem for the autonomy of syntax, only if those sentences were irreducibly ill-formed. But they are not, since both can occur as questions:

(33) a. Every day of the week would she talk about her job?
b. Given any opportunity would he yodel?

So there is nothing wrong with the syntactic structure of (30b) and (31b) per se. It is just a matter of how that structure can be interpreted. As far as the Lakoff and Brugman argument is concerned, it needs to be pointed out that they just assume without discussion that there is a directionality of determination that goes from meaning to form. There is no reason to assume that. One could just as easily restate (32b) as (34):

(34) The nonoccurrence of the main clause event is entailed only given an inversion structure.

That formulation is empirically equivalent to (32b) and fully consistent with the autonomy of syntax.

2.3. Autonomy and minimalism

To read certain recent minimalist publications, one might think that the autonomy of syntax is a dead issue. Consider the following now-famous quote by Hauser, Chomsky, and Fitch:

> We hypothesize that FLN only includes recursion and is the only uniquely human component of the faculty of language (Hauser, Chomsky and Fitch 2002: 1569)

If all that were specific to the computational system were recursion, then syntax would be autonomous by definition. There would be no debate over autonomy at all. But in the approach of every minimalist, there is vastly more than recursion that needs to be posited for the syntax. Among other things, we have the following:

(35) a. Economy principles such as Last Resort (Chomsky 1993), Relativized Minimality (Rizzi 1990) (as well as its cousin, Chomsky and Lasnik 1993's Minimize Chain Links), and Anti-Locality (Grohmann 2003). None of these fall out from recursion per se, but rather represent conditions (however well motivated) that need to be imposed on it.

b. The entire set of mechanisms pertaining to phases (Chomsky 2001) needs to be specified, including what nodes count for phasehood, as well as the various conditions that need to be imposed on their functioning, like the Phase Impenetrability Condition.

c. The categorial inventory (lexical and functional) needs to be specified, as well as the formal features they manifest.

d. The set of parameters (there might be hundreds), their possible settings, and the implicational relations among them, need to be specified. This problem is especially acute, since (35a–c) clearly differ from language to language.

And any one of (35a–d) could in principle be semantically conditioned. In other words, there is nothing inherent to the MP that would diminish the importance of the issue of autonomy, nor would lead to an easy resolution of the issue.

3. Autonomy and evidence

Now where does 'evidence' fit into the picture outlined in the previous section? Given that syntactic systems are autonomous, it does not follow logically that semantic evidence should be irrelevant to their formulation. Nevertheless, from the earliest days of transformational generative grammar there has been a widespread sentiment that such evidence should be avoided to the extent possible. This sentiment has been based to a large extent on pure methodological caution. Since the nature of the form-meaning interface is one of the most difficult problems in linguistics, the worst thing, therefore, would be to *presuppose* that semantic considerations bear on the construction of a syntactic theory. In fact, generativists have generally seen the opposite direction to be a more promising one, that is, to use form-based evidence in constructing semantic theories. Linguistic form, for all of its complications and uncertainties, seems far more tangible and understandable than linguistic meaning. Hence, the idea that it makes more sense to use form to get at meaning, rather than the reverse. As Chomsky put it many years ago: "In general, as syntactic description becomes deeper, what appear to be semantic questions fall increasingly within its scope . . . " (Chomsky 1964: 936). To illustrate, take the passive in *Syntactic Structures.* Chomsky motivated the transformation purely on its formal properties (the occurrence of the morpheme *be+en*, its limitation to transitive verbs, and so on). Contrary to what many believe, the rough paraphrase relation between actives and passives was not one of Chomsky's motivations. In fact, he went on to argue that the fact that transformations are to a large degree meaning-preserving was an empirical discovery. He could hardly have claimed to have explained the meaning-preserving properties of transformations if he had used evidence based on paraphrase to motivate transformations in the first place.

Consider a later example of deeper syntactic description encompassing what has traditionally been called 'semantics'. A highly constrained theory of movement rules led to the Specified Subject Condition and Tensed-S Condition, which led to the trace theory of movement rules, which led to the possibility of surface interpretation of meaning (all of this was in Chomsky 1973), which led to capturing certain aspects of quantifier scope structurally, as in May (1977). Notice the methodology here. There was no starting assumption that it was within the domain of syntax to explain facts about quantifier scope (as was the case in generative semantics) or even that quantifier scope data was necessarily evidence bearing on syntactic theory. Rather, each step of syntactic analysis seemed to lead closer and closer to a syntactic treatment of aspects of quantifier scope.

In other words, in early work in generative syntax, one generally assumed a methodological counterpart to the autonomy of syntax:

(36) Autonomy of Syntax (Methodological Counterpart): Semantic evidence (i.e., judgments of paraphrase, ambiguity, scope, nuances of aspect and the nature of events, etc.) should not in general be used as data in the construction of a syntactic theory.

There is a nice quote from *Aspects of the Theory of Syntax* affirming the autonomy of syntax, both in its theoretical and methodological variants:

> For the moment, I see no reason to modify the view, expressed in Chomsky (1957) and elsewhere, that although, obviously, semantic considerations are relevant to the construction of general linguistic theory ... there is, at present, no way to show that semantic considerations play a role in the choice of the syntactic or phonological component of a grammar or that semantic features (in any significant sense of this term) play a role in the functioning of the syntactic or phonological rules. (Chomsky 1965: 226)

4. The weakening of the autonomy of syntax

Since the 1980s, the autonomy of syntax has become progressively weakened, both theoretically and methodologically, as indicated in (37a–e):

(37) Examples of the theoretical and/or methodological weakening of the autonomy of syntax in mainstream generative syntax:

a. The Theta-Criterion (Chomsky 1981), which demands that the syntax 'know' which syntactic elements bear Θ-roles and which do not.

b. The idea that 'c-selection' (essentially, subcategorization) is derivable from 's-selection' (essentially, the thematic properties of the items involved) (Chomsky 1986).

c. Uniformity of Theta Assignment Hypothesis (UTAH) (Baker 1988). Identical thematic relationships between items are represented by identical structural relationships between those items at the level of D-structure.

d. Lexical decomposition, which derives semantically complex predicates via syntactic movement operations (Baker 1988, 1993; Hale and Keyser 1993, 1997; Borer 2003)

e. The cartography program (Rizzi 1997; Cinque 1999), which appeals in part to semantic motivation for syntactic projections:

> In fact, a restrictive theory should force a one-to-one relation between position and interpretation (p. 20) . . . each projection has a specific semantic interpretation. (p. 132) (Cinque 1999)

f. The triggering of movement (and/or the licensing of configurations) by semantic properties of heads (Rizzi 1991/1996; Haegeman 1995):

> Syntactic movement . . . must be triggered by the satisfaction of certain quasi-morphological requirements of heads. . . . *[S]uch features have an interpretive import (Wh, Neg, Top, Foc, . . .)*: they determine the interpretation of the category bearing them and of its immediate constituents . . . , function as scope markers for phrases with the relevant quantificational force in a local configuration, etc. . . . (Rizzi 1997: 282; emphasis added)

> [The Negative Criterion appeals to] the semantic-syntactic feature NEG. (Haegeman 1997: 116)

One might wonder whether all of (37a–f) are not just good examples of syntax becoming deeper and incorporating semantics. In fact, they are not. What we have in all of (37a–f) are the workings of a dramatically changed theoretical outlook, which in some ways is the antithesis of the methodological counterpart to the autonomy of syntax in (36). (37a–f) do not illustrate pushing back the frontiers of syntax and thereby encompassing aspects of meaning. What they illustrate is the assumption that it is the task of syntax to draw on semantic evidence. The negative consequence, as we will see in the following section, is that it becomes more and more difficult to capture purely formal generalizations.

5. The negative effects of the use of semantic evidence

This section demonstrates the problems inherent in the use of semantic evidence to motivate syntactic theory, drawing on the analysis of English modal auxiliaries (Section 5.1), English derived nominals (Section 5.2), negation crosslinguistically (Section 5.3), and topic and focus projections (Section 5.4). Section 5.5 argues that the categories Noun and Verb are not (necessarily) defined on the basis of semantic evidence and Section 5.6 argues that there is little to be gained by the argument that (non-semantically-motivated) formal patterning is a function of the PF component.

5.1. English modal auxiliaries

There are profound structural generalizations governing the modals (for details, see Huddleston and Pullum 2002):

(38) a. They occur before all other auxiliaries (*must have gone; *have must gone*)
b. They do not occur in sequence (in Standard English) (**might could*)
c. They take neither the infinitive marker nor inflection (**to would; *she woulded*)
d. They must be followed by non-finite form of the verb or auxiliary (**I must had gone*)
e. They invert in questions and are followed by the negative morpheme (*could she run?; she could not run*)
f. All of (38a–e) apply to modals both in their root and epistemic senses:
i. Root *must* = obligation; epistemic *must* = consequence
ii. Root *may* = permission; epistemic *may* = possibility
iii. Root *can* = ability; epistemic *can* = possibility

Consider now some of the current work on English modals, taking the work of Tim Stowell and Karen Zagona as exemplars, since it is the most insightful as well as the most cited (Stowell 2004; Zagona 2007). In this work, capturing (38a–f) plays the most minor role. Rather, the goal is to find ways to represent the subtle scopal differences between root and epistemic modals structurally. So for Stowell the goal is explain the fact that epistemically construed modals and root modals do not pattern alike in how they are interpreted relative to tense. Roughly speaking, the generalization is that tense can take scope over root modals but not over epistemic modals. Zagona argues that modals can be merged above or below Tense, and their position relative to tense determines whether they will have an epistemic or root reading. These semantic differences between roots and epistemics are real, so any comprehensive theory needs to take them seriously. But capturing them in terms of Merge order or difference in projection renders it all the more difficult to account for the fact that in terms of their formal properties, roots and epistemics are just about the same. That is, the more internal syntactic structure one attributes to modals, the more difficult it becomes to provide an elegant account of (38a–f).

I can anticipate an objection here, based on the idea that my arguments are a priori. What principle, one might ask, makes it evident that the computational system should handle, say, the syntagmatic position of modals as a higher priority than accounting for their scopal properties? My reply is based on the assumption that there are phenomena that are clearly syntactic, those that are ambiguously syntactic or semantic (or part of a system interfacing the two), and phenomena that are clearly semantic. The diagram in (39) illustrates:

(39)

(A) PHENOMENA THAT ARE CLEARLY SYNTACTIC	**(B) PHENOMENA THAT ARE AMBIGUOUSLY SYNTACTIC OR SEMANTIC (OR PART OF A SYSTEM INTERFACING THE TWO)**	**(C) PHENOMENA THAT ARE CLEARLY SEMANTIC**
**John has must go(ne)* is an ungrammatical sentence of English	Tense can take scope over root modals but not over epistemic modals	*John will go* entails *John can go*

I take it as a methodological principle that any adequate model of the computational system of a language has the obligation to account for phenomena of type (A) before those of type (B). Otherwise put, a model of the computational system that accounts for (B), while rendering an account of (A) more difficult, is inadequate. Clearly, then, current approaches to modals, which complicate syntactic analysis by admitting evidence based on their semantic properties, are inadequate.

5.2. English derived nominals

Let us examine another interesting area of English syntax, namely, derived nominals (DNs). These are nominalizations exhibiting derivational morphology, as in (40):

(40) refusal, height, aggression, sanity, help, righteousness, worker

In a landmark paper, Chomsky (1970) argued that derived nominals are simply ordinary noun heads of ordinary NPs in underlying syntactic structure. He gave a number of arguments, two of which are purely syntactic. The first is that the structures in which DNs occur resemble noun phrases in every way. (41a) and (41b) have identical structures in relevant respects:

(41) a. Mary's three boring books about tennis
b. Mary's three unexpected refusals of the offer

Notice that the containing phrase can contain determiners, prenominal adjectives, and prepositional phrase complements (as in 42a) but not adverbs, negation, aspect, nor tense (42b–d):

(42) a. the stupid refusal of the offer
b. *the refusal stupidly of the offer
c. *the not refusal of the offer
d. *the have refusal of the offer

Chomsky's second argument is based on the fact that DNs occur in DPs corresponding to base structures, but not to transformationally derived structures. Consider the contrast between the (b) phrases and the (a) phrases in (43–49):

(43) a. Harry appeared to have won.
b. *Harry's appearance to have won (no Raising within DP)

(44) a. Mary gave Peter the book.
b. *Mary's gift of Peter of the book (no Dative Movement within DP)

(45) a. There appeared to be no hope.
b. *there's appearance to be no hope (no There-Insertion within DP)

(46) a. I believed Bill to be a fool.
b. *my belief of Bill to be a fool (no Raising-to-Object within DP)

(47) a. John interested the children with his stories.
b. *John's interest of the children with his stories (no Psych-Movement within DP)

(48) a. Lee is easy to please.
b. *Lee's easiness to please (no Tough-Movement within DP)

(49) a. Mary looked the information up.
b. *Mary's looking of the information up (no Particle Movement within DP)

Chomsky argued that the data in (43–49) follow automatically from the treatment of DNs as deep structure nouns. If one assumes that the domain of movement is S, but not DP, then the ungrammatical (b) phrases are simply underivable. Chomsky's analysis was broadened by others to encompass what came to be called the 'lexicalist hypothesis', namely, the idea that derivational operations are not performed by the computational system.

These profound formal generalizations are all but ignored in a lot of current work. Instead, the goal has become to capture subtle, and in this case I would say mostly nonexistent, semantic generalizations structurally – a goal which, contrary to Chomsky's analysis involves positing a disappearing VP node in the analysis of some or all DNs. Current nonlexicalist analyses appeal to a distinction that was first proposed, I believe, in Grimshaw (1990). Grimshaw divided derived nominals into two classes, which are now often called 'Argument-Structure Nominals (Arg-S-Nominals)' and 'Referential Nominals (Ref-Nominals)'. (50) and (51) illustrate each class:

(50) Arg-S-Nominals
  a. the instructor's (intentional) examination of the student
  b. the frequent collection of mushrooms (by students)
  c. the monitoring of wild flowers to document their disappearance
  d. the destruction of Rome in a day

(51) Ref-Nominals
  a. the instructor's examination/exam
  b. John's collections
  c. these frequent destructions

Grimshaw recognized that the fundamental difference between the two types of nominals is a semantic one, having to do with their associated event properties. Arg-S Nominals have full argument and event readings, while Ref Nominals do not. Grimshaw concluded quite reasonably that such facts are best accounted for in lexico-semantic structure. But Borer (2003), Alexiadou (2001), and others opt for a syntactic account of these semantic differences. For Borer and Alexiadou, Arg-S-Nominals, but not Ref-Nominals, are associated with an underlying VP node. (52b) is Borer's derivation:

(52) a. Kim's destruction of the vase
  b. [$_{NP}$ *-tion*$_{NOM}$ [$_{EP}$ *Kim* [$_{Arg-SPQ}$ *the vase* [$_{VP}$ *destroy*]]]]

In this analysis, for Arg-S-Nominals, each morphological element heads its own categorial projection, itself dominated by the appropriate functional projection. Successive head movements merge the root with affixes to create the appropriate complex lexical item. Ref-Nominals for Borer, on the other hand, project only nominalizing functional structure – no verbal functional structure at all – and they have no internal argument structure.

Significantly, neither of the profound structural generalizations pertaining to DNs follow from (52b). First, it does not account for the fact that the two types of nominalizations manifest the same internal structure (the inflection on the specifier, the positioning of adjectives, the impossibility of adverbs). And this internal structure is the same as for ordinary nouns. The default hypothesis has to be, then, that both have the *same* syntactic derivation. It is just an accident, given (52b), that Arg-S-Nominals and Ref-Nominals end up having the same surface properties. And as far as the fact that we don't find DN's in transformationally-derived structures is concerned, it is compatible with a non-lexicalist analysis like (52b) only with a host of additional assumptions. Once again, the admitting of semantic evidence has complicated syntactic analysis.

Borer and others do in fact give examples of what they consider to be purely morphosyntactic differences between the two types of nominals (many of these were proposed originally by Grimshaw):

(53) Supposed differences between Arg-S-Nominals and Ref-Nominals (Grimshaw 1990; Borer 2003)

a. Arg-S-Nominals have obligatory arguments; Ref-Nominals do not.
b. Arg-S-Nominals always contain affixes attached to verbal or adjectival stems.
c. Zero-derivation nominals can be Ref-Nominals, but not Arg-S-Nominals.
d. Arg-S-Nominals are mass nouns, Ref-Nominals are count nouns.
e. Arg-S-Nominals allow internal 'verbal' modification; Ref-Nominals do not.

The idea is that the properties listed in (53a–e) support a transformational derivation like (52b) of Arg-S-Nominals. However, (53a–e) are wrong from beginning to end. First, there are many Arg-S-Nominals that do not have obligatory arguments (Williams 1985: 301; Law 1997: 43):

(54)
a. Dr. Krankheit's operation (on Billy) took three hours.
b. John submitted himself to her scrutiny.
c. Human rights in third world countries are subject to constant repression.
d. The poor are susceptible to constant repression by the rich.
e. A very strong will for survival helped the villagers sustain such heavy bombardment.
f. Political dissidents in the ex-USSR were under constant surveillance by the KGB.
g. The sea water was sent to the plant for desalination.

h. The analysis needs further refinement.
i. The UN officials appeared to be in constant negotiation.
j. Constant exposure to the sun is harmful to the skin.

Second, there are many suffixless nouns that behave like Arg-S-Nominals in that they manifest the full argument structure and the event reading that Borer attributes to such nominals (Newmeyer to appear-a):

(55) a. Mary's metamorphosis of the house (made it unrecognizable)
b. the IRS's scrutiny of dubious looking tax forms
c. my lab assistant's culture of new forms of bacteria
d. the anathema by the church of those taking part in satanic rituals
e. America's moratorium on helping to support UNESCO
f. Iraq's frequent changeover of its currency (has left its people confused)
g. the constant mischief by the boy
h. Laval's ongoing treason (kept France under the Nazi yoke)
i. the frequent recourse to long discredited methods
j. my impulse to be daring
k. Yahoo's homicide of AltaVista and AllTheWeb
l. Pope's and Swift's persiflage of the Grub Street hacks

Third, are many zero-derivation Arg-S-Nominals (Newmeyer to appear-a):

(56) a. my constant change of mentors from 1992–1997
b. the frequent release of the prisoners by the governor
c. the frequent use of sharp tools by underage children
d. an officer's too frequent discharge of a firearm (could lead to disciplinary action)
e. the ancient Greeks' practice of infanticide
f. my constant need for approval
g. the student's conscious endeavor to improve her grades
h. the constant abuse of prisoners by their guards
i. Smith's consent to accept the nomination
j. Mary's resolve to be more assertive
k. access to the mainframe by qualified users (will be permitted)
l. France's test of nuclear weapons in the South Pacific

And fourth, there are many Arg-S-Nominals that are count nouns:

(57) a. Mary's constant refusals of the committee's offer
b. Paul and Frank's many discussions of modern jazz
c. your interpretations of the new rules
d. the apostle Peter's three denials of Jesus
e. the custom officials' inspections of suspicious baggage
f. (I can't take anymore) rejections of my submissions by the journal *Linguistics Illustrated*
g. Sam's constant attentions toward Susan (were not welcomed)
h. Coca Cola's twelve interruptions of the Super Bowl game
i. Mary's incessant arguments against the theory of Goofy Grammar

Fu, Roeper and Borer (2001) attempt to motivate an internal VP for Arg-S-Nominals by giving examples of where they occur with *do so* (presumptively a VP anaphor), as in (58), and with adverbs, as in (59a–d):

(58) John's destruction of the city and Bill's doing so too

(59) a. While the removal of evidence *purposefully* (is a crime), the removal of evidence *unintentionally* (is not).
b. His explanation of the problem *thoroughly* to the tenants (did not prevent a riot).
c. Protection of children *completely* from bad influence (is unrealistic).
d. His resignation so *suddenly* gave rise to wild speculation.

I would be inclined to attribute phrases like (58) to performance error or to a recency effect. But if (58) argues for a VP node with event nominalizations, then the equal acceptability (or lack of it) of (60) should argue for a VP node with *bare* nominalizations in the plural:

(60) America's attacks on Iraq were even less justified than the latter's doing so to Kuwait.

Yet, these are just the nominalizations for which Borer claims that there is *no* VP node. I find (59a–c) so marginal that it is surely inadvisable to appeal to their grammaticality to prop up a theoretical proposal. In any event, they seem no better or no worse than (61a–c), where it is claimed that there *is no* internal VP node.

(61) a. I must deplore the recourse all too frequently to underhanded tactics.
b. The use – I must say somewhat frighteningly – of mercury to cure gastric ulcers has been condemned by the AMA.
c. Could we arrange for the prisoners' release more gradually than has been the practice?

(59d) is most likely an example of a *so*-phrase modifying a Noun, analogously to the following:

(62) With a heart so pure he will never go astray.

Once again, in other words, what we find in current work is an appeal to semantic evidence to motivate syntactic structure while at the same time ignoring hard-core syntactic facts (for more discussion of DNs, see Newmeyer to appear-a).

5.3. Negation crosslinguistically

The above modals and nominalizations examples were English-based. We find the same problem crosslinguistically. That is, we find the positing of semantically-based projections that render the purely formal generalization all but impossible to capture. I could give many examples, but given space constraints I will confine myself to one, namely, the Neg Phrase projection. The default assumption now is that where we have semantic negation, we find Neg Phrase (for a typical example, see Ouhalla 1991). An immediate problem with such an idea is that negation is almost never overtly phrasal. That is, we almost never find what are rightfully called specifiers or complements with negation. But I will leave that point aside and stress that the only motivation for NegP is semantic and that its positing obscures the formal similarities between negatives in a particular language and other categories with the same formal properties (different for different languages). To illustrate, consider some of the categorial possibilities for negation crosslinguistically:

A. Complement-taking verb (Tongan: Churchward 1953: 56; John R. Payne 1985: 208)

In Tongan, *'ikai* behaves like a verb in the *seem* class (we know there is a complement because *ke* occurs only in embedded clauses):

(63) a. Na'e 'alu 'a Siale
ASP go ABSOLUTE Charlie
'Charlie went'

b. Na'e 'ikai [$_S$ ke 'alu 'a Siale]
ASP NEG ASP go ABSOLUTE Charlie
'Charlie did not go'

B. Auxiliary (Estonian: Blevins 2007)

In Estonian, negative forms pattern with perfects, which are based on a form of the copula OLEMA:

(64)

Property		**Auxiliary/Particle**	**Main Verb Form**
NEG(ATIVE)	NONPAST	*ei*	(UNINFLECTED) STEM
	PAST		PARTICIPLE
PERFECT		OLEMA	

C. Derivational affix (Turkish: John R. Payne 1985: 227)

In Turkish, the negative morpheme patterns with other affixes:

(65) V + Refl + Recip + Cause + Pass + Neg + Possible + Tense/Mood + Person/Number

D. Noun (Evenki: Payne 1985: 228)

In Evenki, *ācin* has a plural form and takes case endings like ordinary nouns:

(66) a. nuŋan ācin 'he is not here'
b. nuŋartin ācir 'they are not here'

E. Adverb (English: Jackendoff 1972; Baker 1991; Ernst 1992; Kim 2000; Newmeyer 2006)

In English, *not* is an adverb in the same class as *never, always, just*, and *barely*. For example, *not*, along with other adverbs of its class, occurs in the auxiliary (67a), but not in pre-subject position set off by comma intonation (67b), nor in post-verbal position (67c), or in post-object position (67d):

(67) a. Mary has not / never / barely begun the assignment.
b. *Not, / *Never, / *Barely, Mary has begun the assignment.

c. Mary left *not / *never /*barely.
d. Mary has begun the assignment *not / *never / *barely.

Furthermore, *not*, like other adverbs of its class, functions as a modifier of an adjective, adverbial element, and prepositional phrase:

(68) a. This is a not unattractive doll in some ways.
b. Harvey was a rarely helpful service employee.

(69) a. Not surprisingly, he is on a diet.
b. She often behaved incompetently, but rarely helplessly.

(70) a. It is hot. But not in your apartment.
b. I've looked in a lot of places for my keys. But never in your apartment.

Not does have properties not shared with adverbs. The most noteworthy is that it triggers the obligatory appearance of *do*-supported tense in the absence of an auxiliary verb:

(71) a. John never opened the book.
b. *John not opened the book.
c. John did not open the book.

Also, *not* cannot precede a finite verb:

(72) a. Mary never left.
b. *Mary not left.

What is illustrated in (71) and (72) are typically considered two separate distinctive properties of *not*. But, in fact, if tensed forms of the auxiliary *do* are generated in English in non-negative and non-interrogative contexts, as I believe to be the correct analysis, then (71) and (72) reduce to one property. I see no reason to question the idea that sentences such as (73) are fully grammatical:

(73) John did leave.

The fact that (73) is typically – perhaps, necessarily – uttered with contrastive stress on *did*, seems irrelevant to the syntax of English, which needs in any event to generate it. If (73) is grammatical, then filter (74) accounts for the ungrammaticality of (71b) and (72b), while not blocking grammatical (71c):

(74) **not* before a finite verb

Filter (74) has the virtue of accounting for the otherwise puzzling fact that *not*, unlike other negative adverbials, does not occur in fronted position with the inversion of the auxiliary:

(75) a. Never has Mary tackled such assignments.
b. *Not has Mary tackled such assignments.

(75b) is a straightforward filter violation.

Another property of *not* that has been argued to distinguish it from adverbs is its ability to license VP ellipsis. Sentences like (76b) are often claimed to be bad:

(76) a. Tom has written a novel, but Peter has not.
b. (*)Tom has written a novel, but Peter has never.

In fact, (76b) seems like perfectly fine colloquial English to me, as do (77a–b), in which ellipsis is licensed by *rarely* and *just*, two adverbs in the same class as *never*:

(77) a. I'll cut corners wherever I can, but Mary will rarely.
b. Tom arrived hours ago, but Mary has just.

In summary, *not* is an adverb in English. The fact that the semantic properties of *not* are quite different from those of other adverbs – in particular the fact that it functions as an operator – gives strong credence to AS, and illustrates that a semantically-motivated Neg Phrase is not the way to go.

5.4. Topic and Focus Phrases

Covert TopicP and FocusP projections, have also been motivated almost entirely on the basis of semantic evidence (see Newmeyer to appear-b). The most serious problem with covert movement to FocusP is that basically *anything* can be in focus, which means that focus movement obeys or violates island constraints willy-nilly. So as noted by Reinhart (1991), the stressed NPs in (78) are contained in strong (ungoverned) islands:

(78) a. [$_{IP}$ [$_{CP}$ That Linda argued with THE CHAIRMAN] is surprising].
b. [$_{IP}$ [$_{NP}$ Even the paper that LUCIE submitted to our journal] was weak].

Extraction of the focused elements should be impossible. Horvath (1999) made similar point with examples of (79) and (80):

(79) Q. Do people wonder where Mary was last night?
A. No, people wonder where [Mary's BOYFRIEND] was last night.

(80) Q. Have you shown Bill the book that I gave you for your birthday?
A. No, I have (only) shown him the book that you gave me for CHRISTMAS.

I would say that covert Focus and Topic projections create even more problems than the NegP projection. There are, however, options for capturing both the formal and semantic properties of topics and focuses that are both more empirically adequate than positing new projections and which are fully compatible with the autonomy of syntax. Basically, the idea is to regard topic, focus, and discourse anaphoricity as interface phenomena, as has been argued by Vallduví 1992; Costa 2004; Reinhart 2006; and Neeleman and van de Koot 2007).

5.5. The question of nouns and verbs

I can anticipate an attempt to construct a reductio against the arguments of the previous sections. One might object that categories that are universally accepted, Noun and Verb, for example, are ultimately based on semantic evidence as well. And if so, wouldn't one have a double standard by accepting Noun and Verb, but rejecting Neg Phrase? However, Noun and Verb are not necessarily defined semantically. The best treatment of categories is Mark Baker (2003)'s book *Lexical Categories,* which provides the following formal definitions of Noun and Verb:

(81) Baker (2003) on Noun and Verb:
a. X is a verb if and only if X is a lexical category and X has a specifier.
b. X is a noun if and only if X is a lexical category and X bears a referential index.

These definitions might be a little confusing, given the term 'referential index'. However, Baker makes it clear that he is using the term in a purely formal way and that it should not be identified with 'semantic reference'. He points out that the relation between having a referential index and bearing reference is very indirect, as is illustrated by examples like *the average man* and *the flaw in the argument.* In fact, Baker gives example after example to show that nouns and verbs cannot be defined notionally. So DP and VP are quite different in their nature from the putative NegP.

5.6. The 'It's all PF' rebuttal

As another possible rejoinder to the above arguments, one might wish to dismiss the formal generalizations discussed as just low-level PF generalizations, not central to the workings of the computational system at all. Or perhaps, one might say, they should be handled by the morphology or in the lexicon. My terse reply is 'Syntax is syntax'. If it did turn out to be correct that the formal facts regarding modals, nominalizations, negation, and so on really are part of, say, PF, then we need a theory of PF syntax that tells us what is possible and what is impossible. Such a theory is all the more necessary, given the sheer amount of syntax that has been attributed to PF in recent years:

(82) Some syntactic phenomena that have been attributed to PF:
  a. extraposition and scrambling (Chomsky 1995)
  b. object shift (Holmberg 1999; Erteschik-Shir 2005)
  c. head movements (Boeckx and Stjepanovic 2001)
  d. the movement deriving V2 order (Chomsky 2001)
  e. linearization (i.e. VO vs. OV) (Chomsky 1995; Takano 1996; Fukui and Takano 1998; Uriagereka 1999)
  f. *Wh*-movement (Erteschik-Shir 2005)

So the 'it's all PF' defense simply will not work as a means of justifying the use of semantic evidence. If most of what has historically been called 'syntax' reassembles itself in PF (or in the morphology or in the lexicon), then we might as well just relabel PF, the morphology, and the lexicon 'the syntactic component' and start from there.

6. Some additional issues

This section treats three issues related to the use of semantic evidence to motivate syntactic theory: the question of why such evidence has increasingly been appealed to in recent years (Section 6.1), the question of whether deeper syntactic description does, in reality, generalize to account for facts about meaning (Section 6.2), and the consequences of the implicit denial that there is something 'special' about syntax (Section 6.3).

6.1. On the question of why semantic evidence has played an evermore important role

It is interesting to speculate why semantic evidence has come to play a greater and greater role in mainstream syntactic theorizing. The answer appeals in part to conceptions and their implementations that were novel to the minimalist program, in particular, the following:

(83) a. There is no optionality in grammar; hence elements move only when they are 'required to'. (Chomsky 1995)
 b. Movement must be triggered by a feature on a functional head. (Chomsky 1995)
 c. "In a perfectly designed language, each feature would be semantic or phonetic, not merely a device to create a position or to facilitate computation." (Chomsky 2000: 109)

The execution of (83a) and (83b) represented a move toward the 'semanticization' of syntax. (83a), in effect, requires that seemingly optional variants have different underlying structures. Since few if any structural variants have the same semantic properties (broadly defined), it seemed reasonable to locate their structural differences in projections with direct semantic relevance. But if projections are semantically defined and, as in (83b), movement is triggered by features of projections, then we are a step closer to the idea that movement is semantically motivated. The quote in (83c) is the icing on the cake. We can disagree with each other profoundly about what a 'perfectly designed language' might look like. But if we do happen to agree with (83c), then we can say good-bye to the methodological counterpart to the autonomy of syntax.

However, I do not think that syntax is drifting in a non-autonomist direction purely as a result of minimalist theorizing. The trend was well underway before the first minimalist publication. I think that the basic problem is that, throughout most of its history, we have not seen a formal semantic theory that has meshed comfortably with mainstream generative syntax. And the main reason for that is that Chomsky, for a variety of reasons, has never shown any interest in such a theory. So the tendency has been to 'go with what we know', that is, to expand syntax to encompass what is naturally the domain of semantic theory.

6.2. On deep syntactic description encompassing semantics

Let us reconsider one of the ideas that has driven generative grammar since its inception: "… as syntactic description becomes deeper, what appear to be semantic questions fall increasingly within its scope …" (Chomsky 1964: 936). So, far, I have not questioned the correctness of the quote. But we should examine it more closely. The idea of deeper syntax encompassing semantics reached its apogee in 1981 with the government-binding theory. One of the major pillars of GB was that the key principles of the theory handled hard-core syntactic facts and facts about construal at the same time. The two most important examples are in (84):

(84) a. The binding theory accounted both for constraints on movement and constraints on anaphora.

b. The Empty Category Principle accounted for both purely structural facts (e.g. *that*-trace, the order of elements in incorporation structures, constraints on the extraction of adjuncts, etc.) and facts about (semantic) scope.

Neither of these generalizations obviously hold today. First, the locality of movement follows from the nature of Merge, but probably not the locality of anaphor binding. In any event, long-distance anaphors (LDA) appear to be the norm in language, not the exception. Within the framework of Optimality Theory, Moon (1995) argued that the thematic role of the antecedent and anaphor in Korean is the major factor determining binding possibilities. As we can see in (85), the purely structural c-command relation is a distant fourth:

(85) Ranked constraints in the binding of Korean long distance anaphors:

a. Thematic Hierarchy Constraint (LDA must be bound by a thematically higher NP)

b. Larger Domain Preference Constraint (Given potential antecedents for LDA in different domains, the more distant the domain, the stronger the preference)

c. Subject-Orientation Constraint (LDA must be bound by a subject NP)

d. C-Command Constraint (LDA must be bound by a c-commanding NP)

e. Discourse Binding Constraint (LDA must be bound by a prominent discourse NP if no sentential antecedent is available)

And second, the Empty Category Principle is not even expressible, given minimalist assumptions.

The failure of deeper syntactic description to generalize to account for semantic generalizations gives us one more reason to be skeptical about the desirability of appealing to semantic evidence to motivate syntactic theory.

6.3. On the 'specialness' of syntax

I close this paper on an extremely speculative note. The one feature that has made generative grammar distinctively different from every other contemporary approach is the claim that there is something 'special' about syntax. And furthermore this 'specialness' of syntax is at the root of the theory of Universal Grammar. Most of the arguments for innateness take as a starting point some syntactic construct and go on from there to argue that it could not have been learned inductively, given the poverty of the stimulus. Opponents of a UG-perspective, that is, most functionalists, cognitive linguists, and artificial intelligence researchers, know this very well. That is, they know that if you give up the autonomy of syntax (both in its conceptual and methodological aspects), the arguments for innateness disappear. What one hears all of the time from such scholars is that the arguments for UG fall through because Chomsky and his associates do not realize how isomorphic syntax is to semantics. Consider, for example, Robert Van Valin (1998)'s attack on the innateness of constraints on extraction. He breaks extraction into its component parts and tries to show that each part admits to a semantic generalization. (Most cognitive linguists are happy to posit innate concepts). I do not think that he is successful, but the blurring of the distinction between form and meaning gives a huge opening wedge to opponents of generative grammar.

Let us return to Chomsky's view of what a perfectly designed language might be like:

> In a perfectly designed language, each feature would be semantic or phonetic, not merely a device to create a position or to facilitate computation. (Chomsky 2000: 109)

That of course is what *opponents* of generative grammar have been saying for decades. For example, consider a quote from one of the most anti-UG papers written in recent years by two of the most anti-UG linguists, Nicholas Evans and Stephen Levinson:

> The core similarities across languages have their origin in two sources: physiological constraints on the sound system and conceptual constraints on the semantics. (Evans and Levinson 2007: np)

There is really very little difference between the two quotes. Now, there are many ways that one might react to the similarity of the two positions. One might well respond by offering the opinion that such is all for the good. After all, the prevailing opinion is that the more convergence one finds between theories, the better off we are. True, but not if one is not forced to give up too much to achieve that convergence. In my view, giving up the autonomy of syntax, and in particular in appealing to semantic evidence along the way, is giving up too much.

7. Conclusion

The autonomy of syntax embodies a substantive component and a methodological one. The former entails that constructs from meaning, discourse, and use do not enter into the formulation of the syntactic rules and principles. The latter prohibits the use of semantic evidence to motivate syntactic theory. I have argued that the abandonment of the latter in much recent work has had serious negative consequences for linguistic theory.

Acknowledgement. I would like to thank Sam Featherston for his helpful comments on the pre-final version of this paper.

References

Adger, David
1992 The licensing of quasi-arguments. In: Peter Ackema and Maaike Schoorlemmer (eds). *Proceedings of ConSole I*), 1–18. Utrecht: Utrecht University.
1994 *Functional Heads and Interpretation*. Ph. D. thesis, University of Edinburgh.

Alexiadou, Artemis
2001 *Functional Structure in Nominals: Nominalization and Ergativity*. Amsterdam: John Benjamins.

Baker, C. L.
1970 Notes on the description of English questions: The role of an abstract question morpheme. *Foundations of Language* 6: 197–219.
1991 The syntax of English *not*: The limits of core grammar. *Linguistic Inquiry* 22: 387–429.

Baker, Mark C.
1988 *Incorporation: A Theory of Grammatical Function Changing*. Chicago: University of Chicago Press.

1993 Noun incorporation and the nature of linguistic representation. In: William A. Foley (ed.), *The Role of Theory in Language Description*, 13–44. Berlin: Mouton de Gruyter.

2003 *Lexical Categories: Verbs, Nouns, and Adjectives.* Cambridge: Cambridge University Press.

Berwick, Robert C. and Amy Weinberg

1984 *The Grammatical Basis of Linguistic Performance.* Cambridge, MA: MIT Press.

Blevins, James P.

2007 Periphrasis as syntactic exponence. To appear in: Farrell Ackerman, James P. Blevins and Gregory S. Stump (eds.) *Patterns in Paradigms.* Stanford: CSLI Publications.

Boeckx, Cedric and Sandra Stjepanovic

2001 Head-ing toward PF. *Linguistic Inquiry* 32: 345–355.

Borer, Hagit

2003 Exo-skeletal vs. endo-skeletal explanations: Syntactic projections and the lexicon. In: John Moore and Maria Polinsky (eds.), *The Nature of Explanation in Linguistic Theory*, 31–67. Stanford: CSLI Publications.

Bresnan, Joan W.

1978 A realistic transformational grammar. In: Morris Halle, Joan Bresnan and George Miller (eds), *Linguistic Theory and Psychological Reality*, 1–59. Cambridge, MA: MIT Press.

Chomsky, Noam

1964 The logical basis of linguistic theory. In: Horace G. Lunt (ed.), *Proceedings of the Ninth International Congress of Linguists*, 914–977. The Hague: Mouton.

1965 *Aspects of the Theory of Syntax.* Cambridge, MA: MIT Press.

1970 Remarks on nominalization. In: Roderick Jacobs and Peter Rosenbaum (eds.), *Readings in English Transformational Grammar*, 184–221. Waltham, MA: Ginn.

1973 Conditions on transformations. In: Steven Anderson and Paul Kiparsky (eds.), *A Festschrift for Morris Halle*, 232–286. New York: Holt Rinehart & Winston.

1981 *Lectures on Government and Binding.* Dordrecht: Foris.

1986 *Knowledge of Language: Its Nature, Origin, and Use.* New York: Praeger.

1993 A minimalist program for linguistic theory. In: Kenneth Hale and Samuel Jay Keyser (eds.), *The View from Building 20: Essays in Honor of Sylvain Bromberger.*, 1–52. Cambridge, MA: MIT Press.

1995 *The Minimalist Program.* Cambridge, MA: MIT Press.

2000 *New Horizons in the Study of Language and Mind.* Cambridge: Cambridge University Press.

2001 Derivation by phase. In: Michael Kenstowicz (ed.), *Ken Hale: A Life in Language*, 1–52. Cambridge, MA: MIT Press.

Chomsky, Noam and Howard Lasnik
1993 Principles and parameters theory. In: J. Jacobs, A. von Stechow, W. Sternefeld and T. Venneman (eds.), *Syntax: An International Handbook of Contemporary Research*. Berlin: Walter de Gruyter.

Churchward, Clerk M.
1953 *Tongan Grammar.* London: Oxford University Press.

Cinque, Guglielmo
1999 *Adverbs and Functional Heads: A Cross-Linguistic Perspective.* Oxford: Oxford University Press.

Costa, João
2004 *Subject Positions and Interfaces: The Case of European Portuguese.* Berlin: Mouton de Gruyter.

Denham, Kristin
2000 Optional Wh-Movement in Babine-Witsuwit'en. *Natural Language and Linguistic Theory* 18: 199–251.

Ernst, Thomas
1992 The phrase structure of English negation. *Linguistic Review* 9: 109–144.

Erteschik-Shir, Nomi
2005 Sound patterns of syntax: Object shift. *Theoretical Linguistics* 31: 47–93.

Evans, Nicholas and Stephen C. Levinson
2007. The myth of language universals. Unpublished paper, University of Melbourne and MPI Nijmegen.

Fu, Jingqi, Thomas Roeper and Hagit Borer
2001 The VP within nominalizations: Evidence from adverbs and the VP anaphor *do so*. *Natural Language and Linguistic Theory* 19: 549–582.

Fukui, Naoki and Yuji Takano
1998 Symmetry in syntax: Merge and demerge. *Journal of East Asian Linguistics* 7: 27–86.

Givón, Talmy
1990 *Syntax: A Functional-Typological Introduction, vol. 2.* Amsterdam: John Benjamins.

Grimshaw, Jane
1990 *Argument Structure.* Cambridge, MA: MIT Press.

Grohmann, Kleanthes K.
2003 *Prolific Peripheries.* Amsterdam: John Benjamins.

Haegeman, Liliane
1995 *The Syntax of Negation.* Cambridge: Cambridge University Press.
1997 The syntax of N-words and the Neg Criterion. In: Danielle Forget, Paul Hirschbühler, France Martineau and María-Luisa Rivero (eds.),

Negation and Polarity: Syntax and Semantics, 115–137. Amsterdam: John Benjamins.

Haiman, John (ed.)
1985 *Iconicity in Syntax*. Amsterdam: John Benjamins.

Hale, Kenneth and Samuel Jay Keyser
1993 On argument structure and the lexical expression of syntactic relations. In: Kenneth Hale and Samuel Jay Keyser (eds.), *The View from Building 20: Essays in Honor of Sylvain Bromberger*, 53–110. Cambridge, MA: MIT Press.
1997 On the complex nature of simple predicates. In: Alex Alsina, Joan W. Bresnan and Peter Sells (eds.), *Complex Predicates*, 29–65. Stanford: CSLI Publications.

Hauser, Marc D., Noam Chomsky and W. Tecumseh Fitch
2002 The faculty of language: What is it, who has it, and how did it evolve? *Science* 298: 1569–1579.

Holmberg, Anders
1999 Remarks on Holmberg's generalization. *Studia Linguistica* 53: 1–39.

Horvath, Julia
1999 Interfaces vs. the computational system in the syntax of focus. In: Hans Bennis and Martin Everaert (eds.) *Interface Strategies*, 183–205. Amsterdam: Royal Academy of the Netherlands.

Huddleston, Rodney and Geoffrey K. Pullum
2002 *The Cambridge Grammar of the English Language*. Cambridge: Cambridge University Press.

Hudson, Richard A., Andrew Rosta, Jasper Holmes and Nikolas Gisborne
1996 Synonyms and syntax. *Journal of Linguistics* 32: 439–446.

Jackendoff, Ray
1972 *Semantic Interpretation in Generative Grammar*. Cambridge, MA: MIT Press.

Kim, Jong-Bok
2000 *The grammar of Negation: A Constraint-Based Approach*. Stanford: CSLI Publications.

Kirby, Simon
1998 *Function, Selection and Innateness: The Emergence of Language Universals*. Oxford: Oxford University Press.

Lakoff, George and Claudia Brugman
1987 The semantics of aux-inversion and anaphora constraints. Unpublished paper delivered to the Linguistic Society of America.

Lasnik, Howard and Timothy A. Stowell
1991 Weakest crossover. *Linguistic Inquiry* 22: 687–720.

Law, Paul
1997 On some syntactic properties of word-structure and modular grammars. In: Anna-Maria Di Sciullo (ed.), *Projections and Interface*

Conditions: Essays on Modularity, 28–51. Oxford: Oxford University Press.

May, Robert
1977 The grammar of quantification. Ph. D. dissertation, MIT.

McDaniel, Dana
1989 Partial and multiple Wh-movement. *Natural Language and Linguistic Theory* 7: 565–604.

Moon, Seung Chul
1995 An optimality approach to long distance anaphors. Ph. D. dissertation, University of Washington.

Neeleman, Ad and Hans van de Koot
2007 Dutch scrambling and the nature of discourse templates. Unpublished paper, University College London.

Newmeyer, Frederick J.
1991 Functional explanation in linguistics and the origins of language. *Language and Communication* 11: 3–28.
2006 Negation and modularity. In: Betty Birner and Gregory Ward (eds.), *Drawing the Boundaries of Meaning: Neo-Gricean Studies in Pragmatics and Semantics in Honor of Laurence R. Horn*, 247–268. Amsterdam: Benjamins.
to appear-a Current challenges to the lexicalist hypothesis: An overview and a critique. In: Simin Karimi, Heidi Harley and Scott Farrar (eds.), *Language: Theory and Practice: Papers in Honor of D. Terence Langendoen*. Amsterdam: John Benjamins.
to appear-b On split-CPs and the 'perfectness' of language. In: Benjamin Shaer, Philippa Cook, Werner Frey and Claudia Maienborn (eds.), *Dislocation: Syntactic, Semantic, and Discourse Perspectives*. London: Routledge.

Ouhalla, Jamal
1991 Functional categories and the head parameter. Paper delivered at the 14th GLOW Colloquium.

Payne, Doris L.
1998 What counts as explanation? A functionalist approach to word order. In: Michael Darnell, Edith Moravcsik, Frederick J. Newmeyer, Michael Noonan and Kathleen Wheatley (eds.), *Functionalism and Formalism in Linguistics*, 135–164. Amsterdam: John Benjamins.

Payne, John R.
1985 Negation. In: Timothy Shopen (ed.), *Language Typology and Syntactic Description. Volume I: Clause Structure*, 197–242. Cambridge: Cambridge University Press.

Prince, Ellen F.
1978 A comparison of *wh*-clefts and *it*-clefts in discourse. *Language* 54: 883–906.

Reinhart, Tanya
2006 *Interface Strategies*. Cambridge, MA: MIT Press.
1991 Elliptic conjunctions – non-quantificational LF. In: Asa Kasher (ed.), *The Chomskyan Turn: Generative Linguistics, Philosophy, Mathematics, and Psychology*, 360–384. Oxford: Blackwell.

Rizzi, Luigi
1990 *Relativized Minimality*. Cambridge, MA: MIT Press.
1991/1996 Residual verb second and the *wh*-criterion. In: Adriana Belletti and Luigi Rizzi (eds.), *Parameters and Functional Heads: Essays in Com parative Syntax*, 63–90. Oxford: Oxford University Press.
1997 The fine structure of the left periphery. In: Liliane Haegeman (ed.), *Elements of Grammar: Handbook of Generative Syntax*, 281–337. Dordrecht: Kluwer.

Stowell, Timothy A.
2004 Tense and modals. In: Jacqueline Guéron and Jacqueline Lecarme (eds.), *The Syntax of Time*, 621–635. Cambridge, MA: MIT Press.

Takano, Yuji
1996 Movement and parametric variation in syntax. Ph. D. dissertation, University of California, Irvine.

Uriagereka, Juan
1999 Multiple spell-out. In: Samuel David Epstein and Norbert Hornstein (eds.), *Working Minimalism*, 251–282. Cambridge, MA: MIT Press.

Vallduví, Enric
1992 *The informational Component*. New York: Garland.

Van Valin, Robert D.
1998 The acquisition of WH-questions and the mechanisms of language acquisition. In: Michael Tomasello (ed.), *The New Psychology of Language: Cognitive and Functional Approaches to Language Structure*. Mahwah, NJ: Lawrence Erlbaum.

Williams, Edwin
1985 PRO and subject of NP. *Natural Language and Linguistic Theory* 3: 297–315.

Yuasa, Etsuyo
2005 *Modularity in Language: Constructional and Categorial Mismatch in Syntax and Semantics*. Berlin: Mouton de Gruyter.

Yuasa, Etsuyo and Elaine J. Francis
2003 Categorial mismatch in a multi-modular theory of grammar. In: Elaine J. Francis and Laura A. Michaelis (eds.), *Mismatch: Form-function Incongruity and the Architecture of Grammar*, 179–227. Stanford: CSLI Publications.

Zagona, Karen
2007 On the syntactic features of epistemic and root modals. In: Luis Eguren and Olga Fernández Soriano (eds.), *Coreference, Modality and Focus*, 221–236. Amsterdam: John Benjamins.

Automated support for evidence retrieval in documents with nonstandard orthography

Thomas Pilz and Wolfram Luther

Abstract. The interdisciplinary project on rule-based search in text databases with nonstandard orthography develops mechanisms to facilitate working with documents containing spelling variants and recognition errors. Even though the quality of optical character recognition has greatly increased in recent years, suboptimal sources like old documents, poor quality texts or texts in historical fonts still severely complicate successful queries. Proper results are the consequence of several intermediate stages of processing: the collection of data (evidences of nonstandard spelling and related standard spelling), the training of specific search modules and, of course, the actual search task. This paper concentrates on automatic support methods that allow for a constant reduction of human intervention. It describes the inherent problems, the process of evidence collection, the underlying methods, their value for linguistic research and how these methods can be implemented in an interface for automatic user support.

1. Spelling variation

While there is a significant amount of historical linguistic material in electronic form on English (OED, Early English Books Online), the equivalent sources for German are just starting to appear. This offers advantages to research but reveals several technical problems. While German texts since the Early New High German period (from 1350) are at least roughly comprehensible to modern speakers, the orthographic conventions of earlier stages of the language were different and far less standardized. The average string edit distance between variants and standard spellings, which can be used as a measure of variance, drops if only slightly from 1.76 (15th century and older) to 1.35 (19th century). The average maximum distance per text decreases from 5.71 edit operations (15th century and older) to 3.43 (19th century). Additionally the total number of spelling variants increases, too. Historical writers also employed specific digraphs like <ů>, <ÿ> or <æ> to represent non-Latin sounds. Such sequences cannot even be reliably displayed in web browsers, not to mention electronic processing. The misinterpretation of characters in optical character recognition

(OCR) is another source of spelling variation. This represents a challenge for electronic searches.

Because the differences between spelling variants and standard spellings bear evidence to differences in orthography, we call a pair consisting of a spelling variant and a standard spelling an *evidence*.

The RSNSR (Rule-based search in text databases with non-standard orthography) project collected 12,758 spelling variants taken from texts dating from 1293 to 1926 and created a database of spelling variants and their related standard spellings. The following findings are based on this database.

2. Detection

Before finding the standard spelling equivalent to a spelling variant, one first has to detect nonstandard spellings in an arbitrary text – in other words, to be able to separate variant and standard spellings. Only then can these spellings be categorized, combined with their related standard spellings and used in training or building a database. As a result, the question arises: Which features are characteristic of spelling variants but not of standard spellings, and vice versa?

It is well known that N-grams are apt to capture letter replacements in context. We assume that spelling variants feature an N-gram distribution that differs significantly from the one of standard spellings. Collecting the bigrams, trigrams and quadrigrams of both spelling variants (Var) and related standard spellings ($\overline{Var}$) in our database, we can examine those differences and decide whether N-grams are an effective means of separation. A measure is required for the relevance of an N-gram in regard to its expressiveness in indicating spelling variation or standard spelling. It should consist of at least two factors: the influence of N-Gram n compared to all N-grams $N = Var \cup (\overline{Var})$ and the strength of n indicating variation or standard spelling, represented by the unconditioned probability $P(n)$. By comparing n to all N we assure a balanced calculation if the cardinalities ($card$) of Var or $\overline{Var}$ differ significantly. Finally, we scale the measure by Pn^2 and get the *discriminants*

$$D(n) = \left| \frac{(card(n \in Var)}{(card(Var)} - \frac{(card(n \in (\overline{Var})}{(card(\overline{Var})} \right| \cdot |P(n) - (1 - P(n))| \cdot P(n)^2; \qquad Var \cap (\overline{Var}) \neq \emptyset$$

$$\overline{D(n)} = \left| \frac{(card(n \in Var)}{(card(Var)} - \frac{(card(n \in (\overline{Var})}{(card(\overline{Var})} \right| \cdot |P(n) - (1 - P(n))| \cdot (1 - P(n))^2$$

We extracted 659 different bigrams, 5,205 trigrams and 14,210 quadrigrams. Since *D(n)* reduces logarithmically, only a comparatively small number of *N*-grams is highly discriminative. Of all 659 bigrams in our database sorted by decreasing *D(n)*, only the first 34 differ by more than 5 percent in their discriminative value from their predecessor. The distinctly most frequent bigram in *Var* with the best discriminatory function is <th> with 1,628 occurrences in *Var* and only 66 in $\overline{Var}$. Since the quadrigrams <thei> and <heil> also occur very frequently, we can assume that <th> originates mainly from the prevalent historical morpheme *-theil-* 'part', found for example in *Mittheilung* 'notification', *Theilnahme* 'participation' or *Vortheil* 'advantage'. Another very frequent historical bigram is <ey>, a representation of the modern diphthong <ei> (584 vs. 0 occurrences). <co>, <ct> and <ci> relate to the standard spelling bigrams <ko>, <kt> and <zi> and demonstrate the variable phonetic representation of the historical grapheme <c> as the voiceless velar plosive [k] and the voiceless alveolar fricative [s]. Both bi- and trigrams reveal the abundance of Latin loanwords in our historical documents. The Latin prefix *con-/kon-* 'with' occurs very frequently, as do the sequences *-ction/-ktion* with the nominalization suffix *-tion*. The bound derivational morpheme *-iren* is also highly distinctive; despite 219 appearances among the spelling variants, there is not a single occurrence in any equivalent standard spelling. Instead *-iert* and *-iere* are typically modern morpheme fragments. Comparing bi-, tri- and quadrigrams we see an increasing correlation between the historical and modern *N*-grams with increasing *N*. Whereas there are only four noticeable relations between the eight most distinct historical and modern bigrams

(1) a. (<co> – <ko>, <ct> – <kt>, <ir> – <ie>, <ci> – <zi>)

which are quite scattered, there are five between the trigrams

(1) b. (<the> – <tei>, <irt> + <ire> – <ier>, <cti> – <kti>, <con> – <kon>)

and seven between quadrigrams

(1) c. (<thei> + <heil> – <teil>, <rthe> – <rtei>, <iren> – <iere>, <erth> – <erte>, <uebe> + <eber> – <über>)

with almost no permutation of order. It is also noteworthy that the historical *N*-grams are more distinctive than the ones derived from standard spellings. The most discriminative historical *N*-grams (4944 occurrences) appear within the standard spellings (346 occurrences) in only 6.99 percent of cases. The most discriminative modern *N*-grams (3591 occurrences), on the other hand, can

bigram

N-gram	*P(n)*	|*n*| in *Var*	|*n*| in $\overline{Var}$	*D(n)*[1]	*N-gram*	*P(n)*	|*n*| in *Var*	|*n*| in $\overline{Var}$	$\overline{D(n)}$
<th>	0.96	1628	66	0.0430	**<kt>**	0.13	76	493	0.0071
<ey>	0.99	584	0	0.0188	**<ko>**	0.18	109	493	0.0049
<co>	0.99	382	0	0.0123	**<ie>**	0.33	705	1431	0.0025
<ct>	0.99	375	0	0.0121	**<ek>**	0.20	73	281	0.0022
<vn>	0.99	304	1	0.0098	**<zi>**	0.21	82	301	0.0022
<ff>	0.85	694	119	0.0091	**<uk>**	0.09	9	91	0.0018
<ir>	0.83	753	159	0.0079	**<ka>**	0.23	86	277	0.0016
<ci>	0.99	224	1	0.0072	**<nk>**	0.22	64	224	0.0015

trigram

N-gram	*P(n)*	|*n*| in *Var*	|*n*| in $\overline{Var}$	*D(n)*	*N-gram*	*P(n)*	|*n*| in *Var*	|*n*| in $\overline{Var}$	$\overline{D(n)}$
<the>	0.95	728	41	0.0088	**<tei>**	0.03	15	495	0.0069
<rth>	0.99	343	2	0.0055	**<ier>**	0.14	126	778	0.0050
<irt>	0.92	320	27	0.0033	**<kti>**	0.02	3	188	0.0029
<ire>	0.93	279	18	0.0032	**<sst>**	0.08	21	246	0.0025
<thu>	0.98	207	3	0.0032	**<übe>**	0.09	25	252	0.0024
<cti>	0.99	184	0	0.0029	**<kon>**	0.09	20	202	0.0019
<con>	0.99	183	0	0.0029	**<ekt>**	0.06	10	154	0.0017
<fft>	0.96	221	9	0.0029	**<bei>**	0.09	28	219	0.0017

Figure 1. Most discriminatory bi-, tri- and quadrigrams in our database

quadrigram

N-gram	*P(n)*	$\|n\|$ in *Var*	$\|n\|$ in $\overline{Var}$	*D(n)*	*N-gram*	*P(n)*	$\|n\|$ in *Var*	$\|n\|$ in $\overline{Var}$	$\overline{D(n)}$
<thei>	0.99	467	4	0.0063	**<teil>**	0.01	4	456	0.0065
<heil>	0.96	468	15	0.0056	**<iert>**	0.06	21	351	0.0039
<rthe>	0.99	224	1	0.0031	**<rtei>**	0.01	0	199	0.0028
<iren>	0.99	219	0	0.0030	**<iere>**	0.09	25	255	0.0023
<erth>	0.99	186	0	0.0025	**<über>**	0.09	22	237	0.0022
<uebe>	0.99	159	0	0.0022	**<tier>**	0.03	5	168	0.0022
<eber>	0.98	160	2	0.0021	**<erte>**	0.11	32	261	0.0021
<auff>	0.98	144	2	0.0019	**<eren>**	0.16	58	306	0.0018

Figure 1. continued

also be found in the spelling variants (1204 occurrences) in 33.55 percent of cases. Therefore, it has to be expected that a standard spelling is more likely to be classified a spelling variant than vice versa if N-grams are used for classification, resulting in a shift.

There are, of course, also multiple N-grams with no discriminative value at all. The 27 most frequent bigrams in our database (for example <en>, <er>, <ch>, <ge>) appear to almost equal extents in both spelling variants and standard spellings.

Considering these findings we can safely assume that spelling variation is by no means a random phenomenon. This is consistent with the statement by Mihm (2007: 195)

> [...] dass die generelle Annahme von Arbitrarität, die ja auch in einem logischen Widerspruch zur Annahme von Konventionalität steht, im Wesentlichen keine Berechtigung besitzt. Vielmehr erwies sich die Mehrzahl der Varianten als regelhaft verteilt [...].

> [that the general assumption of arbitrariness, which stands in logical contradiction to the assumption of conventionality, basically has no justification. On the contrary, the majority of variants [in the sense of variable letters] proved to be distributed with regularity]

If spelling variation is not random, features of spelling variants are not random variables in the sense of frequency probability. Instead, the Bayesian probability, as it is used in spam filters, for example, can be applied to decide whether an unknown spelling is a spelling variant or not. With a Bayesian classifier, it is possible to condition this decision on another feature, in this case the combination of N-grams in a spelling. We are able to calculate the posteriori probability $P(Var|NK_i)$ for the conditioned event "word w is a spelling variant if it contains the N-gram combination NK_i". Even though it is possible to calculate, the total number of N-gram combinations becomes exceedingly large and includes many combinations impossible in natural language. In the same way, a spam filter does not decide whether an email is spam by combining all possible words in it but by calculating the spam probability for each individual word. If we transpose the detection of a spelling variant to single N-grams, we calculate the probability of a word being a spelling variant by determining how likely each of its N-grams is to occur in a spelling variant. As a result we define

- P($NVar$) as the prior probability of the occurrence of N-grams significant for spelling variants
- P(N_i) as the prior probability of "word w contains N-gram N_i".

The a posteriori probability

$$P(NVar|N_i) = \frac{P(N_i|NVar) \cdot P(NVar)}{P(N_i)}$$

allows for the deduction of the conditioned probability of a word being a spelling variant if it contains N_i. In other words, the probability of an N-gram being significant for a spelling variant is based on the relation of the probability of N_i occurring in spelling variants and of N-grams being significant for spelling variants in general to the probability of N_i occurring in any word. According to the law of total probability and the definition of

- $card(N_i Var)$ being the total amount of N_i in all spelling variants,
- $card(N_i \overline{Var})$ being the total amount of N_i in all standard spellings,
- $card(NVar)$ being the total amount of all $N_i Var$ and
- $card(N\overline{Var})$ being the total amount of all $N_i \overline{Var}$,

we rewrite $P(NVar|N_i)$ in the following easily calculable way:

$$P(NVar|N_i) = \frac{\dfrac{card(N_i \overline{Var})}{card(N\overline{Var})} \cdot \dfrac{card(NVar)}{card(NVar) + card(N\overline{Var})}}{\dfrac{card(N_i)}{card(N)}}$$

One of the advantages of a Bayesian classifier is that it not only decides whether a word is a spelling variant or not but also how confident the classifier is that its assumption is correct. For reliable Bayesian classification one has to provide certain values of influence (cf. Graham 2002). The number of *interesting* conditionals defines how many of the conditionals with $P(NVar|N_i)$ farthest away from neutral 0.5 are to be taken into account. It can be set at a surprisingly low value without losing quality, because many spelling variants differ in only one or two N-Grams from their standard equivalent.

To reduce the risk of rare conditionals in the database skewing the results, the definition of a *minimal occurrence* threshold is necessary. If an N-gram is encountered that did not appear in the training material, no probability is available. To handle such conditioners a *preset value* has to be defined. Graham suggests a preset of 0.4 for every unknown word encountered. Shifting the preset value from neutral 0.5 to 0.4 accounts for the reduction of false positives, since it is much better to receive a spam mail than to lose a desirable one. Also, as Graham phrases it, "if you've never seen a word before, it is probably fairly innocent; spam words tend to be all too familiar". It is questionable whether such a shift is advisable when dealing with spelling variants. If one were simply to separate spelling variants and standard spellings, 0.5 would seem to be the best choice. If, however, the results are to be used for the collection of spelling variants for subsequent training, it is much better to lose a variant spelling than to use a standard spelling for training. Also, as we stated above, a standard spelling is more likely to be classified a spelling variant than vice versa, because the N-grams in standard spellings are less distinctive than the ones in spelling variants. Therefore 0.4 is more advisable as a default for unknown N-grams. Conditionals that only appear in Var are set at 0.99, while those solely in $\overline{Var}$ are set at 0.01. The most important values are the upper and lower thresholds for identification, which, in spam filters, are usually set at 0.99 and 0.01. Looking at the distribution of the bi-, tri- and quadrigram probabilities, it is evident that the ability to differentiate between discriminative and indiscriminative conditionals increases with the length of N. While 20.4 percent of bigrams have a probability between 1.0 and 0.95, it is true of 35.5 percent of trigrams and of 46.9 percent of quadrigrams. At the same time, 48.3 percent of bigrams, 29.6 percent of trigrams and 18.1 percent of quadrigrams lie between the probabilities of 0.6 and 0.4.

Once the classifier is trained, arbitrary words can be examined for their probability of being spelling variants. For this purpose, a word is split into its N-grams. For all conditionals that exceed the minimal occurrence $P(NVar|N_i)$ is calculated. If we define

- $N = NVar \cup \overline{NVar}$ the set of all N-grams and
- $NW \subset N$ the set of all N-grams N_i of a word w,

the individual probabilities of the most interesting N-grams can be accumulated to the aggregate probability $P(NVar|NW)$:

$$P(NVar|NW) \approx \frac{\Pi^n_{(i=1)} P(NVar|N_i)}{\Pi^n_{(i=1)} P(NVar|N_i) + \Pi^n_{(i=1)}(1 - P(NVar|N_i))}$$

Of course, we cannot expect to reach the quality of modern spam filters since the transition between standard spellings and spelling variants is fluent. Many N-grams are shared by both alike and therefore have a neutral probability, while spam words are highly discriminative. Additionally, some standard spellings contain historical residuals due to conservatory tendencies in language. Words like *Thunfisch* 'tuna' or *Thron* 'throne' include the distinctly historical grapheme <th> (93.4 percent more frequent in historical texts) and every *Stadt* 'city' contains <dt>, which is typical of the baroque era (74.3 percent more frequent in historical texts between 1550 and 1750).

As was to be expected, quadrigrams separate more decisively than bi- and trigrams. The major proportion of quadrigrams is positioned furthest away from neutrality ($1 > \chi \geq 0.95$; $0.05 \geq \chi > 0$) while most bigrams are centralized around 0.5. This is consistent with the findings stated above and a logical result of N increasing from single letter distribution ($N = 1$) to separate dictionaries for spelling variation and standard spelling (N = max. wordlength).

The classifier was evaluated with a separation task of a mixed set of 4,000 spelling variants from 1293 – 1900 and 4,000 standard spellings (1/3) after being trained on 8,000 spellings (2/3) each. Training and task were repeated ten times and the results averaged. We measured the quality of the classifier according to its

- True positives (TP): spelling variants (SV) correctly classified
- True negatives (TN): standard spelling (StS) correctly classified
- False positives (FP): StS classified SV
- False negatives (FN): SV classified StS
- Unclassified (UCF): unclassified spellings

By adjusting the parameters of the classifier, single values can be slightly raised or lowered. Raising upper and lower thresholds reduces the unclassified spellings but raises true positives, true negatives, false positives and false negatives. If the true positives increase so do the false positives. The quadrigram-based classifier yields the best results. On the other hand, the number of quadrigrams greatly depends on the size of the training set. By adding a dictionary of stan-

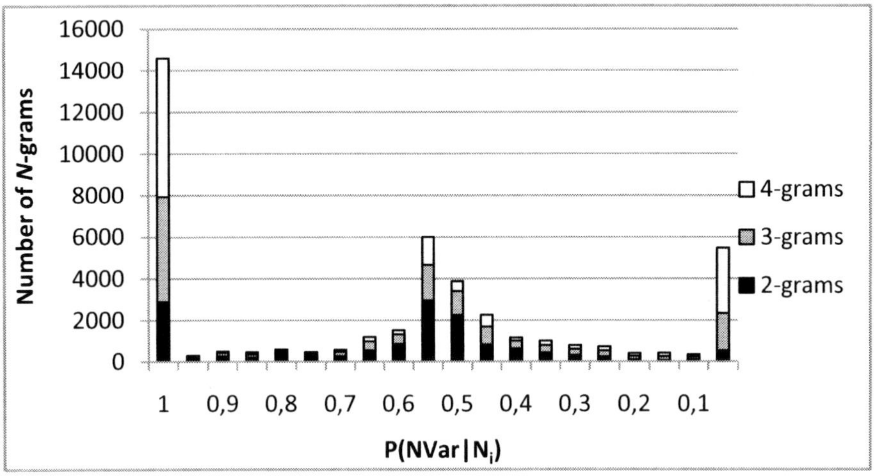

Figure 2. The distribution of *N*-grams in the classification table

dard spellings we expected to further reduce unclassified spellings as well as true negatives, leading to increased true positives and false positives as well. Even though false negatives slightly increase using dictionary and quadrigrams, increased true positives and decreased false positives are much more important.

Using this classifier as a text filter, it is possible to automatically harvest spelling variants in text documents. The low ratio of false positives ensures a reliably clean result set that can be used for further processing.

The classifier was implemented as an interactive filter application in Java. Every spelling whose value exceeds the upper threshold is highlighted in red with the confidence value of the classifier – the distance of *P(NVar|NW)* from 0.5 – represented by the color's saturation. Adjustment of the threshold can be performed in real-time without any noticeable lag. The assigned values can be stored as an annotation layer in the text. Prior to exporting the selected spellings to an SQL- or Berkeley-database or in flat XML manual correction and (de-)selection is possible.

Since the classifier can be easily trained, additional filters can be created and applied to the same text. At the moment our database consists of only 732 training evidences for OCR errors, too few for an acceptable filter. Applied to the separation of Latin and historical German spellings the classifier yields similar results to the ones shown in Table 1.

Table 1. Results of the spelling variant/standard spelling classification task

N	TP in % of spelling variants	TN in % of standard spellings	FP in % of standard spellings	FN in % of spelling variants	UCF in % of all spellings
2	60.80	26.91	04.17	03.88	52.11
3	66.74	52.25	03.19	04.57	36.62
4	70.98	65.33	02.15	05.30	28.12
4+Dict	73.08	78.42	02.06	06.72	19.85
4+Dict²	64.00	80.18	01.13	05.12	24.77

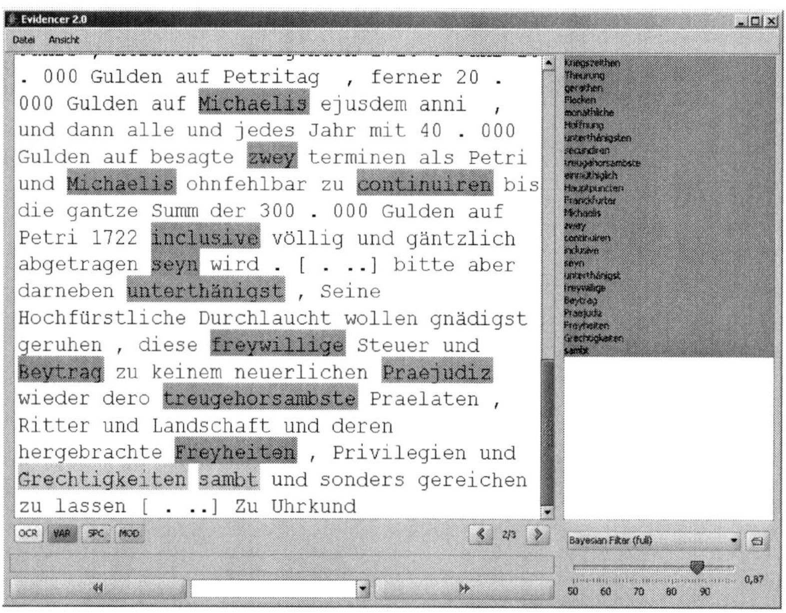

Figure 3. The classification application can filter for historical spellings and optical character recognition errors

3. Temporal classification

Diachronic factors like language fashions or changing norms of the letter inventory or graphematic variation (Mihm 2007, p.196f.) are of indisputable influence on spelling variation[3]. If these factors exhibit certain diachronic characteristics, they can be employed to classify spelling variants and the documents these variants are included in.

As mentioned above, characteristic attributes of New High German are already noticeable in Early New High German text production. Moser identifies a gradual consolidation of writing style since the 8th century due to the small number of Latin letters taken over (Moser 1951: 300). This does not confute the fact that Early New High German is of course far from being as homogeneous as the term might suggest (König 2004: 91f.). As a starting point for the examination of New High German based spelling variation, we therefore chose the – from the perspective of orthography – historically significant milestone of 1250. It is characterized by fundamental differences to earlier Middle High German spelling (Mihm 2007: 232). Early New High German is commonly considered to have originated around 1350, as accepted in numerous related projects (c.f. Lüdeling et.al. 2005, Solms and Wegera 1998). The diachronic periods following are certainly more difficult to separate since several sociopolitical events accumulate and partially overlap: Luther's influences in the first half of the 16th century, the decline of Lower German in the 16th and 17th centuries, the baroque era and the Thirty Years' War, to name only the most important ones. To further subdivide the Early New High German period between 1350 and 1650 without dissecting any significant processes, we follow Mihm who detected a significant drop in the variance of vowel sounds as well as in the inventory of vowel graphemes between 1430 and 1460 (Mihm 2007: 223). The unification of German orthography in 1901 marks the end of the timeframe in our focus. We therefore propose Late Middle High German (1250–1350), Older Early New High German (1350–1450), Later New High German (1450–1650) and New High German (1650–1900) as a diachronic classification of spelling variants.

When working with our historical database, we noticed that the number of spelling variant tokens – as defined by Peirce (1906, p. 4537)[4] – steadily decreased as we approached the present. We manually counted the spelling variants of 54 historical texts between 1293 and 1900 containing 74,781 words, including 13,135 variant tokens. The digital documents were taken randomly from various publicly available sources[5] and mainly involve political, philosophical and religious topics. Given this variety, the homogeneity of the result is surprising. As can be seen in Fig. 4, the number of spelling variant tokens is strictly monotonically non-decreasing from 65 percent in 1300 to ~3 percent

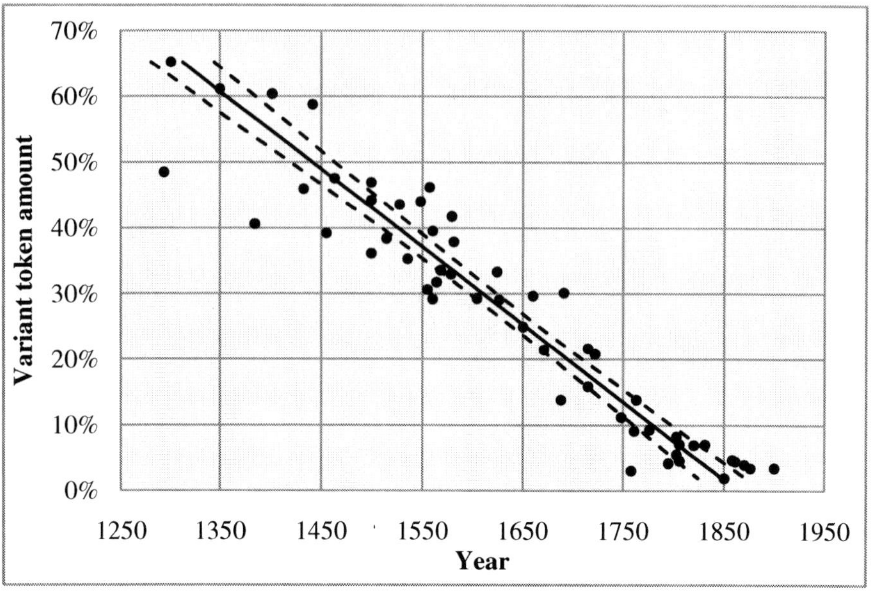

Figure 4. Linear regression and confidence interval of variant token amounts in historical German text documents.

in 1900. The Pearson correlation coefficient with dates $X = (x_1, x_2, \ldots, x_n)$, percentage $Y = (y_1, y_2, \ldots, y_n)$ and the data centroid $(\overline{x}, \overline{y})$ accounts for a very strong decreasing linear relationship of $r \approx -0.95145$. Building a linear regression model minimized to dates allows for the calculation of the estimator $\widehat{x}_i = -847.02+1864.38x_i$, which can be used to predict a document's diachronic classification. Its standard error of estimate $\widehat{\sigma}_{xy} = 49.85$ accounts for ~50 years of error between the data and our estimate. The upper and lower bounds of the 95 percent confidence interval range from ±32.14 years in 1300 to ±13.71 years in 1626 and ±23.50 years in 1850.

To automate the temporal classification of texts, the Bayesian classifier can be employed again. As shown above, given arbitrary German texts it is able to detect spelling variants. In this case, the variants are not exported but their total number in the document is counted. Since the classifier cannot decide the origin of 20–25 percent of all spellings (cf. Table 1), the number of variants found is significantly higher than in manual count. A result of for example 75 percent spelling variants therefore is to be read as 75 percent of the *classified* spellings. The standard error of estimate $\widehat{\sigma}_{xy} = 78.44$ of its linear regression accounts for ~80 years of error between data and estimate. Of course this estimate is of limited reliability but

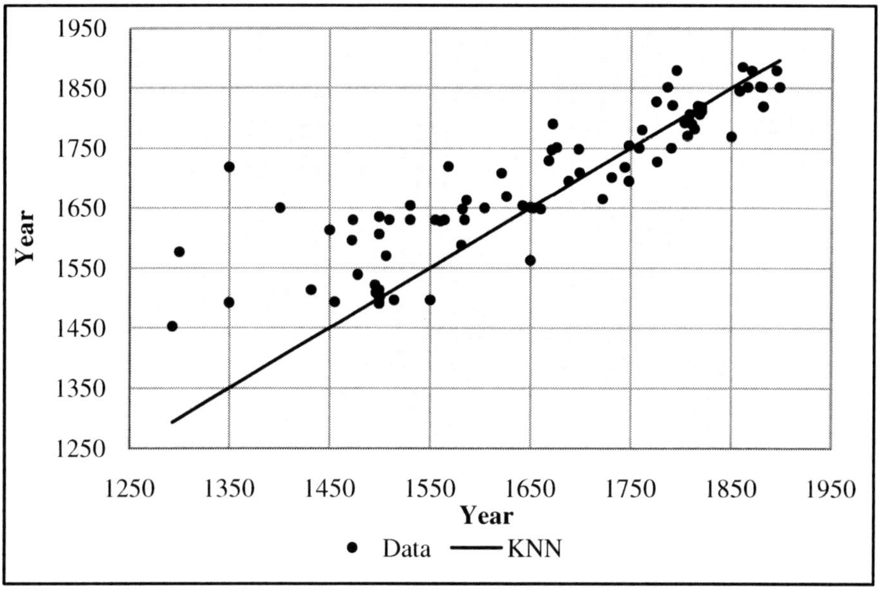

Figure 5. KNN estimation of historical texts

still acceptable for a rough classification. Using more advanced multivariate regression methods like logistic regression will yield better results.

Another approach is the application of the *k*-nearest-neighbor method (KNN), which has been used successfully by Uytvanck (2007) to date and localize Dutch charters of the 13th and 14th centuries on the basis of their orthography. By calculating the document vectors based on the appearance of *N*-grams in full text, the cosine distance is able to measure the distance between training documents and an unknown text. Instead of considering only the document with minimal angle, the *k* nearest documents of the training set are taken into account when estimating the temporal origin of the text being compared. Setting $k = 3$ we were able to minimize the mean error to 64 years. Because of few 14th century documents available to us, classification of texts older than 1450 proves unsatisfying (Fig. 5).

4. Evidence creation

When comparing different spellings of the same word, the question arises: How similar are spellings, and how can their similarity be measured? Is *aufwändig* more similar to *aufwendig* 'elaborate'[6] than *Jngenieur* is to *Ingenieur* 'engineer'? Similarity and difference can both be expressed as a function of distance. However, the distance between words is not fixed. Distance measures can help by calculating the distance or similarity between two words. In contrast to standard measures, like Levenshtein distance, stochastic distance measures are trainable. When assigned a specific training set, such a measure is able to adapt to the letter replacements characteristic of the training data. For example, if we try to find the related standard spelling for the German variant *Saltz*, the Levenshtein algorithm does not differentiate between the correct standard spelling *Salz* 'salt' and *Satz* 'sentence' with respect to the string distance. A measure that takes heed of linguistic knowledge – in this case that <t> can be omitted because <tz> is phonetically identical to <z> – will be able to determine the actual variant from a list of candidates. Dialectrometry commonly makes use of such measures to calculate the distance or similarity between different dialect variants (Heeringa et al 2006: 51). We implemented the learning string edit distance proposed by Ristad and Yianilos (1998). It is based on the expectation-maximization algorithm to build a (locally) optimal set of letter replacements. Using the learning string edit distance, we trained a distance measure for every diachronic category proposed in section 3.

Both methods, Bayesian classification as well as KNN, are able to roughly assign arbitrary historical documents to one of the categories. Using this information, the measure especially trained on data from this category can be automatically selected. This measure is most likely to fit the type of orthography that is prevalent in the document. As was shown in (Pilz et al. 2007), adjusted distance measures lead to better retrieval results. If we use the best fitting measure to calculate the distances between the spelling variants collected (cf. section 2) and a contemporary dictionary, it is possible to create evidences – pairs of spelling variants and standard spellings. Looking at the words that prove to be especially problematic, we notice certain characteristics:

- short spellings variants can hardly be assigned the correct standard spellings (e.g. *vmb* – *um* 'at', *nit* – *nicht* 'not', *eer* – *er* 'he'). Even a single letter replacement changes a high percentage of the word's recognizability
- some words consist of very frequent graphemes, therefore increasing the space of potential matches in standard spelling (for example *hendlen* – *handeln* 'to act' is instead assigned to *enden* 'to end' or *hehlen* 'to trade (with stolen goods)')
- some spelling variants are highly variable (e.g. *eehfig* – *ewig* 'eternal')

Also, if a distance measure is sensitive to word length, differences in length between the standard and the variant spelling can yield diverse results. In the

17th and 18th centuries, for example, extensive use was made of derivational suffixes. Whereas nowadays the adverb *streng* 'strictly' is used, in 1650 Hans Michael Moscherosch used *strängiglich* instead. Normalization by length appears to be a solution to differences in word length, but, as Heeringa et al. (2006) state, it only perverts the measures. Normalization optimizes for minimum normalized length of the replacement path rather than minimum replacement costs (Heeringa et al 2006: 54).

Still, we achieve a precision@1 – the precision that the relevant standard spelling is the best match according to the distance measure – of 58.6 to 60.5 percent. We attached our distance measures to the application mentioned above.

5. Conclusion

The capabilities of the system we have developed are promising. We are able to automatically extract up to almost 3/4 of the spelling variants of an arbitrary text document. The number of digitized documents available increases by the day and already exceeds an amount that can be manually processed. With automatic approaches, these documents can still be dealt with, reducing the amount of human attention required. It therefore is of only minor importance that 1/4 of spelling variants is missed. Due to the low ratio of false positives, the set of collected spellings is clean enough to be used for subsequent processes, like the training of specific distance measures or text classification. In order to increase the quality of evidence creation, we hope to acquire a larger contemporary dictionary and to process compounds.

The automatic classification methods require additional research. The Bayesian classifier, KNN and other techniques used in authorship attribution, like entropy coding, will be combined to increase their reliability. The results of differentially trained Bayesian classifiers in particular, such as classifiers for historical, regional or foreign spellings and OCR errors, have to be combined and calculated crosswise. Sections in Latin are common in older German documents and are often confused with spelling variants. Sequential processing of these cohesive segments is necessary.

Acknowledgements. We would like to thank the Deutsche Forschungsgemeinschaft for supporting this research.

Notes

1. Normalized by the highest values *D(n) = 1330 [bigram], 550 [trigram], 447 [quadrigram]*
2. This classifier with different parameters using quadrigrams and a dictionary is given as an example
3. For another detailed examination of standardization factors and their potencies please consult (Vandenbussche 2007, p. 28).
4. Peirce's definition:
   A Single event which happens once and whose identity is limited to that one happening or a Single object or thing which is in some single place at any one instant of time, such event or thing being significant only as occurring just when and where it does, such as this or that word on a single line of a single page of a single copy of a book, I will venture to call a Token. (...) I propose to call such a Token of a Type an *Instance* of the Type.
5. Bibliotheca Augustana, documentArchiv.de, Hessisches Staatsarchiv Darmstadt
6. Both *aufwändig* and *aufwendig* are standard spellings in modern German.

References

Bibliotheca Augustana
2008 www.hs-augsburg.de/~harsch/augustana.html (online, visited: 26.05.08)

Graham, Paul
2002 A Plan for Spam. paulgraham.com/spam.html (online, visited: 26.05.08)

Digitales Archiv Hessen-Darmstadt
2008 www.digada.de (online, visited: 26.05.08)

documentArchiv.de
2008 www.documentarchiv.de (online, visited: 26.05.08)

Heeringa. Wilbert, Peter Kleiweg, Charlotte Gooskens and John Nerbonne
2006 Evaluation of String Distance Algorithms for Dialectology. In: John Nerbonne and Erhard Hinrichs (eds.), *Linguistic Distances*, 5162. (Workshop at the joint conference of ICCL & ACL) Sydney

König, Werner
2004 *dtv-Atlas Deutsche Sprache*. München: 14th ed. Deutscher Taschenbuch Verlag

Lüdeling, Anke, Thorwald Poschenrieder and Lukas Faulstich
2005 DeutschDiachronDigital – Ein diachrones Korpus des Deutschen. Georg Braungart, Peter Gendolla and Fotis Jannidis (eds.). *Jahrbuch für Computerphilologie*, 6: 19–36, Darmstadt: Mentis

Mihm, Arend
2007 *Sprachwandel im Spiegel der Schriftlichkeit: Studien zum Zeugniswert der historischen Schreibsprachen des 11. Bis 17. Jahrhunderts*. Michael Elmentaler (ed.), Frankfurt a.M.: Lang

Moser, Virgil
1951 *Frühneuhochdeutsche Grammatik*. Lautlehre, Vol 3. Heidelberg: Winter

Peirce, Charles S.
1906 Prolegomena to an Apology for Pragmaticism. *Collected Papers of Charles Sanders Peirce*, 8 volumes. Harvard University Press in 1931–1958

Pilz, Thomas, Axel Philipsenburg and Wolfram Luther
2007 Visualizing the Evaluation of Distance Measures. *Proceedings of the Ninth Meeting of the ACL Special Interest Group in Computational Morphology and Phonology*, 8492, Prague, CZ

Ristad, Eric Sven and Peter N. Yianilos
1998 Learning String Edit Distance. *IEEE Transactions on Pattern Recognition and Machine Intelligence*, 20 (5): 522532. San Francisco

Solms, Hans-Joaching and Klaus-Peter Wegera
1998 Das Bonner Frühneuhochdeutschkorpus. Rückblick und Perspektiven. In: Rolf Bergmann (ed.). *Probleme der Textauswahl für einen elektronischen Thesaurus*. Beiträge zum ersten Göttinger Arbeitsgespräch zur historischen deutschen Wortforschung am 1. und 2. November 1996, 2239. Stuttgart: Hirzel

Urkundenbuch der Stadt Leipzig
2008 Codex Diplomaticus Saxoniae Regiae. Vol.1. isgv.serveftp.org/codex (online, visited: 26.05.08)

Uytvanck van, Dieter
2007 Orthography-based dating and localisation of Middle Dutch charters. Master thesis. Radboud University Nijmegen

Wikisource
2008 de.wikisource.org (online, visited: 26.05.08)

Scaling issues in the measurement of linguistic acceptability

Thomas Weskott and Gisbert Fanselow

Back in 1981, Milton Lodge, a political scientist, published a book which gave researchers from the social sciences a crash course in using the method of magnitude estimation (ME), which he claimed to yield ratio scale type data, and which had, up to that point, been mostly used in psychophysics. Lodge was confident that this method would vastly improve the measurement of attitudes and opinions which was then dominated by the method of Likert-scale type questionnaires (asking participants to give judgments on an n-point scale), which produced only data of nominal or ordinal scale type. In his book, Lodge issued a warning against premature adaptations of the ME method, but also against premature rejection of its usage:

> "If people can make only nominal or ordinal judgments on a dimension, then overspecifying the data as having interval or ratio properties will misrepresent the relations truly implied by their judgments. If, on the other hand, people are capable of making ratio judgments about the intensity of some social attributes, but only interval or ordinal judgments are recorded, the underspecificity will result in the loss of both information and proper access to powerful analytical tools." (Lodge 1981:30)

If we substitute "the intensity of some social attributes" in the quote above with "linguistic acceptability", we get a statement of the set of problems this paper deals with. Given that there exist – at least – three different types of acceptability judgment measures, binary, n-point, and magnitude estimation, we may ask ourselves whether there are differences in the usefulness of these measures for the testing of linguistic hypotheses, and whether we run danger of overspecification or loss of information when we apply the ME method, or fail to apply it. In part, this paper deals with problematic aspects of the ME method also touched upon by Sam Featherston's contribution to this volume (Featherston 2009).[1] Featherston discusses problems of the ME method in more detail than we do here. In this paper, we will restrict ourselves to the comparison of the three measures mentioned above with respect to the naturalness of the task and the informativity of the measure for linguistic hypotheses. We will provide a discussion of the measurement theoretic properties of these measures and the experimental tasks in which they are employed. This will at times be a somewhat tedious exercise, but we are confident that linguists with an interest in validation of their empirical methods will bear with us. Our main emphasis will be on the notion of *informativity* of a measurement scale for a given empirical hypothesis. Before turning to a measurement theoretic discussion of this notion, we will first present the three different types of measures informally and consider the naturalness as well as the cognitive requirements of the tasks that employ these measures. The upshot of this comparison will be that, contrary to what is usually assumed, the three measures do not differ in informativity, whereas the naturalness and cognitive requirements of the tasks do differ to a considerable degree. Instead of giving a recommendation for one type of measure, we will argue for a careful consideration of the measurement-theoretic and task-related properties of different types of judgments from case to case.

In the next section, we will lay out the methodological background and go through the task demands of the three types of measures successively. Section 3 deals with the alleged difference in informativity of different measurement scales and discusses the claim that data from binary and n-point judgment tasks are less informative with respect to linguistic hypotheses than data from the ME task Section 4 presents experimental evidence for the claim that the three measures do not differ with respect to informativity. Finally, section 5 discusses these findings and concludes the paper with an outlook on the implications for the empirical investigation of linguistic hypotheses.

Task demands and naturalness

In order to be able to compare the three type of measures, we must first make sure that everything else in the experimental situations we want to compare is equal, or at least close to equal. Thus, for all three types of measures to be discussed below, we take as the common basis the following type of empirical research question: we want to investigate an empirical hypothesis concerning some disjunct linguistic properties *A* and *B*. The null hypothesis is that the judgments of stimuli instantiating *A* are not different from the judgments of stimuli instantiating *B*. This is the hypothesis we want to falsify. That is, our claim is that the judgments *do* differ depending on whether the stimulus instantiates *A* or *B*. To test this, we present participants with linguistic stimuli and ask them to respond with a judgement which expresses their respective assessment of the acceptability of that stimulus. Instead of asking for acceptability, the judgment task may also be formulated such that the judgment pertains to the grammaticality, or the syntactic well-formednes of the stimulus (depending on what *A* and *B* are). For all three types of experimental task, we assume in what follows that the usual standards of experimental design are adhered to (Cowart 1996: 44–53), including, among other things: that there are clearly defined experimental conditions (avoiding known confounds as much as possible); that each participant is confronted with at least four items (i.e. lexical variants) of each experimental condition; and that a sufficient number of participants takes part in the experiment to allow for robust averaging over both subjects and experimental items. In our own experiments, we employ latin squares to instantiate repeated measures designs. This procedure allows the computation of means for each participant in each condition (averaging over different items), and to compute means for each item (averaging over different participants).

A binary judgment task employs two alternative responses: a *yes* and a *no* answer. Dependening on the question the experiment pursues, these alternative answers can be labelled as "unacceptable"/"acceptable", "ungrammatical"/"grammatical", or as "I would not say something like that"/"I might say something like that".

In a n-point judgment experiment, the participant is presented a scale with *n* points (usually five or seven), the extremes of which are labelled with the labels given above for the binary task. In some cases, the middle point is also labelled (with e.g. "I do not know").

In a ME experiment, the participant is confronted with two stimuli: the so-called *modulus*, which is a stimulus that serves as a reference relative to which all the other stimuli have to be judged, and the stimulus proper. The task of the participant, after having assigned a numerical value (from the set of positive rational numbers) to the modulus at the outset of the experiment, is to assign a numerical value to the stimulus *relative to* the value she has assigned to the modulus. For example, if the modulus is a sentence of medium acceptability and was assigned the value "20", and the stimulus proper is of low acceptability, the participant may choose to assess the acceptability of the stimulus by assigning it the value "5". (Note that for the purposes of statistical analysis, the values assigned to a specific stimulus by different participants are "normalized" by dividing each individual participant's judgment value by the value assigned to the modulus by that participant).

In all three kinds of experiment, the specific assignment of a value to the stimulus is partly determined by the instruction the participant is given at the beginning of the experiment. In the binary task, the instruction is usually given by way of an example: a perfectly acceptable sentence is presented as a sample stimulus, and the instruction states that, if the participant considers this stimulus to be acceptable, then she should assign it the value "acceptable", whereas an unacceptable sample stimulus should be assigned the "unacceptable" value. In the n-point task, the instruction will essentially be the same as in the binary task, but it will possibly also contain a sample stimulus of medium acceptability, together with an assignment of the medium value of the n-point scale to this sentence. In addition, the instruction in the n-point task usually asks the participant to use the full range of the scale in her judgments. In the ME task, participants are first familiarized with the magnitude estimation technique by going through a training period in which they have to give numerical estimates of line lengths. After that, they are given the instructions how to estimate the acceptability of linguistic stimuli; the instructions usually contain a statement of the following form: if you have assigned the modulus (usually a medium acceptable sentence) the value "20", and you consider the stimulus sentence to be twice as bad as the modulus, then you should assign the stimulus sentence the value "10".

A conspicuous difference between the tasks is of course that the first two kinds of judgments force the participant to use only the predetermined values, whereas the ME task grants the participants more freedom: any numerical value which fulfils the perceived relation between the modulus and the stimulus can be used to assess the acceptability of the latter. We will return to this point below.

Let us now look at the task the participant has to perform. In the binary task, the participant has to decide for every item in every condition whether the particular stimulus is acceptable or not, and assign the respective value. In performing this task, the participant has to confront her grammatical knowledge with a yes/no-question: is this sentence acceptable, or is it unacceptable? Note that although this task assumes that each individual decision is an absolute one (i.e., it is made without recourse to any other decisions pertaining to other stimuli), in practice it is not, since in the course of an experiment the individual decisions cannot but influence each other. That is, the judgment is not an absolute one, because each stimulus is couched in a series of other stimuli, and a judgment decision made with respect to one item might influence a decision to be made with respect to another item.[2] But neither is the judgment an explicitly relative one, because the instruction does not demand to judge stimuli relative to another.

In the n-point task, the judgments are given numerically and hence the degree of freedom in assigning a value to a stimulus is higher. But this also complicates the cognitive task the participant has to perform in order to come to a decision: the set of answers to the question posed to her grammatical knowledge is not partitioned in two (as in the binary task), but instead there are *n* partitions of the set, and they are ordered with respect to acceptability. That is, the question posed to grammatical knowledge ("How acceptable is this given *n* ranks of acceptability?") is probably much less natural than the plain yes/no-question. It may help the participant that the instruction has provided examples of full acceptability and plain unacceptability, that is, the extremes of the scale, plus possibly a medial point on the scale. In addition, the participant will (if only implicitly) built up an ordering of the stimuli by herself in the course of the experiment. This, of course, implies that the judgment decisions in the case of the n-point task are prone to influences from the surrounding experimental items much more than in the case of the binary task. In other words, the question the participant poses to her grammatical knowledge in judging the acceptability of a stimulus *x* will be relational in nature: "Given that I have assigned stimulus *y* the acceptability rank *i*, and given the acceptability relation between *x* and *y*, which rank *j* do I have to assume for stimulus *x*?". "Acceptability relation between *x* and *y*" can mean two things here: either a mere qualitative difference (same/different), or a qualitative one which refers to the ranks of the n-point scale: while *y* belongs to acceptability class (= rank) *i*, *x* belongs to acceptability class *j*. According to this latter interpretation, a higher numerical value thus can be interpreted as a higher rank in perceived acceptability. And the ordering of the ranks will even permit a distance interpretation: if the (arithmetic) difference between ranks *j* and *i* assigned to stimuli *x* and *y* is smaller than the rank difference between *i* and *k* assigned to *x* and *z*, then we can take the difference in acceptability between *x* and *y* to be judged as smaller than the one between *x* and *z*. This interpretation makes explicit recourse to the relational nature of the judgments, although the instruction in an n-point judgment task is not explicitly stated in relational terms. The relational nature of the task brings about a further problem: the number of stimuli with respect to which *x* is judged increases over the course of the experiment, and thus complicates the judgment decision even more. Moreover, the participant may be forced to squeeze two or more stimuli into one rank set, although she would want to differentiate between these items further.

It is especially this last problem that the method of ME has been claimed to have a solution for. Since the participant is free to assign the stimulus any numerical value she wants as long as it represents the relative acceptability with respect to the modulus value, the participant can circumvent the problem of squeezing the judgments for two stimuli into the same acceptability class by simply assigning them (if only minimally) differing values. In the ME task, the question posed to the participant's grammatical knowledge hence comes down to the following: "Given the assignment of value *i* to the modulus α, and the assignment of value *j/a* to the stimulus *y*, and the acceptability relation between *x* and *y*, what is the value *k/a* to be assigned to *x*?". It is important to note that it is even less clear what is meant by "acceptability relation between *x* and *y*" here than in the case of the n-point task discussed above. As far as we can see, it could mean at least four different things. Firstly, it could be spelled out as a mere difference in acceptability (i.e. a binary same/different-decision). In this case, the numerical value assigned to *x* should only be different from that assigned to *y*, no matter whether smaller or larger. In fact, the two values would not even have to be numerical; any unique label would do. The second possibility is that the relation between the two stimuli would be cast as a difference in terms of belongingness to different classes of acceptability (i.e., something like the ranks in the n-point task). As noted above, the numerical value assigned to *x* should then express the rank of *x* relative to the rank of *y*: a higher numerical value could then for example be interpreted as a higher rank in acceptability. In addition, rank differences might be interpreted as a distance metric for acceptability. On the third possible interpretation, the "acceptability relation" could be understood as a difference in terms of absolute distance, which would involve comparing intervals rather than ranks: the distance in acceptability of *x* to the modulus α is smaller/larger than the distance in acceptability of *y* to α. In this case, a higher numerical value could be interpreted as indicating a larger or smaller distance in perceived acceptability. Note that the distance metric imposed on acceptability by this interpretation is much more fine-grained than the one based on ranks. Whereas the latter is necessarily limited to the number of ranks, the former can differentiate between as many distances as there are intervals. And finally, according to the fourth possibility, the "acceptability relation" would be translated into metric information proper. That is, the numerical values in the ME task would be taken at face value and be interpreted as not only indicating the distance in acceptability qualitatively (i.e., a smaller or larger distance), but also the *size* of the distance in acceptability. In this case, if the numerical value *i/a* assigned to *x* is two times larger than the numerical value *j/a* assigned to *y*, then this should be interpreted as indicating that *x* was judged to be twice as acceptable as *y*. It is exactly this fourth interpretation of the task that is suggested to the participant by the instruction.

If we now try to compare the naturalness of the three tasks and their respective interpretations, we have to keep in mind that, as yet, we have no clear conception of how the judgment process works, and which of the many dimensions of a linguistic stimulus affect it. That is, we do not know which mental representations enter into the computation of the judgment decision, nor do we know how this computation proceeds in time, and by which factors it can be affected. This would be the subject of psychological theory of linguistic judgment that is still missing. For want of such a theory, we have above made use of the somewhat awkward phrase "pose a question to one's grammatical knowledge". Although it is not clear what this exactly means in procedural terms, it is certainly the case that a subprocess which fits this metaphorical description is involved in the multi-dimensional judgment process. With this caveat in mind, let us look at the different tasks with regard to their naturalness.

The binary task may be rightly called the most natural one, because it comes closest to our natural way of metalinguistic judgment in everyday situations: the yes/no-difference corresponds to our categorical perception of linguistic expressions as "good", or, more often, as "bad" (or, rather, as belonging to the "you can't talk like that"-class). Furthermore, the binary measure is the most direct one, since it does not involve any explicit relational reasoning: the judgment of a stimulus *x* as being unacceptable does not necessarily imply a comparison of *x* with another stimulus *y*. But we repeat here that even in the case of binary judgments, there may be relational influences from preceding decisions.

Compared to the binary task, the n-point task appears to be much less natural. The number of possible answers is much larger: we can imagine that the number of binary judgments is multiplied by *n* (is *x* a "1" or a "2"? a "2" or "3", and so on). It seems obvious that this makes the judgment process much less direct and, as we have seen above, opens the door to the influences of relational reasoning: e.g., if *y* is a "3", then *x* is at least a "4". We should also ask ourselves what sense participants can make of such relational judgments by trying to step into their shoes: what sense does it make to say that a sentence *x* is, say, three ranks higher in acceptability than sentence *y*? Or, if we interpret n-point data on a interval scale, what do we mean by saying that the acceptability difference between sentence *x* and sentence *y* is larger than the one between sentences *u* and *v*? What is the *denotation* of the intervals we compare, [*x,y*] and [*u,v*]? There are domains (such as, for example, pitch in music) where the notion of an interval is well-defined, and even musical laypersons can be trained easily to recognize different intervals (for instance a fifth or a major third) quite reliably. But no such interpretation for the notion of an interval is at hand if we talk about acceptability differences. We might attribute this to the lack of a physical correlate of the stimulus which is continuous and can be divided up into what (Poulton 1989) calls "familiar units".

Still, we think that one can argue in favor of the n-point task by noting two things: first, it seems not to be odd to say that the difference in acceptability between sentences *x* and *y* is smaller or larger than the one between sentences *u* and *v*. Everyone who has a naïve understanding of the notion of acceptability can understand this statement. If not, we can explain it to him or her by rephrasing it by something like the following: "Look, *x* sounds OK, but *y* sounds bad, but while *u* also sounds OK, *v* sounds even worse compared to *u* than *y* compared to *x*." The second point concerns the fact that an increasing number of people is getting used to assess their attitudes towards other people, products, commercials etc. by making use of n-point scales in marketing research surveys. So the task of expressing one's attitude towards the acceptability of a linguistic expression by means of such a scale, although somewhat indirect and prone to influences of other judgments, is not quite as unnatural for many participants as it may seem at first blush.

Turning to the ME task, it strikes us as obvious that it is not a very natural task to assign numerical values to the perceived acceptability of a stimulus sentence. In fact, this point is even conceded by proponents of this method more or less explicitly, as for instance (Cowart 1996), who states – rather cautiously – that "[. . .] not all participants are equally comfortable with numbers [. . .]"(Cowart 1996: 74). This will become even more clear if we bring to mind what kind of mental operation the task demands from the participant. As stated in the instruction, the participant is asked to calculate a ratio from the acceptability values assigned to the modulus and to the stimulus. Recall that the instruction states that something like "If you have judged sentence *x* with a '10' and perceive sentence *y* to be twice as good as sentence *x*, you should judge *y* with a '20'." Multiplication is an operation that is defined for ratio scale data only. Thus, the participant is explicitly advised to calculate ratios, i.e. to treat perceived acceptabilities as ratios of numbers from the set of positive rational numbers. Now, as we have remarked above in connection with the notion of an interval as a denotation of a perceived difference, it is hard to see what sense such a notion makes when applied to the domain of linguistic acceptability – there simply is no physical correlate of the stimulus that would lend itself to an interpretation in terms of relative differences expressed or interpreted as intervals. This point becomes even more problematic if we try to express the differences by ratios, i.e. as quantitative differences. What could be meant by a statement like "Sentence *x* is twice as acceptable as sentence *y*"? It strikes us as rather astonishing that participants in ME experiments apparently are willing to make some (if any) sense of this, and exhibit a judgment behavior that is consistent with an interpretation of the acceptability differences as intervals. This can partly be attributed to the training phase preceding the acceptability judgment task in ME experiments, where participants have to estimate line lengths to familiarize with the task. In the domain of physical length, the notion of an interval is well-defined, as is the notion of a ratio of lengths. The judgment of linguistic stimuli (the estimation of acceptability) is then performed by analogy to the line length estimation task. In a similar vein, the apparent consistency of ME judgments of acceptability across modalities as shown by the cross-modality matching task (Bard, Robertson, and Sorace 1996: 54–60) is hard to explain given the equivocality of the notion of a ratio of acceptability. Nevertheless, participants show a judgment behavior that is consistent across modalities (e.g., numbers and line lengths as estimates of acceptability). As the authors themselves put it rather cautiously:

> "Whatever subjects do when magnitude-estimating linguistic acceptability, and however odd they find the whole process at first, they clearly have this ability in their psychological repertoire, just as they have the ability to give proportionate judgments of brightness or prestige." (Bard, Robertson, and Sorace 1996: 60).

To sum up: the three methods we discussed clearly differ in the naturalness of the judgment task they employ. While the task to give a binary judgment clearly appears to be the most natural one, the task in the n-point judgment is somewhat less natural, although it can be made sense of even if the data are interpreted on an interval level. The naturalness of the task in the ME judgment is reduced by the problem of complete obscurity of the notion of a ratio of acceptability – and recall that the instruction given to the participants in this task presupposes an interpretation of this notion. Furthermore, as even its proponents admit, the oddity of the ME task necessitates a training phase which allows to familiarize the participant with the estimation of acceptability. Note that no such training is necessary for the two other methods.

It should be noted, however, that the unnaturalness of the ME task is not per se an argument against the results an ME experiment produces: first, the results show a consistent pattern across participants, items and even modalities. And it can be adduced in favor of the task that it allows participants more freedom in the assignment of values to perceived acceptabilities. Furthermore, there are many tasks in psycholinguistic experiments that demand processing of linguistic stimuli in a highly unnatural environment (as, e.g., the naming of depicted objects with a simultaneous presentation of distractors over headphones in the picture-word interference task in language production; cf. Levelt 1989, Hantsch, 2003).

We conclude this section by stating that there are clear differences in the naturalness and the cognitive requirements of the tasks which the three measures involve. Whether these differences should be regarded as relevant in the decision which measure to employ in a given acceptability study hinges on the measures being equal with respect to informativity. We will turn to this problem in the next section.

Informativity

It has been claimed by proponents of the ME method that data gained from a binary and n-point judgment task are less informative than those gained from the ME judgment task. This is evident in the quote from (Lodge 1981) cited above, as well as in the following one from (Bard, Robertson, and Sorace 1996):

> "(...) these scales (ordinal, TW&GF) are too low in the series either to capture the information that could be made available or to serve the current needs of linguistic theories." (Bard, Robertson, and Sorace 1996:40).

The claim put forward by these authors simply is that data from a scale type lower than that of ME, which is of ratio type, lose information in comparison to ME type data. This claim deserves closer scrutiny.

In order to compare the three types of measures with respect to informativity, let us first look at the possible outcomes of a series of hypothetical experiments employing the three types of measures.

The results of experiments with a repeated measures design will be condition means of binary judgments (ranging from 0 to 1), or condition means of n-point judgments (ranging from 1 to *n*), or condition means of ME judgments (with no predefined range). Given our empirical hypothesis, we will want to make sure that the means for the conditions which instantiate property *A* and the ones that instantiate property *B* are different, and that this difference is statistically reliable; that is, that the error probability α that the difference we have found in our experimental sample is not present in the population from which the sample was drawn is equal to or smaller than 5 %. Let us further assume that our empirical hypothesis states that the condition instantiating property *A* is fully acceptable, while the condition instantiating *B* is marginal, or mildly unacceptable. What does our hypothesis mean with regard to our three different measures?

For the binary judgments, the hypothesis states that the means of binary judgments for condition *A* is higher than the condition means for *B* (both when aggregating over participants and items). In order for this to be true, the number of participants rejecting an item as unacceptable should be smaller in the *A* condition than in the *B* condition. That is, our hypothesis is now couched in terms of a difference in frequencies of rejections depending on condition.

Turning to the n-point judgments, the hypothesis states that the mean value assigned to condition *A* should be higher than the mean value assigned to condition *B*. In order for this to be the case, the values assigned to condition *A* items should on average stem from the upper end of the n-point scale rather than from the lower end, while the reverse should be true for condition *B* cases. Our hypothesis is now formulated in terms of a difference in mean numerical values depending on condition.

And similarly for the ME judgments: in this case, the hypothesis also states that the mean numerical values should be different for the two conditions, the mean of the values assigned to the stimuli of condition *A* being higher than the mean of the values assigned to condition *B* stimuli.

An important difference between the three types of measures lies in the difference in variability of individual judgment data points. Trivially, binary judgments have only two possible outcomes – each individual data point can take on only one of two possible values ("0" and "1"). In contrast, n-point judgments exhibit a larger degree of variability: each individual judgment may take on one of n different values. For ME judgments, the degree of individual variability is even larger, since there is no restriction on the possible values used to express the acceptability judgment. While this property of ME data is taken to be an advantage from the perspective of the participant in a judgment experiment (and rightly so, as discussed above), it is far from clear what this larger degree of variability means with respect to the informativity of the condition means that enter into the inferential statistics, i.e. the statistical evaluation of the empirical hypothesis vs. the null hypothesis. From the perspective of inferential statistics, the only point that matters is whether the data help us to reject the null hypothesis, and whether they do so with a sufficient degree of reliability. While in the inferential statistics of, for example, an analysis of variance (ANOVA), the p-value informs us about the probability that we have falsely rejected the null hypothesis, the p-value tells us nothing about the variance that underlies the pattern we find in the data. In our example above, we may find that for all three measures, there is a statistically significant difference between the condition means for condition A vs. the condition means for condition B, and hence that we can reject the null hypothesis that there is no difference between the two conditions with an error probability lower than five percent. But given the different degrees of variability in the individual judgments discussed above, this is not informative with respect to possible differences about how this result of the statistical analysis has come about. We may want to know how much of the actual variance in the data can be accounted for by our experimental factor (A vs. B), as opposed to mere random variance or the influence of some other factor which we did not control in our experiment. In the ANOVA procedure, there is a measure for this proportion of variance accounted for, called partial eta-squared (partial η^2; s. Cowart 1996: 123–125). It can take on values between 0 and 1 – a partial η^2 of 0 means that none of the variance in the data set can be attributed to the experimental factor (a rather undesirable outcome of an experiment), while a partial η^2 of 1 would mean that all the variance in the data set is produced by the factor we are investigating (which is rarely the case in the social sciences). A partial η^2 of, say, .60 means that 60% of the variance in the sample can be traced back to the experimental factor, while 40% of variance must be attributed to some other factor, be it random, or some other variable. If we have no hint at what might be responsible for the additional variance, we have to consider this variance as spurious. Partial η^2, which is sometimes also called "estimate of effect size", is exactly the measure that connects the two issues raised above: the issue of differences in informativity of a given measure, and the issue of differences in variability in a data set. In order to assess a difference in informativity between two measures of linguistic acceptability, we will have to compare the partial η^2-values obtained in the two respective analyses of the two data sets.

For illustration, consider the following example: if we investigate a two-level linguistic factor with two measures m_1 and m_2 under the empirical hypothesis that the mean judgments for the stimuli from the two levels of the factor (call them A and B) differ, then we have to compute the partial η^2-value of the experimental factor for each of the two measures to determine to which proportion the variance in the two samples can be explained by the difference between A vs. B. If the two measures differ in informativity such that m_2 is less informative than m_1, we expect the partial η^2 in the analysis of the data obtained with m_2 to be lower than the partial η^2 of the analysis of the sample obtained with m_1. The difference in informativity between the two measures can thus be determined by assessing the amount of spurious variance, that is, variance which cannot be attributed to the experimental factors we have employed and which, thus, is not relevant to our testing of the empirical hypothesis.

Experimental evidence

In the series of experiments we will report below, we performed such an analysis of the informativity of three different measures of linguistic acceptability: binary judgments, judgments on a 7-point scale, and ME judgments. To keep the amount of experimental detail to a minimum, we will report only the results of the comparison of the partial η^2-values and refer the interested reader to (Weskott and Fanselow, to appear) for a detailed description of the experiments.

All participants in the experiments to be reported were native speakers of German from the Berlin-Brandenburg area and were naïve with respect to the experimental factors investigated. The experiments each consisted of a pairing of two judgment tasks for the same set of participants and the same set of materials. One set of participants (N = 48) performed a binary judgment task in one experimental session, and was then asked to do a 7-point judgment task on the same set of materials two weeks later. The second set of participants (N = 48) also performed a binary judgment task on one occasion, and was then asked to rate the same stimuli with the ME method in a second session two weeks later. To control for possible ordering effects, we split each of these two participants sets in half. One half had to perform the binary task first, and then the other task. The other half had the reverse order of task assignment.

The materials we base our analysis on were sentences which served as benchmark sentences in our experiments. These stimuli are included in all our experiments and serve as fixed points in between which the judgment values of the other experimental sentences can locate. In order to fulfill this role, the benchmark sentences have to occupy the extreme points of the acceptability continuum. The benchmark sentences in our experiments came in four conditions (see sample items given below): fully acceptable (1), syntactically defective (2), semantically defective (3), and both syntactically and semantically defective (4).

(1) *Das Auto wurde repariert.*
The car was repaired.
'The car was repaired.'

(2) *Die Suppe wurde gegen versalzen.*
The soup was against oversalted.
'The soup was against spoiled.'

(3) *Der Zug wurde gekaut.*
The train was chewed.
'The train was chewed.'

(4) *Das Eis wurde seit entzündet.*
The ice was since inflamed.
'The ice was since inflamed.'

Each of these conditions was realized in six different lexical variants, yielding an overall of 24 experimental items. Each participant saw the full set of items, which were interspersed between 96 other experimental sentences coming from a wide range of different constructions and instantiating different degrees of acceptability. According to our hypothesis, the fully acceptable sentences of the type exemplified in (1) should get the best acceptability rating; stimuli of type (2) should be judged to be considerably less acceptable than those in (1), whereas those of type (3), while being also judged as not acceptable, should still be judged as being slightly better than the ones in (2). The sentences of type (4), exhibiting both a syntactic and a semantic violation, should be judged as being totally unacceptable.

The data were treated as follows: binary judgments were arcsine-root-transformed to correct for normality of distribution. 7-point judgments were left as is. ME judgment scores, following the standard procedure, were divided by the modulus value and log-transformed.

In Table 1 below, we present the descriptive rating values for the following four variables: *Binary1*, *Binary2*, *7-point*, and *ME*. The first two are the ratings from the binary judgment task, and the second two are the respective 7-point and ME-ratings with which the binary ones were paired. In order to retain maximal comparability between the two groups (Binary1/7-point and Binary2/ME), we report item means only.

Table 1. Item means for the four measures dependent on condition

Measure	Condition 1	Condition 2	Condition 3	Condition 4
Binary1	.99	.06	.14	.00
Binary2	.87	.08	.22	.01
7-point	6.89	1.54	2.22	1.16
ME	1.49	–.60	–.31	–1.11

For each of the measures, we performed an analysis of variance with violation as a repeated contrast ((1) vs. (2), (2) vs. (3), and (3) vs. (4)). As above, the analyses were ran on the item means in order to allow for maximal comparability. Table 2 gives the partial η^2-values of the repeated contrasts for the four measures.

Table 2. Partial η^2 for the four measures dependent on condition

Measure	Cond1 vs. Cond2	Cond2 vs. Cond3	Cond3 vs. Cond4
Binary1	.993	.655	.969
Binary2	.983	.732	.942
7-point	.990	.781	.909
ME	.968	.412	.971

Before turning to the critical comparison of the measures, we want to note that all four of them show the same drop in the effect size estimate in the comparison of Condition 2 and 3: while all other contrasts show exceedingly high partial η^2-values, this contrast is subject to a larger amount of variability. This is the case if we compare the two binary measures only, but also for the comparison of the former with the two measures of higher scale type. This is to say that, for this contrast, variance can only be accounted for in roughly 40 to 80 percent, while the variance entering into the other contrasts seems to be caused by these contrast almost exhaustively (between 90 and 99 percent).

Turning to the critical comparison of the effect sizes, namely the one of Binary1, Binary2 and 7-point vs. ME, we see that there are no substantive differences between the measures for the contrasts of Condition 1 vs. Condition2, and the contrast of Condition 3 vs. Condition 4 – on these contrasts, all four measures perform equally well, accounting for roughly 90% of the variance in the data sets. In the contrast of Condition 2 vs. Condition 3, however, there is a substantial difference between Binary1, Binary2 and 7-point judgment data on the one side, and the ME data on the other. While the former still show a effect size estimate of around 70%, the variance in the ME data can only be accounted for by the contrast between the conditions to 41%.

We interpret these data as follows: firstly, it is not the case that the measures of lower scale type (Binary1 and 2, 7-point) are less informative than ME. All four measures show the same high proportion of variance accounted for in the contrasts between Conditions 1 and 2 and Conditions 3 and 4. Second, taking the partial η^2-values as an indicator of the informativity of a measure with respect to a given hypothesis, we are forced to conclude that for the relatively subtle contrast between Conditions2 and 3, the ME variable contains less information about the experimental contrast than the three other measures.

Conclusion

Given the results of the experiment reported in the last section, as well as a series of similar experiments that we have conducted employing different linguistic factors (see (Weskott and Fanselow: in prep.)), it seems that the claim that measures of linguistic acceptability which are of lower scale type than ME data are less informative with respect to linguistic hypotheses cannot be upheld. Our results clearly indicate that binary judgments and 7-point judgments are equally informative as ME judgments in repeated measures designs with well-defined conditions. In fact, as the contrast between Conditions 2 and 3 showed, there may be cases of subtle differences in which ME data fail to produce effects of a size comparable to the one of the two other measures. This may be due to the inherent variability of ME judgments. While this is clearly an advantage over the other measures from the point of view of the participant, which is not forced to use predetermined values to express her assessment of linguistic acceptability, it may also cause spurious variance in circumstances where participants differ widely with respect to their estimate of acceptability. It remains to be shown by further systematic comparisons of different measures of linguistic acceptability whether there are cases in which ME judgment data show a greater sensitivity to an experimental factor than data of lower scale type. Given the evidence reported here, we are led to conclude that the different measures do not differ with respect to informativity.

A dimension along which the measures do differ is the naturalness of the task in which the measures figure, and the cognitive effort that they require from the participant in a judgment experiment. As we have argued in section 2, the task in an ME experiment is the least natural one of the three task we have looked at, a point conceded even by proponents of the ME method. We have also noted that this in itself is not an argument against employing ME in a rating study, because many psycholinguistic experimental settings are not what one would consider "natural" in any sense, and nevertheless do produce reliable and theoretically valuable data. The question whether one should put up with the unnaturalness of the ME task then essentially hinges on the question whether an experimental setting involving a more natural task would fail to produce equally robust statistical effects. As we have argued here, the more natural tasks of judging linguistic acceptability in a binary fashion or on a 7-point scale do not produce less robust statistical effects. Given a repeated measurements design with a sufficient number of experimental items and participants, as well as sufficiently well-defined factors and thoroughly controlled materials, the scale type of the measure of acceptability is of secondary relevance, and the naturalness of the task may ultimately be decisive in the choice of method.

Notes

1. We want to thank Sam Featherston for making available to us the manuscript of his contribution in advance. A paper and a poster discussing issues closely related to the ones presented here were presented at the Linguistic Evidence 2008 conference by Markus Bader, Tanja Schmid, and Jana Häussler (see 37–60), and by Brian Murphy and Carl Vogel (see Murphy and Vogel, 2008). Furthermore, we want to point the interested reader to a paper by Jon Sprouse which is concerned with further problems of the ME method (see Sprouse 2007).
2. This is one of the reasons why in each experiment (irrespective of the method employed), there should be a sufficient number of filler items interspersed with the experimental materials. The ratio of experimental items to fillers should at least be 1 : 2; see Cowart 1996:93.

References

Bader, Markus, Tanja Schmid, and Jana Häussler
2009 Optionality in verb cluster formation, this volume.

Bard, Ellen Gurman, Dan Robertson, and Antonella Sorace
1996 Magnitude estimation of linguistic acceptability. *Language* 72(1): 32–68

Cowart, Wayne
1996 *Experimental Syntax. Applying Objective Methods to Sentence Judgments*. Thousand Oaks: Sage Publishers.

Featherston, Sam
2009 A scale for measuring well-formedness: Why syntax needs boiling and freezing points. In: Sam Featherston and Susanne Winkler (eds.) *The Fruits of Empirical Linguistics. Volume 1: Process*, 47–73. Berlin: de Gruyter.

Hantsch, Ansgar
2003 *Fisch oder Karpfen? Lexikale Aktivierung von Benennungsalternativen bei der Objektbenennung*. MPI Series in Cognitive Neuroscience 40. Leipzig: Max-Planck-Institut für neuropsychologische Forschung.

Levelt, Willem J.M.
1989 *Speaking. From Intention to Articulation.* Cambridge, MA: MIT Press.

Lodge, Milton
1982 *Magnitude Scaling. Quantitative Measurement of Opinions*. Newbury Park, CA: Sage Publishers.

Murphy, Brian, and Carl Vogel
2008 *An empirical comparison of measurement scales for judgements of acceptability*. Poster presented at the Linguistic Evidence 2008 conference. Tübingen.

Poulton, E.C.
1989 *Bias in Quantifying Judgments*. London: Erlbaum.

Sprouse, Jon
2007 Continuous Acceptability, Categorical Grammaticality, and Experimental Syntax. *Biolinguistics* 1: 118–129.

Weskott, Thomas and Gisbert Fanselow
in prep. On the informativity of different measures of linguistic acceptability. Ms, University of Potsdam.

Conjoint analysis in linguistics – Multi-factorial analysis of Slavonic possessive adjectives

Tim Züwerink

1. Introduction

Linguistic variation may be considered the "central problem" of modern linguistics (Labov 2004: 6). Variation is defined as the choice between "two alternative ways of saying the same thing" (Labov 2004: 6). Decision processes between formally different but semantically comparable language structures are complex and influenced by a variety of factors. Some of these are associated with the speaker or hearer, others with the utterance or with the situation of communication. Though language variation is in primary focus of modern linguistics, comparably little effort has been made (exceptions see e.g. Gries 2001) on developing research techniques to reveal the relative importance of single grammatical, functional-stylistic or sociolinguistic factors in multi-factorial designs. Instead of examining the importance of many factors at the same time, researchers normally focus on one or a small number of factors in a single study. However, the multi-factorial approach has two main advantages. On the one hand the importance of decision factors can be determined relative to others. This is impossible in a study that examines only one factor at a time. On the other hand a large spectrum of occurrences of grammatical structures under many different and controlled circumstances is evaluated to draw more general conclusions.

The conditions of alternation between the attributive genitive and the "Possessive adjective" (PA) in particular Slavonic languages have been characterised as very complex (see e.g. Corbett 1995, Corbett 1987 and Ivanov et al. (ed.) 1989). The aim of three online surveys conducted by the author with more than 1100 Russian, Czech and Croatian native speakers respectively, was a multifactorial analysis of the decision process between the PA and the substantive in the genitive case without a preposition. This analysis was conducted under varying lexical (PA and head nouns of noun phrases), grammatical (different case, number and gender of noun phrases), functional-stylistic (different social spheres and registers of communication) and also sociolinguistic (respondents' characteristics) circumstances.

Conjoint Analysis (CA), which apparently has not been used in linguistics before, was applied as the survey technique. In market research, where it is most common and very widespread, this type of analysis breaks down the customer's decision between products, showing the importance and preference impact of different product attributes (Green/Rao 1971, Cattin/Wittink 1982, Kohli 1988, Klein 2002). When confronted with a large number of decisions between varying product offers, the researcher will ideally be able to determine the importance of a particular factor in the customer's eyes. The analysis is based on a regression presupposing that every object (e.g. car) can be understood as the sum of its relevant factors (e.g. colour, brand, price and others). The result is an estimation of so called part-worth utilities for every factor value (e.g. "red", "Mercedes", "EUR 30,000"). For the purpose of this analysis, it was assumed that language variation, just like choosing a product, is influenced by numerous factors, some of which can be varied systematically to show their relative importance and the preference impact of factor values for the speaker's decision between synonymic syntactic structures.

Apart from presenting the results of the survey, the following questions will be brought up: What benefits does CA offer for linguistic purposes in comparison to other research techniques? What specific issues arise when one applies CA to language material? How can the statistical evaluation procedures of CA be optimised for testing factors of linguistic variation?

The objective of this paper is not least to prepare the ground for future applications of this research technique in linguistics.

2. Conjoint Analysis – assessing factors of decision-making

2.1. Origin and basic principles of Conjoint Measurement

At first Conjoint Analysis ("CONsider JOINTly") was developed and applied in psychology (Luce/Tukey 1964). Since the 1970s Conjoint Analysis found its way into market research (Green/Rao 1971, Cattin/Wittink 1982). Today CA is a standard procedure in determining customer preferences (Wittink et al. 1994). Many pricing and product development projects are conducted with the aid of this research design to gain information about customers' preferences. To illustrate the basic principles of CA a fictitious example from market research in the automotive industry shall be given.

The question underlying the survey is this: Which factor values (e.g. different brands or colours) are more or less valuable than the others? Which factors are most important in the decision-making process of the respondents? The

Table 1. Fictitious example of Conjoint stimuli in market research

	Object 1	Object 2
Brand	X	Y
Price	EUR 38,000	EUR 36,000
Power	110kw	140kw
Colour	green	black

Conjoint Analysis procedure allows for the calculation of a so-called Part-worth utility for every factor value, which is estimated in a linear regression. The underlying assumption is that the overall utility of every object (in this case, a car) can be understood as the sum of all part-worth utility values of the respective factor values. Thus, the estimation is based on the following equation (y_k is the estimated overall utility of the stimulus k; β_{jm} is the part-worth utility of the factor value m of the factor j; x_{jm} is 1 when the factor j has the value m for stimulus k, otherwise it is 0):

$$y_k = \sum_{j=1}^{J} \sum_{m=1}^{M_j} \beta_{jm} \cdot x_{jm}$$

The higher the part-worth utility is above zero, the more positively the respective factor value influences the preference for the given stimulus. Consequently, if the part-worth utility of a factor value is negative, it more or less strongly prevents

Table 2. Results of fictitious market research example

Factor	Factor level	Partworth utility	Standard error	Confidence interval	
				Upper 95%	Lower 95%
Brand	X	2.3	0.19	2.7	1.9
	Y	–0.1	0.12	0.1	–0.3
	Z	–2.2	0.07	–2.1	–2.3
Price	EUR 30,000	5.0	0.03	5.1	4.9
	EUR 32,000	1.6	0.02	1.6	1.6
	EUR 34,000	–0.1	0.15	0.2	–0.4
	EUR 36,000	–2.5	0.04	–2.4	–2.6
	EUR 38,000	–4.0	0.04	–3.9	–4.1
Colour	green	–0.3	0.12	–0.1	–0.5
	red	2.1	0.03	2.2	2.0
	brown	1.2	0.04	1.3	1.1
	yellow	–3.0	0.13	–2.7	–3.3

Table 3. Relative importance from fictitious example

Factor	Range	Relative importance
Brand	4.5	24.2%
Price	9.0	48.3%
Colour	5.1	27.4%
Total	18.6	100.0%

the respondents from choosing the car. Note that the part-worth utilities of all levels of a particular factor equal out.

The relative importance of a discrete factor *j* (e.g. price of the product) is calculated by the range of part-worth utilities from the highest to the lowest value (e.g. 2.3 for "X" and –2.2 for "Z", which equals a range of 4.5 = 2.3 – [–2.2]) divided by the sum of the ranges of part-worth utilities of all factors *J*.

$$IMP_j = 100\frac{RANGE_j}{\sum\limits_{j=1}^{J} RANGE_j}$$

2.2. Chances and challenges of CA's application in linguistics

Although CA is applicable to all multi-attributive objects of preference, it has not been adopted as a research technique in linguistics. Presupposition for every CA is the assumption that the object of interest can be described as a set of attributes. These objects (e.g. a car), though, have to serve a common objective. In the case of a car, the main function of all these automobiles is largely the same. In the case of language elements one has to find objects that serve the same communicative objective. Language variants have to be presented to the respondents as the basis for their decision. They decide between the variants based on attributes of the different objects, but not because they prefer the semantics of one of the alternatives to the semantics of the other alternative. Even if absolute synonymy is not possible, these differences should be reduced as far as possible.

3. Survey report: Usage factors of Slavonic "Possessive Adjectives"

3.1. Slavonic Possessive Adjectives – potential usage factors

Slavonic Possessive Adjectives are cited a prime example for the fact that morphological structures are often very similar within the Slavonic language family (Hock 1998: 17). They are derived mostly from animate nouns (Corbett 1995: 269) with a suffix and show archaic "short" inflexional paradigms that distinguish them from many other adjectives although in some of their word forms the "long" pronominal endings have replaced them.

Table 4. Examples of Possessive Adjectives and attributive genitive

	Possessive Adjective	Attributive genitive
Russian	*комиссар-ов-а сестра*	*сестра комиссара*
Czech	*komisař-ov-a sestra*	*sestra komisaře*
Croatian	*komisar-ov-a sestra*	*sestra komisara*
Translation	'the commissar's sister'	'the sister of the commissar'

PA with the suffixes *-ov-/-ev-* and *-in-/-yn-* are described to refer to an individualized and concrete entity (e.g. a definite commissar, table 4) in all Slavonic languages[1]. This means that the referent of the PA – with only few exceptions – must be identifiable to the producer as well as to the recipient.

The role of PA is not the same in all in Slavonic languages. Some of them, like Slovenian, Czech or Serbo-Croatian, still show a very dominant position of PA in comparison to the attributive genitive. In other Slavonic languages the PA has declined over the past centuries and its use has become more and more restricted. Table 5 provides an overview of the results of a study on the usage frequencies of PA in Slavonic languages that was conducted in the 1970s (Ivanova 1975: 151). Although the selection of the texts analysed is surely not representative, this overview can put the languages analysed in our study in context.

Apart from general observations on *how often* PA are used, little effort has been made to empirically determine *why* PA are being used or not being used in different languages. Therefore, the primary objective of our survey was to detect important factors for choosing between PA and the attributive genitive.

The research literature on the Possessive Adjectives revealed possible factors, like in Russian the "functional-stylistic" sphere or in all Slavonic languages of the PA's root noun type (e.g. Bräuer 1986, Corbett 1995). Additionally, the noun

Table 5. Usage frequency of Possessive Adjectives and attributive genitive in Slavonic languages

Language	"Possessive adjective"	Attributive genitive
Slovenian	98.2%	1.8%
Czech	94.3%	5.7%
Serbo-Croatian	93.1%	6.9%
Slovakian	83.0%	17.0%
Belorussian	64.6%	35.4%
Ukrainian	48.9%	51.1%
Russian	22.3%	77.7%
Polish	5.8%	94.2%
Average	63.8%	36.2%

phrases were put in different cases, numbers and genders to reflect the whole spectrum of word forms of the adjectives. The objective of representing all PA word forms suggests the application of a multi-factorial approach like CA. The author argues that only by testing a large spectrum of word forms of PA we are in fact able to draw conclusions on this word group. If one were only to focus on one or few factors the results for these factors and would leave a factor like case or gender constant, the results would be valid only for this particular case and gender of PA noun phrases. The strength of CA is therefore to include these potential influence factors into one multi-factorial design. The decision situation is the following: a native speaker is confronted with the alternatives Possessive Adjective and attributive genitive in his or her language. The respondent can not modify the stimuli, which means every influence factor was therefore fixed. Respondents of course were not able to modify her age, gender, level of education or the intensity of use of her native language as well. In this study the population does not consist of speakers but of situations in which two grammatical synonyms can be applied by native speakers. Sociolinguistic factors were also considered influence factors and not distinguished from other factors in the stimuli. In every single decision, a native speaker chose between two grammatical synonyms based on attributes which he or she could not modify.

3.2. Research design of CA for Russian, Czech and Croatian PA

The first step in setting up the research was to find factors which could be decisive when speaker chose between the Possessive Adjectives and the attributive genitive. So the research literature was consulted to compile potentially important factors. Next, PA had to be found which are typical for their respective suffix type and their particular type of root noun. For example, PA derived with the suffix *-in-* and with a kinship term as root noun type had to be found.

In the "National corpus of the Russian language" (*Nacional'nyj korpus russkogo jazyka*, http: //www.ruscorpora.ru), words that fulfilled these characteristics were evaluated concerning their usage in comparison to occurrences of their root noun. The Russian words *дядин* 'PA (uncle)', *матушкин* 'PA (mother *hyp.*)', *тетушкин* 'PA (aunt *hyp.*)' were chosen as the representatives for this class of PA, because the quotient of their occurrences and the occurrences of their root nouns was close to the average in the respective suffix and root noun class (see the underlying equation in image 1; for technical details about the selection procedure in German consult Züwerink 2008). Table 6 illustrates the chosen PA in Russian. We observe that some cells remained empty. This is why the factors suffix and semantics of PA root nouns were later merged to the factor "word formation category". This was possible because the gender of the root noun determines the particular suffix with which the PA is formed.

$$\textit{Relative occurrence of PA} = \textit{Occurrence of PA} \div \textit{Occurrence of PA root noun}$$

Figure 1. Equation for relative occurrence of PA in national corpora

Next the online questionnaire was designed. It consisted of two parts. On the introductory page the respondents were asked to state their age, level of education and gender. Additionally, they were asked if they use their native language more frequently than any other language in everyday life and, correspondingly, if they spent the most of their last ten years in their home country or abroad. This was done in order to determine their exposure to their native language that later should turn out to be an important factor in the decision process. Respondents were also asked how many years they had spent in a city with more than 20,000 inhabitants. This was done mainly to exclude Russian respondents who originate from a rural surrounding, because they are thought to be capable of communicating in standard Russian with a lower probability than urban Russians.

After all data were provided by the respondent, she or he could proceed to the second part of the online questionnaire, which contained the stimuli themselves. The stimuli were structured identically in all languages (image 2). At first, the situation of communication was described. The respondent learned with whom he was talking (mother/father/brother, supervisor/colleague/subordinate, unknown person on the street who is older/of the same age/younger as/than the respondent).

Additionally, information was provided about the register of communication (standard language, colloquial language, different dialects; e.g. "Your conversa-

Table 6. Word formation category of Russian PA tested (the meaning of its root noun is attached to each PA in the table; "hyp." means "hypocoristic")

Semantics of PA root nouns	Suffixes			
	-ov-	*-ev-*	*-in-*	*-yn-*
First names	*Петров*[2] 'Petr'	–	*Ванин* 'Vanja', *Иринин* 'Irina', *Леночкин* 'Lenočka', *Наташин* 'Nataša', *Ольгин* 'Ol'ga'	–
Kinship terms	*дедов* 'grand-father', *отцов* 'father'	*деверев* 'brother-in-law', *тестев* 'father-in-law'	*дядин* 'uncle', *матушкин* 'mother (*hyp.*)', *тетушкин* 'aunt (*hyp.*)'	*племянницын* 'niece', *сестрицын* 'sister (*hyp.)*'
Common nouns referring to persons	*попов* 'Pope (Russian Orthodox Church)'	*государев* 'monarch', *царев* 'czar'	*кухаркин* 'female cook', *старухин* 'aged woman'	–
Common nouns referring to animals	*воронов* 'raven'	–	*кошкин* 'cat', *кукушкин* 'cuckoo'	*курицын* 'chicken'

tional partner uses 'literary' (or standard) language"). It should be stressed that this type of information is different from real life information on the register of communication, but the Russian, Czech and Croatian results show some interesting differences. Then the two utterances were presented between which the respondent could choose. One contained the Possessive Adjective. The semantically identical alternative contained the attribute genitive. The stimuli were generated with an *Excel*-tool in Visual Basic.

In Russian, twenty-four PA and forty-six head nouns were combined to 274 (sensible) noun phrases which were then put in different cases, numbers and genders and then combined with different remarks on the register of communication. In this way more than 45,000 stimuli were created in the Russian survey and randomised in order. Then the stimuli were transferred to an SQL-database and inserted into HTML-format using a php-script. The respondents could simply access an html-page and fill in the questionnaire online.

Situation	
Register of communication	
Remark about identifiability of PA referent	
Alternative A	Alternative B
PA – head noun – semantically neutral verbal phrase.	Head noun – attributive genitive – semantically neutral verbal phrase.
Rating scale	

Figure 2. Structure of stimuli

The respondents stated a preference for one of the language variants on a 10-point Likert-scale where -10- was the most explicit preference for the PA and -1- was the most explicit preference for the attributive genitive, thus the most explicit refusal of the PA. Also, if they felt that one of the alternatives was "wrong", they could click a special button and this resulted in a missing value. This means that if the respondents decided to vote for one of the alternatives they implicitly accepted the other but stated a preference for the one they chose. After the respondent rated 30 stimuli the questionnaire ended and she or he was thanked for her or his participation.

The respondent base does not reflect the overall population. Especially older people, people without higher education and people in remote locations without internet access are underrepresented in the respondent base. But given the fact that the most important characteristics of the respondents were identified, generalizations are possible with regard to a fictitious population. An overview on the characteristics of this fictitious population is provided in table 7.

The questionnaire was checked with native speakers to ensure the comprehensibility of the scale, the decision task and the questions about the characteristics of the respondents. To gather respondents, multiple approaches were used

Table 7. Overview on respondent base

	Russian survey	Czech survey	Croatian survey	Total
Total respondents	720	226	229	1,175
Higher education	87.5%	81.9%	83.4%	85.6%
No higher education	12.5%	18.1%	16.6%	14.4%
Female	63.2%	66.4%	67.3%	64.6%
Male	36.8%	33.6%	32.8%	35.4%
Lived home	73.3%	79.2%	74.2%	74.6%
Lived abroad	26.7%	20.8%	25.8%	25.4%

to diversify the respondent base. In Moscow, St. Petersburg, Prague and Zagreb leaflets with the URL of the online questionnaire were distributed among students with the request to pass on the information to friends and relatives. Emails to universities, mailing-lists and personal friends were sent and messages were distributed via social networking sites. The survey results were evaluated in a three-step analytical approach. I first tested if the differences in responses for different factor values (e.g. cases of the noun phrases, word formation categories etc.) could be generalized with regard to the fictitious population.

The non-parametric Mann-Wilcoxon-U-test and Wilcoxon signed rank tests were applied. The Mann-Wilcoxon-U-test assumes two *independent* samples whereas the Wilcoxon signed rank test is used for testing the differences in two *dependent* samples (Mann/Whitney 1947, Wilcoxon 1945)[3]. In this analysis these two procedures were used in combination because the respondents were not given identical questionnaires. Doing so would have caused an exceedingly long questionnaire for each respondent. The entire catalogue of approximately 45,000 stimuli in the Russian survey was distributed randomly over all respondents. Each respondent had to rate at least 25 stimuli and 30 stimuli at most. Factors for which no significant effect on the respondents' decision could be detected were left out in the further course of the analysis. In the following step the statistically significant factors were tested on their orthogonality – that is on their mutual independence. If influence factors show contingencies – that is they are dependent on one another – there is no chance to assign the effects to a particular one of these factors. To test the mutual independence of the influence factors, the Cramer-V contingency coefficient was calculated. If contingence of two factors was detected, they were merged into one factor. For example, the intensity of use of the respondent's native language was, of course, lower if he or she spent most of the last ten years abroad. These two factors (intensity of use of mother tongue and location of residence) were merged into "exposure of respondents to their native language". The same happened with the factors "suffix" and "root noun type" which were merged to "word formation category".

Finally, the SPSS-CONJOINT-procedure was applied to estimate the part-worth utilities with an *Ordinary least squares regression* (OLS). As the respondents had been given different questionnaires, in the SPSS-CONJOINT-procedure the dependence of the answers had to be neglected. So *Non-overlapping block bootstrap* was used on an OLS-Regression as well as a *Mixed effects model*. The latter procedures which account for the dependence of data largely confirmed the results of the SPSS-CONJOINT-procedure.

3.3. Analysis and interpretation of results of linguistic CA on Slavonic PA

First let us have a look at general figures about the survey results. There is a great difference between the shares of the respondents' decisions for the PA in the languages analyzed. In the Russian survey only 35.7% of all decisions were in favor of the PA, in the Czech and Croatian surveys this figure was 63.9% and 76.2% respectively.

Table 8. Share of respondents' decisions for PA and overall medians

	Russian	Czech	Croatian
Overall share of decisions for PA	35.7%	63.9%	76.2%
Median of scale values	3	8	9

We will omit the results of the first two steps of the statistical procedure, because they were merely prerequisites for detecting factor significance and orthogonality. The interesting results are the part-worth utilities and relative factor importance from the SPSS-CONJOINT-procedure. The latter are presented in table 9.

Table 9. Relative importance of factors

	Russian	Czech	Croatian
Word formation category	57.2%	51.1%	52.2%
Exposure of respondents to native language	5.6%	15.9%	32.4%
Case of noun phrases	8.2%	17.1%	n. a.
Register of conversational partner	17.8%	n. a.	n. a.
Level of education	3.6%	15.9%	n. a.
Syntactic semantics	2.6%	n. a.	n. a.
Social sphere	4.9%	n. a.	n. a.
Age of respondents	n. a.	n. a.	15.4%

The word formation category – including the highly interrelated factors suffix and root noun type – is by far the most important factor in all analysed languages. It can be observed that among the root noun types PA derived from first names are ranked highest, whereas PA derived from common nouns referring to animals where chosen most infrequently (table 10). Also PA with kinship terms as their root nouns tended to rank higher than PA derived from other common nouns referring to persons. These findings are coherent with the observations in research literature. It is argued here that the regularity in which

Table 10. Word formation category of Possessive Adjectives[4]

Language	Factor level		Partworth utility	Standard error	Confidence interval	
	Semantics of PA root noun	Suffix			Upper 95%	Lower 95%
Russian	First names	*-ov-*	–0.95	0.10	–0.76	–1.15
		-in-	2.13	0.05	2.22	2.04
	Kinship terms	*-ov-*	–0.36	0.07	–0.23	–0.50
		-ev-	–1.09	0.08	–0.94	–1.24
		-in-	2.12	0.06	2.24	2.01
		-yn-	–0.45	0.08	–0.30	–0.60
	Common nouns referring to persons	*-ov-*	–0.97	0.12	–0.74	–1.20
		-ev-	0.24	0.08	0.40	0.07
		-in-	0.98	0.07	1.12	0.83
	Common nouns referring to animals	*-ov-*	–1.02	0.12	–0.78	–1.26
		-in-	0.75	0.08	0.91	0.59
		-yn-	–1.37	0.13	–1.12	–1.62
Czech	First names	*-ův-*	1.45	0.10	1.64	1.26
		-in-	0.65	0.10	0.85	0.44
	Kinship terms	*-ův-*	1.43	0.09	1.61	1.26
		-in-	–0.12	0.12	0.12	–0.35
	Common nouns referring to persons	*-ův-*	0.38	0.08	0.54	0.21
		-in-	–1.04	0.09	–0.86	–1.23
	Common nouns referring to animals	*-ův-*	–1.37	0.12	–1.13	–1.61
		-in-	–1.37	0.17	–1.03	–1.72
Croatian	First names	*-ov-*	1.08	0.08	1.24	0.93
		-ev-	0.75	0.10	0.95	0.55
		-in-	1.07	0.10	1.26	0.88
	Kinship terms	*-ov-*	0.92	0.09	1.11	0.74
		-ev-	–0.86	0.08	–0.71	–1.01
		-in-	0.24	0.15	0.53	–0.05
	Common nouns referring to persons	*-ov-*	–0.36	0.07	–0.23	–0.49
		-ev-	–0.37	0.08	–0.22	–0.52
		-in-	–0.50	0.07	–0.37	–0.63
	Common nouns referring to animals	*-ov-*	–0.44	0.11	–0.22	–0.67
		-ev-	–1.85	0.05	–1.74	–1.95
		-in-	0.31	0.06	0.42	0.20

the root nouns occur in a definite meaning is the reason for this ranking. The more likely the root noun is to appear in a definite reference (e.g. first names and kinship terms) the more common it is to derive PA from these root nouns.

Regarding the ranking of the derivational suffixes it has to be noted that in the Russian survey the PA with the suffix *-ov-/-ev-* were chosen much less frequently than those with the suffix *-in-*. This observation is valid for every type of root noun and confirms the remarks in research literature about the perpetual decline of especially those PA with the suffix *-ov-/-ev-* in Russian.

By far the most important sociolinguistic factor turned out to be the exposure of the respondents to their native language (table 11). Only a part of the respondents consisted of native speakers who had spent the last ten years of their lives predominantly in their home country and who use their native language predominantly in their everyday life. Other respondents had spent the last ten years abroad and/or use their native language less frequently than in their everyday life. These circumstances were merged into the factor "exposure of respondents to their native language". In the Croatian survey the respondents with weak exposure to their native language much less frequently chose the PA. The Czech survey showed the same result, however the effect is weakened in comparison to Croatian. In the Russian survey there was only a low importance of this factor. Here the native speakers who had spent the last ten years abroad and/or do not use their native language most frequently in their everyday life chose the PA more frequently than their counterparts. This may be explained by the position that PA hold in the different language systems. In Croatian the overall usage of PA in the survey showed the highest frequency. If a Croatian native speaker is influenced by another language environment, which does not use grammatical structures like the PA, her or his use of these words will decline to a greater extent, than in Russian, where the use of these words is not all that dominant as in Croatian. In Russian, inversely, the PA are at the "outskirts" of the language system. Those native speakers, which have spent a longer period of time outside of her or his native environment, will be more likely to use these words frequently than someone who knows about the restrictive use of the PA from the everyday experience with his mother tongue.

The case of the noun phrases built with PA and the head noun was a visible factor in the Russian and Czech surveys (table 12). While PA in the instrumental case in both languages received the lowest rating, those which appeared in the genitive case were rated high in both languages. The high rating for PA in the genitive case is not surprising because the alternative would have resulted in a noun phrase of head noun and PA root noun in the genitive case (e.g. in Russian *sestry Iriny*) which seems to have been avoided by the participants.

The low ratings for the instrumental could be explained by the theory of markedness (e.g. Jakobson 1936). Complex grammatical structures tend to decline at first in marked cases, like in the instrumental. The Czech survey is widely coherent with this explanation because both locative and dative rate low,

Table 11. Word formation category of Possessive Adjectives[4]

Language	Factor level	Partworth utility	Standard error	Confidence interval	
				Upper 95%	Lower 95%
Russian	Strong exposure	–0.14	0.03	–0.08	–0.20
	Modest exposure	–0.07	0.04	0.00	–0.14
	Weak exposure	0.21	0.04	0.29	0.12
Czech	Strong exposure	0.47	0.06	0.58	0.36
	Modest exposure	–0.06	0.08	0.10	–0.21
	Weak exposure	–0.41	0.07	–0.27	–0.56
Croatian	Strong exposure	0.98	0.06	1.09	0.87
	Modest exposure	–0.14	0.07	–0.01	–0.27
	Weak exposure	–0.84	0.06	–0.73	–0.95

Table 12. Exposure of respondents to native language

Language	Factor level	Partworth utility	Standard error	Confidence interval	
				Upper 95%	Lower 95%
Russian	Nominative	–0.11	0.05	–0.01	–0.20
	Genitive	0.24	0.05	0.33	0.14
	Dative	0.16	0.05	0.25	0.06
	Accusative	–0.11	0.05	–0.02	–0.21
	Instrumental	–0.27	0.05	–0.17	–0.36
	Prepositive	0.10	0.05	0.19	0.01
Czech	Nominative	0.15	0.09	0.32	–0.02
	Genitive	0.13	0.08	0.30	–0.03
	Dative	–0.03	0.08	0.13	–0.20
	Accusative	0.42	0.08	0.59	0.26
	Instrumental	–0.52	0.09	–0.35	–0.69
	Locative	–0.16	0.08	0.01	–0.32

while the non-marked cases nominative and accusative are showing the highest part-worth utilities. Since we have included the case, number and grammatical gender as potential influence factors in our analysis we know both their relative importance and can draw general conclusions on PA word forms of all cases, numbers and genders. I regard this to be a great advantage to regressions with only one independent variable.

Table 13. Case of noun phrases

Language	Factor level	Partworth utility	Standard error	Confidence interval	
				Upper 95%	Lower 95%
Russian	Standard language	–0.64	0.03	–0.57	–0.70
	Dialect	0.18	0.05	0.28	0.09
	Prostorečie	0.45	0.03	0.52	0.38

Table 14. Register of conversational partner

Language	Factor level	Partworth utility	Standard error	Confidence interval	
				Upper 95%	Lower 95%
Russian	Private sphere	0.16	0.03	0.22	0.10
	Professional sphere	–0.14	0.03	–0.08	–0.20
	Encounters with strangers	–0.02	0.03	0.04	–0.08

Only the Russian survey revealed a decisive impact of the register of the addressee that the respondents were asked to imagine (table 13). As described in research literature, the standard language triggers the use of PA to a far lesser extent than non-standard varieties, like regional dialects or *prostorečie*, a pan-regional non-standard variant of Russian (Sussex/Cubberley 2006: 553). The sphere of communication corresponds with this finding as well. In situations where the use of standard language is least mandatory (e.g. in family interaction/communication) the PA were chosen more frequently (table 14).

4. A promising approach for ranking factors of linguistic variation

For the first time the factors of decision making between PA or *definite adjectives* and the attributive genitive in Russian, Czech and Croatian could be revealed empirically. A catalogue of many thousand stimuli was presented to more than 1,000 respondents and the results confirmed some of the observations made in research literature. Other observations were made for the first time. Although CA seems to not have been applied to linguistic data yet, this research technique seems very promising to rank decision factors in any case of language variation. If a simple regression with one independent variable had been used in this analysis, an assessment of the importance of more than one variable relative to the others could not have been made.

CA could be applied wherever there are "two different ways of saying the same thing", that is, wherever different language means can serve to fulfil the same referential function in communication. CA allows for:

- evaluating a representative catalogue of the occurrences of language means in different semantic, syntactic, grammatical and situational contexts;
- taking into account many possible influence factors instead of leaving them fixed or uncontrolled;
- representing a large spectrum of potential occurrences of language means in order to draw more general conclusions;
- assessing the preferences of the respondents without presupposing any knowledge of the respondents about the object of scientific interest;
- providing an easy to complete and little time-consuming questionnaire;
- accessing respondents in remote locations using online questionnaires;
- ranking linguistic factors by their importance for the speakers' decision between language variants;
- prioritising linguistic research to focus on factors of major importance.

It would be preferable to develop a single statistical analysis instead of the three-step approach which was applied here. This aim should be the subject of further investigations.

Notes

1. Overview on Slavonic languages: Ivanov (ed.) 1989: 133–140, Topolińska 1981: 122; Old Church Slavonic: Huntley 1984: 217; Old Russian/Russian Church Slavonic: Marojević 1981: 106, Marojević 1983: 60, Russian: Bräuer 1986: 51, Mel'čuk 1998: 471, Pavlov 1995: 158–159; Polish: Petr 1971: 35; (Serbo-)Croatian: Gaweł 2006: 150–151, Mićanović 2000: 113–114, Zlatić 2001: 237; Czech: Lamprecht/Bauer 1985: 297–298, Šmilauer 1972: 96, Sorbian: Corbett 1987: 302, Corbett 1995: 268.
2. For this class in Russian only *Петров* 'PA (Petr)' was chosen, because the use of this PA type is very restricted in Russian. The results for this PA affirmed this notion.
3. The Wilcoxon signed rank test was used on the medians of one respondent's ratings of a certain attribute. For example, if one respondent rated stimuli that included PA with the suffix *-ov-* twice with -4-, once with -5- and once with -8-, her or his overall rating of this suffix as an attribute of PA, namely the median of the single ratings, was

4.5. The medians for different suffixes of one respondent were compared and it was tested if a difference between the ratings of two suffixes is statistically significant on a 95% (Bonferroni-adjusted for multiple comparisons) significance level. Then, as the respondents had received different questionnaires in which the stimuli had been randomly distributed across all respondents, the Mann-Whitney-U-test was used on the single responses of the participants on a very conservative (Bonferroni-adjusted for multiple comparisons) significance level of 99.9%.

4. The surveys in Russian, Czech and Croatian were conducted separately. "Language" is of course not an influence factor. Part-worth utilities for one factor in one language add up to zero.

References

Bräuer, Herbert
1986 Die possessiven Adjektiva auf -*ov* und -*in* des Russischen der Gegenwart und ihre Possessivität. *Zeitschrift für slavische Philologie* XLVI: 51–139.

Cattin, Philippe and Dick R. Wittink
1982 Commercial Use of Conjoint Analysis: a Survey. *Journal of Marketing* 46: 44–53.

Corbett, Greville
1987 The Morphology/Syntax interface: Evidence from Possessive Adjectives in Slavonic. *Language* 63: 299–345.
1995 Slavonic's Closest Approach to Suffixaufnahme: The Possessive Adjective. In: Frank Plank (ed.), *Double Case. Agreement by Suffixaufnahme*, 265–282. Oxford: Oxford University Press.

Gaweł, Alicja
2006 Kategoria posesywnoœci w jêzyku starochorwackim na przykładzie zabytku *Koluniœev zbornik. Studia z filologii polskiej i słowiańskiej* 41: 139–153.

Green, Paul E. and Vithala R. Rao
1971 Conjoint Analysis for Quantifying Judgmental Data. *Journal of Marketing Research*, 13: 355–363.

Gries, Stefan T.
2001 A Multifactorial Analysis of Syntactic Variation: Particle Movement Revisited. *Journal of Quantitative Linguistics* 8 (1): 33–50.

Hock, Wolfgang
1998 Das Urslavische. In: Peter Rehder (ed.), *Einführung in die slavischen Sprachen (mit einer Einführung in die Balkanphilologie)*, 17–34. Darmstadt: Wissenschaftliche Buchgesellschaft.

Huntley, David
1984 The distribution of the denominative adjective and the adnominal genitive in Old Church Slavonic. In: Jacek Fisiak (ed.), *Historical syntax*, 217–236. Berlin: Mouton.

Ivanov, Vjačeslav V. et al. (ed.)
1989 *Kategorija posessivnosti v slavjanskich i balkanskich jazykach.* Moskva: Nauka.

Ivanova, Tat'jana A.
1975 Nekotorye aspekty sopostavitel'nogo analiza posessivnych konstrukcij (na materiale sovremennych slavjanskich literaturnych jazykov). In: *Slavjanskaja filologija. Sbornik statej*, 148–152. Leningrad: Izdatel'stvo leningradskogo universiteta.

Jakobson, Roman
1936 Beitrag zur allgemeinen Kasuslehre. Gesamtbedeutungen der russischen Kasus. *Travaux du Cercle Linguistique de Prague 6*: 240–288.

Klein, Markus
2002 Die Conjoint-Analyse: Eine Einführung in das Verfahren mit einem Ausblick auf mögliche sozialwissenschaftliche Anwendungen. *ZA-Information* 50: 7–45.

Kohli, Rajeev
1988 Assessing Attribute Significance in Conjoint Analysis: Nonparametric Tests and Empirical Validation. *Journal of Marketing Research* 25 (2): 123–133.

Labov, William
2004 Quantitative Analysis of Linguistic Variation. In: Ulrich Ammon et al. (eds.), *Sociolinguistics*, 6–21. Berlin/New York: Walter de Gruyter.

Lamprecht, Arnošt and Jaroslav Bauer
1985 *Historická mluvnice češtiny*, Praha: Štatní pedagogické nakladatelství.

Luce, R. Duncan and John W. Tukey
1964 Simultaneous Conjoint Measurement: A New Type of Fundamental Measurement. *Journal of Mathematical Psychology* 1: 1–27.

Lyons, Christopher
1999 *Definiteness,* Cambridge: University Press.

Mann, H. B. and D. R. Whitney
1947 On a test of whether one of Two Random Variables is Stochastically Larger than the Other. *The Annals of Mathematical Statistics* 18 (1): 50–60.

Marojević, Radmilo
1981 Oppozicija opredelennych i neopredelennych form pritjažatel'nych prilagatel'nych (k voprosu î prirode imen tipa Vьsevoložaja v drevnerusskom jazyke). *Voprosy jazykoznanija* 5: 106–118.
1983 Posessivnye kategorii v russkom jazyke (istorija razvitija i sovremennoe sostojanie). *Filologičeskie nauki* 5: 56–61.

Mel'čuk, Igor' A.
1998 *Kurs obščej morfologii, tom II, čast' vtoraja: morfologičeskie značenija*, Wien: Gesellschaft zur Förderung Slawistischer Studien.

Mićanović, Krešimir
2000 Posvojni pridjevi i izražavanje posvojnosti. *Suvremena lingvistika* 25/26: 111–123.

Petr, Jan
1971 Posesívní adjektiva v současné polštině. *Slavica pragensia* XIII: 33–44.

Šmilauer, Vladimir
1972 *Nauka o českém jazyku*, Praha: Štatní pedagogické nakladatelství.

Sussex, Roland and Paul Cubberley
2006 *The Slavic languages*, Cambrigde: University Press.

Topolińska, Zuzanna
1981 *Remarks on the Slavic noun phrase*, Warsaw: Wydawnictwo polskiej akademii nauk.

Wilcoxon, Frank
1945 Individual comparisons by ranking methods. *Biometrics Bulletin* 1: 80–83.

Wittink, Dick R. et al.
1994 Commercial Use of Conjoint Analysis in Europe: Results and Critical Reflections. *International Journal of Research in Marketing* 11: 41–52.

Zlatić, Larisa
2001 The Syntactic Status of Slavic Possessives. Gerhild Zybatow et al. (eds.), *Current issues in formal slavic linguistics*, 236–246. Frankfurt/Main: Peter Lang.

Züwerink, Tim
2008 *Possessivadjektive in slavischen Sprachen. Morphosyntax und pragmatische Empirie*, München: Otto Sagner.